Economic Sanctions

Economic Sanctions

Panacea or Peacebuilding in a Post–Cold War World?

EDITED BY

David Cortright
and George A. Lopez

WITH A FOREWORD BY
Ronald V. Dellums

Westview Press
BOULDER • SAN FRANCISCO • OXFORD

Copyright © 1995 by Westview Press, Inc.

Published in 1995 in the United States of America by Westview Press, Inc., 5500 Central Avenue, Boulder, Colorado 80301-2877, and in the United Kingdom by Westview Press, 12 Hid's Copse Road, Cumnor Hill, Oxford OX2 9JJ

Library of Congress Cataloging-in-Publication Data
Economic Sanctions : panacea or peacebuilding in a post–cold war world?
    / edited by David Cortright and George A. Lopez.
        p.   cm.
    Includes bibliographical references and index.
    ISBN 0-8133-8908-9. — ISBN 0-8133-8909-7 (pbk.)
    1. Economic sanctions.   2. Economic sanctions—Case studies.
I. Cortright, David, 1946–   .   II. Lopez, George A.
HF1413.5.E27   1995
337—dc20   95-2899
                                                                                              CIP

Printed and bound in the United States of America

 The paper used in this publication meets the requirements of the American National Standard for Permanence of Paper for Printed Library Materials Z39.48-1984.

10   9   8   7   6   5   4   3   2   1

Contents

Foreword

When I first arrived in the United States Congress in 1971, I introduced legislation into the House of Representatives that would impose economic sanctions against the racist apartheid regime in South Africa. I believed that a U.S. determination to sever economic links with South Africa, and to strengthen the effect of that resolve by pressing for international sanctions that would economically isolate the regime, provided the surest and most morally compelling avenue to end the consistent pattern of gross violations of internationally recognized human rights imposed under apartheid doctrine.

Fifteen years later, amid a national hue and cry for economic disinvestment from South Africa, the Dellums bill to impose sanctions against South Africa finally passed the House of Representatives and sanctions became United States law over the veto of then President Ronald Reagan. I believe to a certainty that the passage of the sanctions law and the heightening of international efforts to isolate South Africa's apartheid government contributed significantly to the watershed political changes that have occurred on that portion of the African continent.

As I stood in Pretoria to witness the inauguration of President Nelson Mandela, I reflected on the positive contribution that the international sanctions effort had made in accelerating the inevitable coming to power of a government in South Africa based on the principle of nonracial democracy. What also seemed clear was that the timely and deliberate use of economic sanctions had mitigated against the possibility that this inevitable celebration might have come as a result of a further protracted and deadly violent armed struggle, fought to a bitter conclusion with all of the lingering consequences that would militate against reconciliation and national development.

In a very different context, I also supported the use of an internationally based economic sanctions strategy to dislodge the Iraqi forces from their conquest and illegal occupation of Kuwait. In the congressional debate about whether to authorize President Bush's undertaking of offensive military actions against Iraq, I pleaded that sanctions be given the opportunity to achieve their objective. To do that, I argued, would mean giving sanctions at least the twelve to eighteen months recommended as a minimum by experts to create enough economic pressure on the Iraqi regime to persuade its military to leave Kuwait without allied forces having to commence offensive military operations.

Thankfully the fearful predictions of massive allied casualties in the war that followed did not come to fruition. Nonetheless, tens of thousands of Iraqis were killed, a dramatic loss of life that may have been avoided had we abided the appropriate period of time to see whether the sanctions would obtain their stated objective.

Sanctions in a Changed World

The eventual and nearly unanimous world condemnation of South Africa, and sanctions against that country, were notable exceptions to the Cold War–era split that had divided the world community into East, West, and the nonaligned. This split often prevented the use of concerted worldwide action to meet humanitarian, peacekeeping, and human rights challenges and thereby forestall armed conflict. The sanctions against Iraq were trumpeted as part of the "new world order" (a phrase that means many different things depending on one's vantage point) made possible by the end of the Cold War.

There seems to be a consensus that the last decade of this century will be seen as a historic turning point for humanity. We have witnessed the end of the costly, dangerous, and sometimes deadly standoff between East and West. Former declared enemies of the West—the Soviet Union and the Warsaw Treaty Organization—have dissolved. Democratic governments have emerged where they had not previously existed throughout Europe, as they have also in Africa, Asia, and the Americas. Despite having faced each other for decades across mine- and barbed wire–laden military lines, U.S. and Russian troops now train and deploy together in peacekeeping operations. Much of Eastern and Central Europe and the former Soviet Union have now joined with the North Atlantic Treaty Organization in new "partnerships for peace" that promise to promote stability within the region.

Yet the post–Cold War years have also brought new challenges to the forefront of international politics. Civil wars, gross human rights abuses, regional conflicts, "ethnic cleansing," starvation and famine, and environmental catastrophes all pose challenges to international norms and place important demands on national and international systems. These demands require unprecedented and innovative responses from political and economic organizations that are themselves in transition. Much of this turmoil reflects the legacy of the Cold War and of the scores of conflicts of the past forty years.

The end of the Cold War era has instilled new life and potential viability into the United Nations, our most important international institution. No longer paralyzed by almost automatic superpower vetoes in the Security Council, the United Nations is finally able to frame a more constructive and increasingly complete set of responses to violations of international norms of behavior. On August 6, 1990, for example, Resolution 661 banned UN member exports to Iraq of any conventional military equipment or technology, as well as imports of oil from Iraq. Not only was this a clear signal of international condemnation of Iraq's invasion of Kuwait, it was an attempt to reverse the transgression by means other than war.

The September 1991 overthrowing of Haiti's first democratically elected president, Rev. Jean-Bertrand Aristide, catalyzed a trade embargo by the Organization of American States against the Haitian military dictatorship and coup leaders within a month. In response to the complex and dynamic horror occurring in the former Yugoslavia, over fifty United Nations resolutions have been passed, several applying some form of economic sanctions to constrain the violence of the war and the incidence of outrageous human rights abuses. Partial sanctions regimes have also been imposed recently against Somalia, Libya, Liberia, and areas of Cambodia.

All these multilateral sanctions regimes suggest a recent trend to find effective international responses, short of military action, to violations of accepted norms of behavior—invasions, coups, terrorism, racism, and human rights abuses. They are one aspect of the diplomatic, political, and economic efforts that constitute part of what I have called "preventive engagement."

Sanctions: A Record of Success

In 1959 African National Congress President Albert Luthuli argued that the international community was duty-bound to impose an economic embargo on South Africa to "hasten the end of the hateful system of apartheid." Three years later the United Nations General Assembly passed its resolution calling for a ban on exports to and imports from South Africa. In 1986, the United States adopted economic sanctions, responding to a massive, domestic antiapartheid movement. While it took thirty-five years from Luthuli's statement for Nelson Mandela to be sworn in as president of a nonracial South Africa, it took less than five years from the adoption of U.S. and complete international sanctions to achieve the release of Nelson Mandela from prison, placing South Africa on an irreversible path to fulfillment of Luthuli's declaration. I believe it is clear, even to those who were initially skeptical, including the American and international divestment campaign, that economic sanctions significantly hastened South Africa's historic political transition. As I noted above,

South Africa's relatively peaceful final transition to democracy serves as proof that nonviolent methods, given sufficient time to work, can achieve the objective of ending the crisis in a manner calculated to promote long-term stability and reconciliation among parties.

Some would argue against the effectiveness of sanctions, saying that these actions will solidify a nation against the international interference, and that populations may be politically mobilized by these embargoes. Skeptics point to the embargo on Serbia and Montenegro where, despite years of hyperinflation, enormous unemployment, and the almost complete devaluation of the Serbian currency, the population pulled together to support President Slobodan Milosevic and the Bosnian Serb war. I would submit that the eventual decision by the Serbian government to cut off their confreres in Bosnia (when the rump Bosnian Serb parliament rejected for the third time the "Contact Group" peace plan of July 6, 1994) proves the effectiveness of sanctions as a strategy. As I have argued on the floor of the House of Representatives, sanctions do take time to achieve their objective.

Sanctions: The Remaining Problems

There are many examples of sanctions regimes undertaken this century and, although we are beginning to better understand this mode of international operation, there is still a need to analyze past experiences to establish more sophisticated practices. That task is advanced nicely by the essays in this book. From a policy point of view, several issues are central to this inquiry.

First, who should participate? Most sanctions regimes have been implemented unilaterally by one country against another. Such actions, while sometimes calculated to achieve noble purposes, can be burdened by national self-interest and distorted by the relative power of the nations involved.

Since the end of the Cold War, however, more actions have become multilateral, a development that is to be heartily embraced. Multinational embargoes and boycotts are usually more effective than unilateral efforts because the economic impact on a nation being embargoed by most or all major trading partners is of course much greater than if only one or two partners participate. Multinational sanctions regimes also provide fewer options for target nations to find alternate sources for fuel, arms, and other embargoed commodities. Equally important, multilateral sanctions, especially those instituted through a United Nations mandate, can claim a moral authority unencumbered by national or regional self-interest, thereby increasing the likelihood of international solidarity, compliance, and secondary enforcement for sanctions violators.

Second, what type of embargo or sanctions regime should be undertaken? Sanctions regimes can range from very limited cutoffs of a single commodity, such as oil or weapons, to restrictions much more expansive in nature. This must be decided on a case-by-case basis, depending on the nature of the target government and the character of the crisis. As with warfare itself, sanctions should be imposed only to the degree that it is necessary to achieve the objective of securing compliance with international norms of behavior.

Related to this, and very important, is the need to carefully understand the humanitarian implications of any sanctions effort. Boycotts, blockades, and embargoes can have devastating consequences on innocent civilian populations, with varying results. By 1994, for example, Iraqi living standards under the prolonged sanctions regime had declined by at least one-third since the 1991 Gulf War. To focus sanctions on governments and elites and to shield innocent civilians from unnecessary suffering, the United Nations has attempted in Iraq, Haiti, and elsewhere to exempt food and medicines. However, we need to know more about how to coerce the key targets of sanctions while protecting, as best we can, the innocent.

Third, once an economic action is implemented, how do we effectuate enforcement? A declared trade or arms embargo is of little effect if it cannot be enforced by the sanctioning countries or organizations. Thus, the arms and trade embargoes on the former Yugoslavia have had mixed results as leakage has occurred along the Danube River and other border areas. The same has been true with the transport of goods across the Dominican Republic/Haiti border and the transshipment of goods through Jordan to Iraq. What may be required to ensure minimal leakage is to provide economic assistance to innocent third party states whose own economies are put at risk by an embargo. Such assistance may be necessary to forestall hardship on the citizens in third party states.

Fourth, what is the scope and strategy for implementing sanctions? It appears that sanctions are most effective when implemented quickly and comprehensively, although the authors in this volume differ on this matter. For example, the sanctions on Haiti were gradually expanded over three years—from an early cutoff of U.S. foreign assistance to an OAS– and UN–imposed embargo on arms and fuel and then finally to a comprehensive prohibition on all trade, commercial air traffic, and financial transactions. If these sanctions had been comprehensive right after the military coup, or at least from the moment of the coup leaders' repudiation of their obligations under the Governors Island Agreement of July 3, 1993, the sanctions regime would have likely been much more effective and expeditious in restoring democracy and ending the vicious reprisals by the regime.

To be most effective against targeted regimes and populations, and least harmful to innocent civilians and other countries, each sanctions regime must be carefully tailored to the individual case. Information drawn from the expanding reservoir of experience that has produced this very inexact science can be helpful in shaping specific sanctions regimes. What is clear, however, is that effective and affordable alternatives to military force are needed now if the international community is to resolve the many ethnic, religious, racial, territorial, and other conflicts of our time with positive solutions. New and diverse approaches to economic development, environmental restoration and protection, conflict mediation and resolution, and economic sanctions—from limited commodity boycotts, to full trade and arms embargoes—will provide viable mechanisms between diplomatic and military actions that can help to achieve these goals. Such an effort will require engagement by all nations, not isolationism, and a commitment to live by the increasingly mature body of law that will develop as we move into the next century.

In this volume, *Economic Sanctions: Panacea or Peacebuilding in a Post–Cold War World?* George Lopez and David Cortright have brought together a group of academics and policy analysts whose work provides a most welcome addition and stimulus to contemporary thinking on these important problems. The authors herein do not always agree on the effectiveness or utility of sanctions regimes, nor do they all agree on the modalities of implementation. Nevertheless, they provide thoughtful and informed analysis on many past and several current sanctions episodes. And they agree that there must be more nonmilitary and less violent, indeed nonviolent, and more effective solutions to the fundamental challenges facing our new world. Serious scholarship regarding such solutions, of which sanctions are a part, is essential to our future. This book advances that agenda and challenges other scholars and policymakers to do likewise.

Ronald V. Dellums
U.S. House of Representatives

Acknowledgments

Because the material included in this volume comprises part of a larger project on economic sanctions involving dozens of experts, we have accumulated many debts in producing this book. First, we would like to thank a number of people who provided financial support for a systematic investigation of the scope, impact, and utility of economic sanctions. These include Kennette Benedict of the John D. and Catherine T. MacArthur Foundation, whose generous grant in the spring of 1993 financed a large part of this project's first phase. George Perkovich of the W. Alton Jones Foundation provided support for the second phase of this effort in which we studied sanctions as a potential tool for the control of weapons of mass destruction. Tom Graham of the Rockefeller Foundation supported a series of visiting scholars to the Joan B. Kroc Institute for International Peace Studies who have investigated the utility of sanctions for denuclearization in South Asia and the Middle East.

We are especially grateful to Congressman Ronald Dellums for taking the time to write the foreword of this book.

The authors of the chapters of this volume have also been particularly cooperative and understanding. Because our goal was to bring research and policy concerns together, we pushed academic scholars to be more sensitive to policy concerns and urged practitioners to be more grounded in academic research. The sound mix of these approaches evident in the book results in no small measure from the authors' efforts to be self-conscious in this matter. Because of their involvement in the ongoing debate about sanctions in Iraq, Haiti, and the former Yugoslavia, a number of the authors were in faraway locales as we were editing their manuscripts. They performed herculean feats, sometimes under adverse circumstances, in revising and rechecking their chapters. To each we owe a special debt of thanks.

Our colleagues at the Joan B. Kroc Institute for International Peace Studies, at *The Bulletin of the Atomic Scientists,* and at the Fourth Freedom Forum deserve special note. Raimo Väyrynen, director of the Kroc Institute, and institute fellows Patricia Davis, Robert C. Johansen, and Alan Dowty have provided a challenging and supportive environment for this project. Our work was greatly aided by the logistical support and organizational skills of Becky Loggins and Midge Holleman at the Kroc Institute and Jennifer Glick, Ann Miller, and Miriam Redsecker at the Fourth Freedom Forum. Bibliographic research and the editing of chapters for the special issue of *The Bulletin* and this volume were skillfully performed by Notre Dame graduate students Jaleh Dashti-Gibson, Abir Khater, and Brenda Markovitz. Special recognition goes to Laura Gerber of Goshen College, who interned at the Fourth Freedom Forum and did an enormous amount of reference work for the entire book, especially the chapters on Haiti, Yugoslavia, and South Africa.

We are grateful as well to Mike Moore, editor of *The Bulletin of the Atomic Scientists,* and his staff for their editing and production of the November 1993 special issue, "Sanctions: Do They Work?" which gave prompt dissemination to the abridged versions of eight of these chapters. Reactions from *The Bulletin* readers to that issue and continued interaction of the editors and the authors of essays helped us crystallize what we wanted to accomplish in a full scholarly volume on sanctions. This is a better book because of Mike's and *The Bulletin*'s emphasis on policy concerns.

This volume could not have come to fruition without the diligent work of Jennifer Glick, who transformed the chapters and our editorial comments into a serious manuscript and then labored over the development of the camera-ready version to ensure prompt production of the book. Her patience with us and chapter authors was exceeded only by her professional competence. Ann Miller, administrative director of the Forum, handled a plethora of tasks and worked with people across continents to secure their full participation in the project. Last, but certainly not least, Mr. Howard Brembeck, founder and chairman of the Forum, provided continuous moral and financial support throughout this venture. We hope that this volume serves as a worthy affirmation of his vision that sanctions are a potentially powerful tool for resolving conflict and promoting norms in the emerging international order.

With so many talented people associated with such a project, it is difficult to admit that there are some flaws and gaps in this volume. We as editors know there are and we accept responsibility for whatever shortcomings the volume may have. Because serious scholarship and policy analysis about sanctions seem particularly difficult to find in recent years, especially when compared to the dominance of sanctions in contemporary thinking and policy about post–Cold War actions, we believe the chapters in this volume represent a solid contribution to increasing the quality of that thinking and policy.

David Cortright and George A. Lopez
Notre Dame, Indiana

About the Contributors

Bashir Al-Samarrai, past research associate at the Center of Middle Eastern Studies at the University of Chicago, lectures frequently on the Middle East and is a member of the Iraqi Democratic Opposition.

Drew Christiansen, S.J., is director of the Office of International Justice and Peace of the U.S. Catholic Conference. He is coeditor of *Morals and Might: Ethics and the Use of Force in Modern International Affairs* (1995).

David Cortright is a visiting faculty fellow at the Joan B. Kroc Institute for International Peace Studies at the University of Notre Dame and is president of the Fourth Freedom Forum, Goshen, Ind.

Jennifer Davis, a native South African, is director of the American Committee on Africa and The Africa Fund.

Ronald V. Dellums has served in the U.S. Congress since 1971, represents California's 9th Congressional District, and has been the chair of the House Armed Services Committee.

Lloyd (Jeff) Dumas is professor of economics and political economy at the University of Texas, Dallas, and has written extensively on issues of national and international security.

Ivan Eland, the principal author of the Government Accounting Office report *Economic Sanctions: Effectiveness as Tools of Foreign Policy* (1992) is a former staff member of the House Foreign Affairs Committee. He is currently on the staff of the Congressional Budget Office.

Kimberly Ann Elliott is a research associate at the Institute for International Economics in Washington, DC, and the coauthor of *Economic Sanctions Reconsidered* (1990).

Dmitry G. Evstafiev is a research fellow at the Center for International Security of the U.S.A. and Canada Institute in Moscow. He has written a number of papers and articles on the issues of regional security, economic sanctions, military-political developments in the Middle East, and ethnic and subethnic conflicts in post-Soviet Eurasia.

Christopher C. Joyner is professor of government at Georgetown University and has published extensively on the legal implications of using force in foreign policy. Currently he is director of the American Society of International Law's project on the United Nations and the International Legal Order.

William H. Kaempfer is associate chair of the Department of Economics at the University of Colorado, Boulder, and a fellow at the Center for Economic Policy Studies at the Claremont Graduate School. He is coauthor of *International Economic Sanctions: A Public Choice Perspective* (1992)

Alexander Konovalov is the director of the Center for Military Policy and System Analyses at the U.S.A. and Canada Institute in Moscow, and is the chairman of the advisory board of the Center for National Security Problems and International Relations, an independent consulting organization.

Sonja Licht is cochair of the Helsinki Citizens' Assembly, the director of the Soros Yugoslavia Foundation in Belgrade, and is a grantee of the Research and Writing Program of the John D. and Catherine T. MacArthur Foundation.

George A. Lopez is faculty fellow and professor of government and international studies at the Joan B. Kroc Institute for International Peace Studies at the University of Notre Dame. He is coeditor of *Morals and Might: Ethics and the Use of Force in Modern International Affairs* (1995).

Anton D. Lowenberg is professor of economics at California State University, Northridge and coauthor of *International Economic Sanctions: A Public Choice Perspective* (1992). He has published extensively in the areas of sanctions, apartheid, economic regulations, and constitutional economics.

James C. Ngobi is secretary of the United Nations Sanctions Committees and has been with the United Nations in various capacities since 1965.

Sergey Oznobistchev is director of the Center for International Security of the U.S.A. and Canada Institute in Moscow, and is deputy director of the Center for National Security and International Relations of the Parliament of the Russian Federation. He is the author of several works on defense and disarmament.

Jack T. Patterson is director of the Conflict Resolution Program of the New York Metropolitan Regional Office of the American Friends Service Committee (AFSC) and was a member of the AFSC working group on international economic sanctions.

Gerard F. Powers is foreign policy advisor for the U.S. Catholic Conference and has published articles on the use of force in Central America and Iraq, the right to self-determination, and the role of religion in the conflicts in Northern Ireland and former Yugoslavia.

David E. Reuther is a career foreign service officer with 24 years of experience in East Asian and Middle East issues. The coordinator of U.S. policy toward Iraq and Iran from 1991-93, he is currently a country director in the office of the Secretary of Defense in the Pentagon.

Claudette Antoine Werleigh is the former minister of social affairs of the Haitian government and was advisor to the Prime Minister of the interim Haitian government in 1991. She is the former director of the

Washington Office on Haiti and is currently the minister of foreign affairs for the Haitian government.

Susan L. Woodward is a visiting fellow at the Brookings Institution and a former national fellow at the Hoover Institution. She is currently working on a book on the Yugoslav civil war as a paradigm for future conflicts.

Economic Sanctions

PART ONE

International and National Experiences with Sanctions

1

Economic Sanctions in Contemporary Global Relations

George A. Lopez and David Cortright

Economic sanctions have been integral to the repertoire of coercive foreign policy measures for centuries. Throughout this time, the imposition of sanctions has involved the dynamic interaction between the policies of implementation and maintenance, on the one hand, and various political and economic calculations of effectiveness on the other. As interstate commerce expanded and the technology of war placed a premium on control of the seas, scholars, advisors to kings, and international jurists formulated theories, strategies, and policies for waging various forms of economic coercion.[1] With each new episode of trade-based diplomacy, new concepts and frameworks of interstate relations and economic thought developed. These concepts and theoretical frameworks had a dual purpose: to describe and evaluate current actions and to prescribe how more effective economic actions might be undertaken in the future.[2]

In the post–Cold War world, the prominence of economic sanctions as a tool of national and multinational diplomacy has increased.[3] Yet descriptions, evaluations, and prescriptions of their place in the new international environment have been much less apparent. Some of this disparity between application and analysis can be attributed to the unprecedented pace and diversity of sanctions episodes. This is illustrated in a series of recent international events that epitomize both the potential and the pitfalls of sanctions use.

In 1992 the United States began a halfhearted policy of invoking sanctions against the military dictatorship of Raoul Cedras in Haiti. By spring and summer of 1994 international and regional pressure pushed the U.S. and the United Nations Security Council to tighten the sanctions and set deadlines for the departure of the junta. At the same time, the U.S.

threatened serious sanctions against North Korea for refusing to permit full inspection of suspected nuclear weapons activities. In Haiti, sanctions fell short of their goal of overthrowing the dictatorship and ultimately were combined with coercive "gunboat" diplomacy to return democratically elected President Jean-Bertrand Aristide to power. In North Korea, a combination of the threat of economic sanctions, high-level diplomacy and a series of technological and economic incentives (what some have called "positive sanctions") led to an agreement that greatly reduced the likelihood of new nuclear weapons production.

Contemporary with these events, debate was renewed about the U.S. embargo against Cuba. Following a tightening of sanctions by the U.S. Congress through passage of the so-called Cuban Democracy Act, the General Assembly of the United Nations voted overwhelmingly to condemn the U.S. action. Despite dramatic economic dislocation in Cuba and the imminent demise of Fidel Castro's rule, U.S. officials maintained that the thirty year embargo would remain firmly in place. In Iraq pressure mounted for an easing of the U.N. embargo. Despite a brief show of force near the Kuwaiti border in October 1994 that raised fears of new military confrontations, Iraq officially recognized the sovereignty and redrawn borders of its neighbor to the south. This Iraqi concession followed a flurry of diplomatic visits by Moscow.

During this time the first black President of South Africa, Nelson Mandela, completed a tour of the United States and gave addresses before both the U.S. Congress and the United Nations General Assembly. Among a number of themes Mandela emphasized, none was more pronounced than his plea that the U.S. and the international community reverse decades of economic sanctions against South Africa and sustain his fledgling majority-rule democracy with an influx of investment, trade, and aid.

Unlike the dynamic linkage between sanctions theory and policy in earlier historical periods, contemporary scholarship and policy analysis lags behind the current plethora of sanctions episodes. Our knowledge of the full ramifications of sanctions use is incomplete. Scholars and policymakers readily acknowledge that judgements about current sanctions cases are made on the basis of ill-defined generalizations. The dearth of detailed analysis of the intricacies involved in imposing sanctions leaves ambiguity and uncertainty. Are sanctions a panacea for coping with the challenges of the post–Cold War world, or an effective tool for a new era of international peacebuilding?

Sanctions as Post–Cold War Policy

With the creation of the League of Nations and then the United Nations, economic sanctions took on new importance in international affairs. The imposition of sanctions is structured directly into the UN Charter as one central means by which the organization and its member states can respond to military aggression or other charter violations. Sanctions are meant to provide a serious and harm-inflicting response to aggression, while also serving as an alternative to collective military force that is considerably stronger than mere diplomatic protest. During the super-power-dominated Cold War era, the pattern of sanctions use was striking. Of the more than sixty sanctions cases between 1945 and 1990, a rate averaging better than one new action per year, more than two-thirds were initiated and maintained by the United States. Three-quarters of these cases involved unilateral U.S. action without the participation of other countries. In the first four decades of the United Nations, multilateral sanctions were imposed by the UN only twice, against Southern Rhodesia in 1966 and against South Africa in 1977.

Since 1990 the pattern of sanctions use has changed. The number of episodes has increased, and all the major cases have been multilateral, usually under the auspices of the UN. The Security Council has approved partial or comprehensive sanctions against Iraq, former Yugoslavia, Libya, Somalia, Liberia, the Khmer Rouge-held areas of Cambodia, and Haiti. This trend toward multilateralism has coincided with a reduction in the resort to unilateral sanctions. Several factors account for these developments. First and foremost, the end of the Cold War has created significant new possibilities for cooperative security arrangements. The threat of great power veto has diminished, and the prospects for concerted action to respond to serious threats to peace, or to affirm shared international norms, has increased. Foreign policy in the United States and Russia in particular has been freed from Cold War constraints, allowing a more cooperative, less ideological approach to international security challenges.

Another factor bolstering the recent use of sanctions has been the enormous increase in the volume of international trade. The annual level of world exports has increased from $134 billion in 1960 to $3.94 trillion by 1992.[4] These figures are likely to grow as the once centrally managed economies of former communist countries become more integrated into the global trading system. Because the nations of the world are more deeply involved in trade, they are more vulnerable to discontinuities in these exchanges resulting from sanctions. On the other hand, as Kimberly Elliott notes in her contribution to this volume, the increase in global trade and economic interdependence also means that more states must agree to comply with sanctions if they are to be effective.

Increased sanctions use also reflects a preference among citizens and policymakers for alternatives to the use of military force. Although this is certainly not a universally held belief, many now recognize that the destructiveness of modern warfare reduces its attractiveness as a means of redressing grievances. Economic sanctions serve as a less-destructive alternative generally and are less likely to provoke a dangerous military counterstrike. Further, the international community has become more concerned with the manner in which violations of widely held international norms, such as nuclear nonproliferation or the protection of human rights, comprise a threat to peace. The willingness to use sanctions is further sustained by a new recognition that the concept of absolute sovereignty enshrined in the traditional Westphalian system has gradually eroded.[5]

Finally, these noticeable trends are reinforced by some realities that are less easily recognized. Sanctions permit nations with quite different foreign policy views a kind of "minimax" opportunity to forge a shared policy response in crises where they might otherwise disagree. Sanctions give national leaders the ability to "do something," while allowing them to refrain from high-risk engagements that might result if more aggressive foreign policy tools were used.

Sanctions also serve as a means for revitalizing the United Nations. At one level they provide the Security Council with various opportunities to forge a consensus on collective action. Over time such consensus building will strengthen the council. Moreover, sanctions fit comfortably within the UN structure for handling disputes and threats to peace as understood in the charter. By providing a graduated and escalatory response to conflict, but in a softer, nonmilitary mode, sanctions fit the lofty ideals of the United Nations as peacekeeper and peacemaker.[6]

What Do We Know About Sanctions?

Despite the increased resort to sanctions and their growing appeal in the 1990s, many questions remain about their utility. As one summary document of a recent conference on economic sanctions noted, "clearly, sanctions are not a tool for all seasons."[7] For what ends and under what conditions should sanctions be employed? What factors account for their success or failure? How can national leaders translate the economic impact of sanctions, that which harms a target nation's economy, into political success, producing new and more acceptable behavior in that nation?

These questions are not new to scholarly investigators, nor are they different from what policymakers seek to know. In response to the multilateral sanctions imposed on racist regimes in southern Africa and the series of U.S.–directed sanctions that continued into the 1980s (e.g., Cuba, the Soviet Union, Vietnam, Iran), a serious literature developed to provide the foundation of much of the thinking (and some empirical generalization) that can inform answers to the queries posed above.[8] These studies were given added weight by the theoretical insights provided by David Baldwin's 1985 classic, *Economic Statecraft*.[9] Both Baldwin's work and the resurgence of sanctions in the post–Cold War era stimulated a series of more recent studies.[10]

From this body of research, which now spans more than a quarter of a century, we can glean a set of central controversies and findings. The bottom-line question for many policy elites has always been, "do sanctions work?" The response of the researchers has been diverse, cautious, and qualified. Nincic and Wallensteen summarize the conventional view that generally, "the effectiveness of economic sanctions seems rather doubtful."[11] Margaret Doxey, the dean of sanctions studies, states emphatically that "sanctions will not succeed in drastically altering the foreign and military policy of the target."[12] Even scholars of the world-order school remain skeptical, as Richard Falk concedes, "the difficulty with sanctions is that they cannot be effective, or that it is hard to make them effective."[13] Yet the major empirical study in the field, undertaken by Hufbauer, Schott, and Elliott at the Institute for International Economics (IIE), shows a success rate among all sanctions cases of 34 percent.[14] Analysts may be cautious about sanctions because they consider this rate simply too low.

We believe that sanctions success rates would be more credible (and that such rates might even increase) if analysts gave greater attention to the purposes for which sanctions are imposed and were more clear about what constitutes success. As Alan Dowty has noted, "the 'success' of sanctions depends on what goals they are measured against."[15] To their credit, the IIE analysts distinguished success rates of sanctions across diverse primary goals.[16] But even with this qualification, their study failed to recognize that sanctions may have important goals beyond those embodied in the instrumental outcome. Sanctions often serve multiple purposes, each of which needs to be assessed when calculating impact. The official or publicly declared purpose of sanctions, usually defined as a specific policy change in the targeted state, is often considered the primary goal.[17] Yet other objectives can always be identified, among them establishing deterrence, demonstrating resolve to allies or domestic constituents, and sending symbolic messages.[18]

The dominant focus of sanctions literature has been on primary goals, in the narrow sense, and only on the success of the instrumental objectives. In the case of the initial sanctions against Iraq, the primary goal was to force Saddam Hussein to withdraw from Kuwait. In the case of U.S.–led sanctions against Libya, the goal has been to coerce the Qaddafi government to extradite the individuals who allegedly engaged in airline terrorism. If the analysis of the effectiveness of sanctions remains literal regarding primary goals, then sanctions do indeed have limited effectiveness. The record demonstrates that by themselves sanctions are seldom able to roll back military aggression, have limited ability to impair a targeted regime, and never are able to topple a dictator. This reality has led the U.S. General Accounting Office to conclude that "the primary goal of sanctions is usually the most difficult to achieve."[19]

Such assessments are not without their flaws, however. For example, in the IIE study, the sanctions imposed against South Africa were not rated as successful because the declared primary goal of ending apartheid was not achieved. In 1990, when the second edition of the study was undertaken, such a judgment might have seemed reasonable. Yet a more nuanced examination clearly shows that sanctions, which had begun to toughen in the early 1980s, made major contributions to fundamental political change within South Africa by the end of the decade. From this perspective, the sanctions imposed against the white South African regime can be judged a partial and important success. Further, because these changes in South Africa then set the stage for other internal events that led to the dismantling of apartheid—three years after the IIE study was published in its second edition—one might judge the sanctions as a qualified, albeit indirect and slow, success.

Measuring the effectiveness of other purposes of sanctions is equally difficult. The U.S. grain embargo against the Soviet Union following the 1979 invasion of Afghanistan was designed, in part, to deter further Soviet encroachments against the more strategic regions of Iran, Pakistan, and the Persian Gulf. Similarly, whatever primary message the UN community has sought to send to Serbian authorities directly about their aggression in the Yugoslav civil conflict, a further meaning of the ongoing sanctions is that such aggression would not be tolerated against Kosovo and Macedonia. Without engaging in a logical fallacy, it is difficult to posit the effectiveness of the deterrent message of sanctions in either of these cases. That a particular objectionable policy was not pursued by a target simply cannot serve as proof of the instrument's effectiveness. But the temptation to recognize the sanctions potential here is a strong one, especially in policy circles.

The symbolic and signaling goals of sanctions may be the simplest to understand, yet they also elude easy analytical evaluation. When a leader joins in imposing sanctions to satisfy domestic concerns that the nation "do something," public opinion polls can be used to determine whether such a policy is successful. When sanctions are meant as a signal of international disapproval of a particular regime or support for an international norm being violated, leaders can often cite the solidarity of many states in imposing sanctions as a manifestation of success.[20] Yet because these criteria are often subjective and imprecise, a clear definition of success is difficult to obtain.

While recognizing the uncertainties involved in such assessment issues, we believe that the scholarly literature offers a number of empirical findings about sanctions that shed light on policy options and that now must be scrutinized in a post–Cold War environment. Historically, sanctions achieve their economic goal (i.e., they have an impact that damages the target economy) when:

- the cost of the sanctions to the target economy exceeds 2 percent of the GNP;
- there is a large economic size differential between the primary sender and the target (a GNP ratio of ten to one);
- there exists a high total trade concentration for the target with the sender (greater than 25 percent of target's total trade);
- they are imposed quickly, with maximum harshness and with the full cooperation of those trading partners who otherwise might circumvent such restrictions;
- the ongoing cost of sanctions to the senders is low.[21]

Related to these empirical generalizations are other trends of interest. Sanctions which involve primarily financial restrictions, such as the freezing of loans and assets held in foreign banks, have a higher political success rate (41 percent) than do the more widely imposed trade sanctions (25 percent).[22] The forms of economic pressure that are most likely to produce the desired political changes within the target government are those that can be effectively targeted against the economic groups which benefit from that regime's existing policies. When elite groups feel the pinch they are more likely to lobby for political change and may even help orchestrate it.[23]

Regarding the time necessary for sanctions to be effective, the cases of the last forty years show that sanctions take nearly three years to achieve their political goal.[24] Analysts are quick to point out, however, that the greatest impact of sanctions economically (and thus by extension politically) occurs in the first year.[25]

Despite these empirical generalizations, recent experience shows that even when economic sanctions devastate a target economy, this does not guarantee that the desired political changes will result. Compliance and changed behavior are difficult to achieve through the exclusive use of sanctions, particularly if it is assumed that the leaders of the targeted state will behave "rationally" as defined by the states that impose sanctions. This tension between the political dilemma and the economic reality of sanctions means that many of the answers to essential questions about sanctions remain uncertain, and in need of further analysis.

The Essays in This Volume

The diverse cases of sanctions use in the post–Cold War era provide a rich body of experience for evaluating the conclusions and generalizations drawn from earlier work. Each new sanctions episode raises anew the myriad dilemmas associated with the use of the instrument in the past. These range from the traditional difficulty of ensuring the necessary international cooperation to maintain the sanctions, to doubts about their economic and political effectiveness, to debates regarding the "morality" of sanctions, i.e., how to protect innocent civilians from the harm of sanctions, while maintaining the pressure needed to exert pressure on decision makers in the target country.

The essays in this volume take aim at these core issues and provide essential detail regarding these and other aspects of the imposition of economic sanctions in the post–Cold War world. In this initial section of the book we include three complementary essays on the experience of sanctions from national and international vantage points. Mr. James Ngobi, Secretary to the United Nations Sanctions Committees, sketches the historical and legal dimensions of UN sanctions activities and analyzes their strengths and weaknesses in a variety of the cases in which they have been in force in the 1990s. Ngobi clearly demonstrates that we have entered an era in which a sanctions regime has emerged. This places a premium on the need for carefully defined principles to guide sanctions imposition, monitoring, and evaluation. This new regime also begs for additional means to strengthen the institutional capacity of the UN and other agencies tasked with carrying out this policy.

In the next chapter, Ivan Eland, former sanctions analyst for the General Accounting Office, examines how the foreign policy and domestic goals of sanctions often diverge from one another, thus making powerful nations rather unpredictable in their use of sanctions. Eland poses succinctly the inherent tension in the political and economic dimensions of sanctions. Whereas past sanctions studies are correct in demonstrating that swiftly imposed, coordinated sanctions produce the greatest economic impact, policy elites may be more likely to opt for graduated sanctions, including the use of threat and then delivery of stiffer sanctions later, because this approach has greater political payoffs at home and in the target state. Eland's particular insight regarding the latter is persuasive: escalating sanctions slowly minimizes the rally-around-the-flag impact of sanctions in the target, while providing time for the imposing state(s) to assist local opposition groups within the target nation to mount an internal campaign against the practices that led to sanctions.

The chapter by Sergey Oznobistchev and his colleagues Alexander Konovalov and Dmitry Evstafiev at the Center for National Security of the USA–Canada Institute in Moscow explores the ambivalence and caution evident in current Russian thinking about sanctions. The experience of Russian history, both in its Soviet and pre-Soviet periods, raises skepticism about situations where economically powerful states use sanctions to bring about changes in the internal politics of a target state. Recent Russian foreign policy adopts a rather strict view of sanctions. Sanctions should be only one of a number of available UN–initiated mechanisms for reducing conflict and defusing crises. They should be imposed during extraordinary situations rather than as routine instruments of diplomacy. Any imposition of sanctions should clearly specify a set of conditions or behaviors which, when achieved, lead to the immediate removal of such sanctions. This latter perspective helps to explain why Russia favors a lifting of sanctions against long-time targets of UN action, such as Iraq.

In Part Two of the book, contributors explore a number of controversies surrounding sanctions. In Chapter Five Kimberly Elliott provides a thorough analysis of the work she and her colleagues at the IIE have undertaken. She also poses penetrating questions regarding sanctions in the 1990s. Elliott believes that a combination of the end of the Cold War and increasing global interdependence signals the end of unilateral sanctions as effective means of coercion. Yet it remains uncertain whether this new era bolsters or stifles the prospects for multilateral cooperation in the use of sanctions. Elliott's observation that sanctions in the post–Cold War world require subtlety, skill, and creativity in their formulation and implementation is an essential recommendation for policymakers.

In Chapter Six William Kaempfer and Anton Lowenberg, two economists of the "public choice" school, discuss the economic conditions associated with the success of sanctions. They also differentiate rather clearly between the manner in which sanctions can work to accomplish their economic objectives (i.e., how sanctions decrease wealth in the target country) and yet not achieve their political objectives. Kaempfer and Lowenberg also point out, in situations as diverse as the sanctions against South Africa and the former Soviet Union in the 1980s, that all of the economic clout that might be gained by the immediate and full imposition of sanctions can be dissipated through the incrementalism of policymakers who fear the domestic political repercussions that may result when sanctions pinch economic interests in their own nation.

In the next chapter Christopher Joyner of Georgetown University builds on themes presented in the Ngobi chapter to assess the political and economic effectiveness of sanctions against the backdrop of international law. Joyner emphasizes what policymakers and scholars often overlook: the balance sheet on sanctions success is quite good. While sanctions have not been successful in overthrowing dictators (a point mentioned by Ivan Eland as well), the success rate of 34 percent noted by Elliott and her colleagues is at least as high as that of military interventions in the Cold War era. Moreover, sanctions that fall short of their full objectives nonetheless can still produce modest policy changes and may lead to further negotiation. Of critical importance for Joyner is that sanctions are an orderly tool of national and international law that can control the escalation of force as a means of resolving conflict. Sanctions are an approach to enforcement in which international law and emerging norms are sustained.

Particularly unique in this section are two chapters which analyze the consequences of sanctions through an ethical lens. This is a theme increasingly prevalent in policy discussions, but one which to date has been absent in serious scholarly analysis of sanctions.[26] Jack Patterson of the American Friends Service Committee and Drew Christiansen, S. J., and Gerard Powers of the U.S. Catholic Conference present complementary frameworks for assessing when and whether sanctions are hurting innocent people in a target state, and what actions can be taken to protect the innocent.

Patterson's discussion emerges from the experience of the Quakers in supporting and continually evaluating (sometimes reevaluating) sanctions in a diverse set of situations, most especially in South Africa and Iraq. From this empirical base, Patterson asks a series of perplexing questions, the most important of which may be how national and international action can ensure that sanctions provide the possibility of bringing about the desired change in the target while also being a realistic alternative to war. Patterson's message is clear: sanctions should constitute "a threshold for peace," not a "trap door for war."

Powers and Christiansen examine the ethical dimensions of sanctions through the application of the theological understandings of the just-war doctrine. The authors work through a number of difficult issues, among them how sanctions must be responsive to the notion of civilian immunity and the obligation of sanctioning nations to meet the basic human needs of the population in the target country. Powers and Christiansen do not shy away from the reality that sanctions often involve powerful economic actors imposing their desires on weaker states. They establish a set of criteria that sanctions policy must meet if it is to be judged morally acceptable rather than a cover for big power coercion. In the final analysis the authors are cautiously optimistic that a morally legitimate sanctions regime can be achieved. This demands an honest confrontation with basic moral questions, however, the most central of which is whether achieving the goal of sanctions compensates for their inevitable (even if unintended) harmful effects on innocent and vulnerable populations within the target nation.

Part Three examines specific sanctions cases of the 1990s, focusing on conflicts in Iraq, the former Yugoslavia, and Haiti. The final chapter of this section provides an analysis of the role of sanctions in bringing about the beginnings of political change in South Africa. Each of these essays provides invaluable insights for both policy and scholarly analysis.

The question of how sanctions may differentially impact a leader and a population is addressed in contrasting analyses of the Iraqi situation. David Reuther, who served in the Northern Gulf Affairs division of the U.S. State Department during the Persian Gulf crisis, outlines the recent and past U.S. government position toward Iraq and why sanctions have been maintained even years after the Persian Gulf War. Somewhat in opposition, Bashir Al-Samarrai of the Iraqi Democratic Coalition calls for a reexamination of sanctions against Iraq. Two essential elements in Al-Samarrai's analysis should give pause to UN decision makers: (1) the ineffectiveness of sanctions in loosening Saddam Hussein's grip on power, and (2) the devastating impact they have had on the quality of life of the Iraqi people.

The theme of how to exert coercive pressure on government leaders without harming innocent people also pervades the two chapters devoted to sanctions against the former Yugoslavia. In Chapter Twelve Susan Woodward of the Brookings Institution offers a complex but compelling argument. While the intentions of the UN in imposing sanctions against former Yugoslavia may have been worthy, the evidence suggests that these sanctions reinforced the causes of war in that disintegrating state and sustained the power of the very leaders they were meant to coerce. In her chapter, Sonja Licht of the Soros Foundation in Belgrade provides additional evidence in support of Woodward's analysis. Licht demonstrates how the economic scarcities that developed as a result of sanctions permitted the Milosevic regime to thrive on the growing economic chaos and poverty and to tighten its hold on power. Economic deprivation and international isolation of Serbia made it practically impossible for local groups opposed to Milosevic and the continued war to argue against either as an acceptable future for Serbia.

In Chapter Fourteen Claudette Werleigh, foreign minister of the democratic government of Haiti, assesses whether sanctions contributed to the return of democracy in Haiti. She provides a damning portrayal of what must be considered a classic case of a sanctions-based policy being stillborn. From the beginning sanctions were imposed incrementally and halfheartedly, first by the Organization of American States, then by the U.S. and the UN. Sanctioning states did not tighten the embargo in a serious way until the summer of 1994. The preferred option of targeting economic pressures on the elite through a freeze of overseas financial assets was not employed until the very end of the crisis. At the last hour a "failed policy" of sanctions gave way to a negotiated interposition of U.S. troops to return Jean-Bertrand Aristide to power.

A much different tale about sanctions unfolds in Chapter Fifteen. Jennifer Davis of the American Committee on Africa provides a scintillating analysis of the dynamic interaction that occurred among private, nongovernmental and governmental organizations within and outside of South Africa to mobilize economic sanctions against the apartheid regime. This case raises the important issue of how to apply economic pressures in a manner that empowers local political groups who oppose the objectionable policy or situation. The Balkans case demonstrates that unless such sensitivity and empowerment become part of sanctions policy, local opposition groups will be isolated and delegitimized through the rally-around-the-flag effect in the target state. In South Africa, by contrast, the international divestment and sanctions campaign provided crucial support for the ultimately successful struggle of the African National Congress and its allies for a nonracial democracy.

In the final part of the book two chapters explore the future of sanctions. Lloyd (Jeff) Dumas argues for the creation of a new UN Council on Economic Sanctions and Peacekeeping to maximize the chances that sanctions imposed by the UN will achieve their stated goals. Dumas' proposal calls for an operating agency that would both monitor compliance of states when sanctions are imposed and assess the effect of sanctions on both the targeted elites and the general population. Regarding the latter, the proposed agency would be particularly sensitive to the adverse humanitarian consequences of sanctions and would be better able than any current mechanism to recommend action to the UN and other bodies when civilian hardship develops.

In our concluding chapter we explore areas where scholarship and policy making should converge to produce a greater understanding of sanctions use. First is the need for a more sophisticated analysis of the context, both domestic and international, in which sanctions are being employed. We also urge a more serious examination of the various methods for improving sanctions effectiveness—in both their political and economic sense. Perhaps most importantly, we recommend that policymakers give greater emphasis to the use of carrots rather than sticks, positive sanctions rather than negative ones. Such incentives are less well understood than sanctions, but they may be more effective as a means of ensuring compliance with international norms and standards of behavior.

Notes

1. A succinct review of the use of economic warfare and coercion since the Seven Years' War can be found in Tor Egil Førland, "The History of Economic Warfare: International law, Effectiveness, Strategies," *Journal of Peace Research,*

Vol. 30, No. 2, pp. 151–62; and Stephen C. Neff, "Boycott and the Law of Nations: Economic Warfare and Modern International law in Historical Perspective," in Ian Brownlie and D. W. Bowett, eds., *The British Yearbook of International law, 1988* (Oxford: Oxford University Press, 1989), pp. 135–45.

2. Although less than a decade has passed since its publication, the classic analysis of this interaction between economic thought and economic policy is found in David A. Baldwin, *Economic Statecraft* (Princeton, New Jersey: Princeton University Press, 1985), especially Chapters 4 and 5.

3. Throughout this chapter our working definition of sanctions parallels that of scholars. We consider economic sanctions to be essentially a coercive foreign policy action of a nation(s) in which it (they) intentionally suspends customary economic relations such as trade and/or financial exchanges in order to prompt the targeted nation to change its policy or behavior. Such sanctions and the desired behavior of the target are publicly announced. See Margaret P. Doxey, *Economic Sanctions and International Enforcement* (New York: Oxford University Press, 1980), pp. 1–4; and Miroslav Nincic and Peter Wallensteen, eds., *Dilemmas of Economic Coercion: Sanctions in World Politics* (New York: Praeger, 1983), pp. 3–5.

4. Statistical Department of the United Nations, *International Trade Statistics Yearbook*, Vol. 1 (New York: The United Nations, 1992).

5. Discussions on this issue abound, but some of the best clarification of the changing understandings of sovereignty and what these fluid views mean for international cooperation in processes such as the imposition of sanctions can be found in Jarat Chopra and Thomas G. Weiss, "Sovereignty is No Longer Sacrosanct: Codifying Humanitarian Intervention," *Ethics and International Affairs*, Vol. 6 (1992), pp. 95–118; R.B.J. Walker and Saul H. Mendlovitz, eds., *Contending Sovereignties: Redefining Political Communities* (Boulder: Lynne Rienner Publishers, Inc., 1990); Kurt Mills, *The New Sovereignty: The Changing Humanitarian Agenda in the Emerging Global Order* unpublished dissertation (University of Notre Dame: January 1995); and Lori Fisler Damrosch and David J. Scheffer, eds., *Law and Force in the New International Order* (Boulder: Westview Press, 1991), especially part three on intervention.

6. The distinction among these terms as part of the political environment of the post–Cold War world was defined by UN Secretary-General Boutros Boutros-Ghali in *An Agenda for Peace* (New York: The United Nations, 1992). The 'soft' or 'idealist' side of sanctions has drawn some serious criticism. See, for example, M. S. Daoudi and M.S. Dajani, *Economic Sanctions: Ideals and Experience* (London: Routledge & Kegan, 1983).

7. The Stanley Foundation, *Political Symbol or Policy Tool? Making Sanctions Work. Report of the Twenty-Fourth United Nations Issues Conference*, The Stanley Foundation, February 19–21, 1993, p. 9.

8. While a full listing of these critical sources is available in the bibliography, the most influential of this period are Doxey, *Economic Sanctions and International Enforcement*; Nincic and Wallensteen, *Dilemmas of Economic Coercion*; Robin Renwick, *Economic Sanctions* (Cambridge: Harvard Studies in International Affairs, 1981); James M. Lindsay, "Trade Sanctions as Policy Instruments: A Reexamination," *International Studies Quarterly*, Vol. 30, No. 2 (June 1986), pp.

153–73; Margaret P. Doxey, *International Sanctions in Contemporary Perspective* (New York: St. Martin's Press, 1987); David Leyton-Brown, ed., *The Utility of International Economic Sanctions* (New York: St. Martin's Press, 1987); and William H. Kaempfer and Anton D. Lowenberg, "The Theory of International Economic Sanctions: A Public Choice Approach," *The American Economic Review*, Vol. 78, No. 4 (September 1988), pp. 786–93.

9. Baldwin, *Economic Statecraft*.

10. Most notable among these are William H. Kaempfer and Anton D. Lowenberg, *International Economic Sanctions: A Public Choice Perspective* (Boulder: Westview Press, 1992); Patrick Clawson, "Sanctions as Punishment: Enforcement and Prelude to Further Action," *Ethics and International Affairs*, Vol. 7 (1993), pp. 17–38; and Lisa L. Martin, *Coercive Cooperation: Explaining Multilateral Economic Sanctions* (Princeton, New Jersey: Princeton University Press, 1994).

11. Nincic and Wallensteen, *Dilemmas of Economic Coercion*, p. 6.

12. Doxey, *International Sanctions*, p. 92.

13. Richard Falk, "The Use of Economic Sanctions in the Context of a Changing World Order" A paper delivered at the Conference on International Economic Sanctions in the Post–Cold War Era, Philadelphia, Pennsylvania, October 17, 1992, p. 1.

14. See Gary C. Hufbauer, Jeffrey J. Schott, and Kimberly Ann Elliott, *Economic Sanctions Reconsidered: History and Current Policy*, 2d ed. (Washington, D.C.: Institute for International Economics, 1990), p. 2.

15. Alan Dowty, "Sanctioning Iraq: The Limits of the New World Order," *The Washington Quarterly*, Vol. 17 (Summer 1994), p. 192.

16. See Hufbauer et al., *Economic Sanctions Reconsidered*, p. 93ff.

17. *Economic Sanctions: Effectiveness as Tools of Foreign Policy* (Washington, D.C.: U.S. General Accounting Office, 1993), p. 11.

18. James Barber, "Economic Sanctions as a Policy Instrument," *International Affairs*, Vol. 55, No. 3 (1979), pp. 367–84.

19. *Economic Sanctions: Effectiveness as Tools of Foreign Policy*, p. 11.

20. This reality has led Nincic and Wallensteen to observe that, "of all the ends that sanctions can plausibly be intended to promote, it is here that such policies may be most effective." Nincic and Wallensteen, *Dilemmas of Economic Coercion*, p. 8.

21. The sources for these generalizations include Hufbauer et al., *Economic Sanctions Reconsidered*, pp. 49–73; GAO, *Economic Sanctions*; Doxey, *Economic Sanctions and International Enforcement*, pp. 77–83; and Lindsay, "Trade Sanctions."

22. Hufbauer et al., *Economic Sanctions Reconsidered*, p. 63ff.

23. See Kaempfer and Lowenberg, "The Theory of International Economic Sanctions," pp. 792–93.

24. Doxey, *Economic Sanctions and International Enforcement*, p. 101.

25. Nincic and Wallensteen, *Dilemmas of Economic Coercion*, p. 109.

26. Among the latter are American Friends Service Committee, *Dollars or Bombs: The Search for Justice Through International Economic Sanctions* (Philadelphia: American Friends Service Committee, 1993); and Pax Christi International, *Economic Sanctions and International Relations* (Brussels: Pax Christi International, 1993).

2

The United Nations Experience with Sanctions

James C. Ngobi[1]

Economic sanctions have gained wide currency and attracted a great deal of attention in the international community, particularly during the last few years. There is a growing awareness that sanctions can provide an efficacious medium for promoting the commonweal of the international community through peaceful means. That would sit well with the vision of the founding fathers of the United Nations (UN). Unfortunately, one too often hears epithets such as sanctions don't work, or sanctions hurt the wrong people, or sanctions are intended only as a political token, rather than as an instrument of deliberate coercive policy. I believe that the founding fathers would cringe at this last characterization of their otherwise seriously conceived method of regulating international behavior through peaceful means. For them, sanctions were to be the last means of coercion before using force. The rationale is that the consequences of sanctions are likely to be less devastating than the injury to persons and damage to property caused by the ravages of open warfare. One has only to look at the recent proliferation of sanctions regimes to see that there is a reliance on sanctions as a viable mechanism for promoting order in the international community. In the first forty-five years of its existence, the United Nations imposed mandatory sanctions only twice. Since 1990 the Security Council has used sanctions at least six times[2] to regulate and redress the accepted norms of behavior among nations through peaceful means. The United Nations first promulgated a regime of mandatory sanctions in 1966 against the rebel United Kingdom–dependent territory of Southern Rhodesia. At the time, Rhodesia was not even a state member of the organization. In 1977 South Africa was the next country against which the Security Council imposed mandatory sanctions.

The Security Council did not resort to the use of sanctions again until the early 1990s. It imposed the first range of mandatory sanctions against Iraq in August 1990 (Resolution 661) in response to that country's invasion of neighboring Kuwait. The invasion was characterized by the council as a blatant act of aggression. In September 1991 the council established an arms embargo against former Yugoslavia (Resolution 713) by prohibiting the supply of any weapons and military equipment to any of the constituent parts of what was previously the Socialist Federal Republic of Yugoslavia. In May 1992 the council imposed various mandatory sanctions against two republics of the former Socialist Federal Republic of Yugoslavia, Serbia and Montenegro (Resolution 757), charging that those two republics were responsible for aiding and exacerbating the ethnic conflict in Bosnia and Herzegovina. In Resolution 748 (1992), the Security Council established selective mandatory sanctions against Libya (the country calls itself the Libyan Arab Jamahiriya) for the continued refusal of the government of that country to hand over certain persons resident there who are suspected of having committed criminal acts against civil transport aircraft. In Resolution 733 (1992) the Security Council established an arms embargo against Somalia by which it prohibited the supply of weapons and military equipment to that country. This action reduced the intensity of factional fighting and, hopefully, will end the devastating civil strife in that country. Similarly, in November 1992 (Resolution 788) the Security Council decreed a mandatory embargo against Liberia, a country in West Africa, where a similar civil war is currently raging. Finally, there has been a massive United Nations operation to restore order in Cambodia. In this country, ravaged by civil war, one of the factions is reneging on the agreement signed by all constituent parties. The Security Council thus adopted a resolution clearly intended for this errant faction (Resolution 792). This resolution was not, however, adopted under Chapter VII of the Charter.

Thus, since 1990 there has been a flurry of activity in the United Nations to use sanctions as a tool for regulating international behavior. One cannot rule out the possibility of yet other countries that may attract the invocation of sanctions against them in the future. Some people have attempted to explain this development as a consequence of the end of the Cold War, where the conduct of international relations has ceased to be characterized by the rivalry between superpowers and the pursuit of parochial interests by blocs of countries with opposing political or economic structures. It is worthy to note that since the beginning of the year 1990, the period when all of the new sanctions regimes have been established, the right of veto has been exercised only twice out of some 150 resolutions adopted by the Security Council, and neither of the two vetoes was directed against the establishment or expansion of the sanctions regimes. The Security Council has now come to realize that the use of sanctions is a viable last alternative to the use of military force, in conformity with the convictions of the founding members of the UN.

The Concept and Nature of Sanctions

To proceed to a methodical treatment of the topic of sanctions, it is first necessary to clearly identify the field of sanctions which concerns us. We must, therefore, consider the concept and nature of sanctions as a coercive instrument of policy and then concentrate on the most relevant of the various types of sanctions.

The idea of sanctions is probably as old as the earliest organization of human society. Many famous writers have examined the role of law in society. They have asserted that the essence of a viable legal system in an organized society is the existence of a central authority that can promulgate the law, and all members of the society ready to obey that law, with punishment to any errant members inflicted by the central authority or its agents. It is a matter of philosophical argument whether obedience to the law is prompted by the fear of punishment, or is based upon a high code of moral conduct to maintain good order in the society. Whatever it is, its result is a positive influence on the conduct of the members and the development of events in the society. The relevant question is whether these principles can be extended to apply at the international level.

Various types of sanctions can be identified. There can be unilateral or multinational sanctions. The sanctions applied against Cuba by the United States over the years are examples of unilateral measures. The sanctions established by the Coordinating Committee for Multilateral Strategic Controls (COCOM) countries to ensure nonprovision of certain classified materials or technology to the former Soviet bloc and certain other countries were an example of regional sanctions. The success of unilateral or regional sanctions depends on the degree of dependence by the target country on the country or group of countries imposing the sanctions, and on the speed and ease with which the target country can alter that dependency. For instance, Cuba at the time of Fidel Castro's rise to power, conducted almost three-quarters of its trade with the United States alone. However, within only a few years of the imposition of the United States sanctions, Cuba was able to divert virtually all of that trade to countries of the former Soviet bloc.

High stakes then are placed on multinational action for effecting a successful sanctions policy. At the international level of the United Nations, however, collective responsibility sometimes becomes an abstract concept, particularly for those states whose national interest is not threatened; the farther away they are removed from the theater and influence of events, the more they are likely to pay lip-service to calls for collective action. As evidence of this, one has only to count the number of responses received from governments to requests from the United Nations for information on the measures they have taken to carry out the mandatory measures decreed by the Security Council. It is a rare occasion when the tally rises to more than one-half the membership in the organization, and of those responding, only a small minority provides details of the measures actually put into force. Often when a dispute in question involves the interests of one or more big powers, the small powers feel inhibited to take measures that may publicly show them pitted with one big power against the other(s); in these circumstances, silence or inaction remains golden.

The Role of the Security Council

The objectives in organizing societies at national and international levels are coincident, namely to facilitate the pursuit of individual goals in an atmosphere of security, peace, and good order. Accordingly, there must be someone or some mechanism at the national level responsible for guaranteeing those conditions. Sanctions (in the modern sense of the word) take the form of punishment at the international level. Whether or not one believes in the retributive theory of punishment, the practical use of sanctions at the international level is intended to transcend such theories and focus on the preservation of peace in the society concerned.

All of the United Nations resolutions establishing mandatory multilateral sanctions are passed by the Security Council under the authority of Chapter VII of the charter. This chapter deals with threats to the peace, breaches of the peace, and acts of aggression.[3] It is for the Security Council to decide when, where, and whether such situations exist or are latent, and to decide the measures that must be employed to stop them or to forestall their occurrence. That role of the Security Council is clearly stated in Article 39 of the charter.[4] To date, the council has adopted close to fifty resolutions based on Chapter VII, and approximately half have dealt with some form of sanctions programs.

There are those who argue that the central role of the Security Council should not be used to encroach on national sovereignty, to intervene in the domestic affairs of states, or to draw in what they consider extraneous matters such as issues of human rights. They cite the protection expressed in Article 2 (7) of the charter.[5] However, the same article has an important proviso that is sometimes ignored, namely that the principle of noninterference in the domestic jurisdiction of states "shall not prejudice the application of enforcement measures under Chapter VII." It was under this proviso that the Security Council took action against South Africa for that country's policy of apartheid. As an institutionalized facet of national policy, the practice of apartheid had already been denounced by the General Assembly of the United Nations as being contrary to the charter and to the Declaration of Human Rights. Moreover, the efforts of the indigenous people of South Africa to resist apartheid often prompted the government of South Africa to mount what it regarded as preemptive strikes against certain neighboring countries under the pretext that the antiapartheid activists were being harbored or trained there with the eventual aim of infiltrating the country for subversive activities. Those strikes alone were sufficient for the Security Council to find situations that warranted measures under Chapter VII of the charter on account of their threat to international peace and security by virtue of their encroachment on other countries' national sovereignty.

The Security Council has dealt with similar situations in other areas as well. In Iraq, the council demonstrated its concern for human rights, said to be denied to the Kurds in the North and to the Shiite population in the marshlands of the South, by adopting Resolution 688 (1991) and by employing measures under the authority of previous relevant resolutions. First, the council condemned the repression of the Iraqi civilian population in many parts of the country and insisted that Iraq allow immediate access by international humanitarian organizations to all those in need of assistance in the country. Second, the Security Council established a no-fly zone by Iraqi aircraft, which the council believed were being used by Iraq to strafe the marshland areas. The straddling of Kurds and Shiite populations across the borders would have again provided sufficient ground for the Security Council to decide that a potential breach of international peace and security existed in the area, and to act accordingly.

Regarding the situation in former Yugoslavia, the Security Council often has denounced the policy of so-called ethnic cleansing and the barbaric methods used to implement it in Bosnia and Herzegovina. In fact, by Resolution 808 (1993), the Security Council established an impartial Commission of Experts to examine and analyze information about reported war crimes in former Yugoslavia, with a view for the council to establish subsequently a War Crimes Tribunal. On March 31, 1993, the Security Council adopted a new resolution (Resolution 816, 1993) authorizing the use of force to enforce its ban on unauthorized flights over the territory of Bosnia and Herzegovina. These developments, while affecting activities within the domestic jurisdiction of states, also demonstrate the increasing trend by the Security Council to effect enforcement of its decisions under a central authority, rather than leave such enforcement to the exclusive performance of individual states.

Enforcement of Sanctions

The Security Council has consistently declared or implied that the responsibility for implementing the sanctions it establishes lies with states (and international organizations, where applicable). This position probably springs from the realization that acts violating sanctions will be committed in the jurisdiction of some state, which must then investigate and/or prevent the act and deal with the guilty parties as appropriate under national laws, if so proven. This is in conformity with the principle of national sovereignty.

For most of the sanctions regimes promulgated, the Security Council also establishes a committee, usually composed of all fifteen council members, with a specific mandate. That mandate usually involves monitoring the application of the sanctions by states (and international organizations, where applicable), assisting states (and international organizations) in trying to implement the sanctions, and submitting reports to the Security Council on the progress of this implementation. The council also makes recommendations about how the implementation can be made more effective. To facilitate their work, the committees often draw up a set of guidelines, which they share with all states and international organizations for their own benefit. Much of the committees' day-to-day work consists of passing information to and from states that might help in investigating possible violations of the sanctions, and in advising states on the type of conduct or activity that might or might not violate the sanctions.

The committees conduct their business behind closed doors. There is no obsession with secrecy intended, but it has been found that open discussion of reports of suspected or actual violations of the sanctions makes states uncomfortable; they fear that the mention of such violations within their jurisdiction will immediately result in branding such states as violators of the sanctions, even before investigations of the reports have been concluded and their culpability proven or dispelled. To be shown or presented to the international community as a sanctions violator is something many states would like to avoid, even if it may require going to certain lengths to conceal such an imputation. Also, the committees try to keep the perpetrators unaware of the investigation trail after them, so that they may not tamper with incriminating evidence.

The United Nations, acting in conformity with Chapter VIII of the Charter on Regional Cooperation, also encourages sanctions implementation by regional organizations. For many years during its existence, the Security Council Committee on Sanctions against Southern Rhodesia cooperated closely with the Organization of African Unity (OAU), which had sanctions committees of its own on Southern Rhodesia and South Africa. Today the Security Council Committee on Yugoslavia is benefiting from its ever-increasing cooperation with the Commission of the European Community, the Conference on Security and Cooperation in Europe (CSCE), the North Atlantic Treaty Organization (NATO), and the Western

European Union (WEU) in monitoring and facilitating the implementation of the arms embargo against the Republics of former Yugoslavia and the general sanctions against Serbia and Montenegro. The Security Council further watches with interest the progress of the sanctions imposed by certain of the regional organizations, such as those by the Economic Organization of West African States (ECOWAS), currently in force against Liberia.

Shortcomings and Possible Improvements

What follows are several personal observations of what I consider to be the shortcomings of the sanctions programs and suggestions for some possible improvements. First, *sanctions generally should not be employed as a permanent feature of policy against any targeted country because the damage they are likely to cause to the long-term infrastructure of that country may far exceed the extent of the wrong committed.* They should be decisive and swift in producing the desired objective in the shortest possible time. The history of sanctions programs shows that many of them have been applied much too selectively, much too gradually and without immediate mechanisms to monitor their effective implementation. Such a recipe gives the targeted country enough time to make the necessary adjustments to withstand the impact of the sanctions and defeat or delay their objective.

Regarding Southern Rhodesia, the Security Council determined on November 12, 1965, that the unilateral declaration of independence by that territory's minority regime constituted a threat to international peace and security, but merely called upon states not to give it any diplomatic recognition (Resolution 216). It was not until after a year later (December 12, 1966) that the council invoked Chapter VII of the charter to impose the first range of sanctions against the rebel territory (Resolution 232). And only on May 29, 1968, did the council create a committee to monitor the implementation of the sanctions (Resolution 258). It took more years and more resolutions before the sanctions could contribute to the capitulation of the rebel regime.

In the case of South Africa, the first two Security Council Resolutions of 1963 (181 and 182) were not adopted under Chapter VII and were only voluntary. The mandatory arms embargo was imposed against South Africa on November 4, 1977 (Resolution 418), but a committee of the council to monitor the implementation of the embargo was not created until after a month later (through Resolution 421) and then only after some prodding. In more recent times, one notes that the Committee on Yugoslavia was created to monitor the arms embargo almost three months after the establishment of the embargo; the Committee on Somalia after nearly six months of establishing the arms embargo against that country; and the

Security Council has yet to create a committee to monitor the arms embargo established against Liberia on November 19, 1992. One also notes, regarding Iraq, that between August 2, 1990 and October 2, 1992 the Security Council adopted a total of twenty-three resolutions under Chapter VII. The vast majority of these resolutions have dealt with various aspects of the mandatory sanctions in force against that country.

Second, *exclusive reliance on states for imposing sanctions means that the Security Council committees do not have an independent external mechanism to implement sanctions or to verify that the investigations undertaken by governments are sufficient and conclusive.* As previously mentioned, protection of national honor may sometimes tempt governments to give little more than lip service to profound investigations that may lead to a discovery of sanctions violations. It is amazing how often the committees forward information to governments sufficient to charge companies within their borders of sanctions violations in ordinary courts of law. However, when governments report back, they declare that "after careful and thorough investigations" of the companies in question, there is no truth whatever in the allegations made. If governments were to rise above the traditional principle of sovereignty and domestic jurisdiction and accept the assistance of independent, external experts during the investigations, a large number of violations of sanctions would be avoided.

Third, *the question of retribution must be a serious claim.* The Security Council declared that Iraq's invasion of Kuwait was a deliberate act of aggression. Iraq must therefore pay compensation for the damage it caused to the people, the environment, and the property of Kuwait and other countries. Furthermore, the council has decided that Iraq must meet certain costs incurred by the United Nations in making adjustments after the Gulf War, such as the cost of inspections inside Iraq and the elimination of weapons of mass destruction, and partial payment of the costs for marking the international boundary between Iraq and Kuwait.

Fourth, *there should also be measures to punish the offenders who continue to trade with a sanctioned country.* If necessary, secondary sanctions can be instituted against companies or persons frequently mentioned or actually convicted of violating the sanctions. Their names could be blacklisted, and eventually they could be prohibited from engaging in international trade for the duration of the sanctions. If it is found that the countries in which such companies or individuals reside are not exercising sufficient control or restraint on their national entities, a threat of secondary sanctions against such countries would likely yield amazing results in the field of compliance.

Often the use of merchant vessels of convenience comes into question. Many of these are registered in countries that do not pay as much attention to all the international criteria and regulations for flagging a merchant vessel as to the amount of fees they charge for granting the registrations. The result is that many such ships engage in reckless transportation of contraband merchandise, making it difficult to track them for possible violations of the sanctions. They change their names and flag almost at will.

Fifth, *steps need to be taken to alleviate the suffering of innocent people in the sanctioned country.* The purpose of sanctions is to force the people in charge of the formulation of repugnant national policies to change those policies. Unfortunately, it often happens that such people are the least affected by the sanctions, while innocent people in the target country suffer. The Security Council has recognized the need to alleviate this suffering of ordinary people by permitting exceptions to the sanctions so that medicines, foodstuffs, and other items of essential human need can still be exported there. Regarding the population at large, sometimes a paradox appears. The people engaged in campaigns against colonial oppression or subjugation have often insisted that, in spite of the difficulties to them, they prefer the sanctions to be maintained and tightened. The Freedom Fighters in Southern Rhodesia very often raised that plea, and in South Africa many opposition parties there continued to advocate the maintenance of sanctions against South Africa until the last moment. In other sanctions situations, such as in Iraq and former Yugoslavia, the Security Council has recognized the need to alleviate the suffering of ordinary people by allowing exceptions to the sanctions. The committees, especially those on Iraq and Yugoslavia, spend a great deal of their time in evaluating the humanitarian nature of the goods requested as supplies to those countries.

As for the hardships caused at the national level, the Charter of the United Nations has a mechanism by which such countries can apply to the Security Council for consultations on how they can cope with the economic difficulties they face resulting from their enforcement of the sanctions. However, Article 50 of the charter only confers that right of consultation. It does not necessarily mean that the Security Council is obliged to come up with answers. In fact, the council does not appear to have ready answers. In cases where such applications have been lodged, the council has appealed to the international community and to international financial institutions to offer generous assistance to such countries. Sometimes the results are good, as in the twenty-one countries that have applied because of the sanctions against Iraq. It is now known that besides soft loans by international financial institutions, the European Community has distributed a total of some $1.2 billion to those countries. Three countries have so far applied to the Security Council because of the sanctions against former Yugoslavia, and it is expected that the council will proceed in a similar manner.

Security Council Efforts
Toward More Effective Implementation of Sanctions

Finally, *attention should be drawn to a growing trend in the Security Council toward prescribing how the sanctions should actually be implemented by states.*

In the case of sanctions against former Yugoslavia, the council has authorized states, acting nationally or through regional agencies under the authority of the Security Council, to halt and inspect vessels in the Adriatic Sea and on the relevant portion of the Danube international waterway to ensure strict implementation of all the sanctions. Previously, in the aftermath of the Gulf War, the council authorized those states cooperating with Kuwait to mount a blockade in the Gulf area for similar purposes. Most recently, the Security Council called upon states to use such measures to ensure strict adherence to the arms embargo against Somalia and the sanctions against Haiti.

A sanctions regime can be used as an effective tool to regulate international behavior before resorting to the use of force. The Security Council of the United Nations should continue to be the central authority for detecting the situations and areas where international peace and security are threatened. The present practices in implementing sanctions fall rather short of achieving the intended objectives. More attention should be paid to devising measures that can make the application of sanctions as effective as possible, achieve their objectives in the shortest possible time frame, and minimize the suffering to the unintended, vulnerable sections of the population in the target countries. This would include the ordinary civilians: women, children, the old, the infirm, and the disabled. Appropriate measures should also be devised so as to avoid, minimize, or alleviate the economic difficulties of the third countries affected by the sanctions.

Notes

1. The views expressed in this article are solely those of the author and do not represent the official position of any organ of the United Nations Organization mentioned.

2. As of August 31, 1994, three more sanctions regimes have been established by the Security Council: against Haiti (Resolutions 841, 875, and 917), Angola—only against the UNITA political movement there (Resolution 864), and against Rwanda (Resolution 918).

3. Some decisions of the Security Council under Chapter VII of the charter may be recommendatory or nonbinding, i.e., when their operative paragraphs are introduced by emotive words such as "The Security Council, . . . *requests, invites, appeals, urges,* etc." Mandatory or obligatory measures, on the other hand, constitute those adopted under Chapter VII of the charter and introduced by

command words such as: "The Security Council, . . . *demands, determines, orders that, calls upon,* etc."

4. Article 39 reads: "The Security Council shall determine the existence of any threat to the peace, breach of the peace, or act of aggression and shall make recommendations, or decide what measures shall be taken in accordance with Articles 41 and 42, to maintain or restore international peace and security."

5. Article 2(7) reads in part: "Nothing contained in the present charter shall authorize the United Nations to intervene in matters that are essentially within the domestic jurisdiction of any state."

3

Economic Sanctions as Tools of Foreign Policy

Ivan Eland

Nations have used economic sanctions as foreign policy tools for centuries and yet, despite the efforts of many analysts, it is not easy to tell whether an episode of sanctions has been a "success." One problem with measuring effectiveness is that analysts usually try to decide whether sanctions have been successful only after they have been in effect for a certain length of time or after they have been removed. One, two, or ten years from the initiation of the episode, it is easy to overlook the complexity of the environment surrounding the imposition of the measures. A second problem is how to define success. Whereas sanctions usually have multiple, and often hidden, goals, the media, and therefore analysts and the public, form too simplistic a view of what goals the sanctions were originally designed to achieve. Because the nation that is the target of sanctions has usually committed some unacceptable act, the focus becomes whether the measures will cause that nation to cease or retreat from the objectionable behavior, that is, comply with the wishes of the sanctioning nation(s). Realistically, however, when analyzing an episode of sanctions, the analyst must go back to the time they were imposed to get a full flavor of the international and domestic environments from which they sprang and the multiple goals they were usually designed to achieve.

Bluntly stated, most of the times a nation imposes sanctions on another country, it has few other policy options. The target nation usually has committed an unacceptable act and intense domestic pressure, particularly in democratic states, to "do something" can persuade the government in the sanctioning nation to respond by imposing sanctions to meet goals other than target compliance. The sanctioning nation may wish to punish the target nation, uphold international norms, demonstrate solidarity with allied nations or the internal opposition in the target nation, or deter worse behavior by demonstrating the will to escalate to a stronger response. These pressures to take some action stronger than a diplomatic response often collide with the reality that more drastic responses, e.g., covert action and military intervention, may not be commensurate with the target's unacceptable behavior or may involve severe costs. Thus, because nations have limited policy options to influence the behavior of other nations and because sanctions occupy the middle ground between diplomatic and paramilitary/military action, they are often selected as the means to pressure a target nation.

Purposes: Symbolic and Instrumental

Because many in academia and the media have analyzed the effectiveness of sanctions episodes using the most difficult goal to achieve (the goal of target compliance), they conclude that the measures are not usually effective. Yet, when a target nation misbehaves, policymakers in government usually disregard the preponderance of negative literature on previous episodes and impose yet another set of sanctions! The recent rash of sanctions episodes (against Iraq, Haiti, and Yugoslavia) indicates that policymakers believe sanctions have utility as foreign policy tools, even if stated compliance goals are not likely to be met. Here the analysis of policymakers may be ahead of the academic community.[1]

Policymakers have known for some time that sanctions can and usually do have multiple goals, both instrumental and symbolic. Once this is recognized, analyzing whether an episode of sanctions is effective becomes much more complex. For example, the common perception is that the grain embargo that President Carter imposed against the Soviet Union for its invasion of Afghanistan failed because the Soviets had not withdrawn their forces by the time Ronald Reagan lifted this embargo. This perception of failure is derived from using target compliance as the main criterion for success. Yet statements by President Carter at the time seem to suggest that he wanted to use sanctions to demonstrate U.S. resolve and to deter the Soviets from further aggression into more strategic areas such as Iran, Pakistan, and the Persian Gulf. It is difficult to determine whether the Soviets intended to take further military action against these other nations or whether U.S. sanctions deterred them from doing so. Yet, in light of the strategic nature of the Near East and the level of U.S. concern about the invasion, the sanctions could be viewed as a vital symbolic response.

Despite the inflated rhetoric of policymakers at the time they impose sanctions, analysts should maintain realistic expectations of what the measures can accomplish and look deeper into the environment surrounding their imposition to explore the policymakers' more modest real goals. Policymakers may publicly embrace the goal of making the target retreat from its objectionable behavior, but they may not really believe that sanctions alone will achieve this ambitious objective. They may have overstated what sanctions could do to sell them domestically[2] or to stake out a strong bargaining position vis-à-vis the target nation.[3] Instead, the policymakers may believe they can only achieve some aforementioned more modest symbolic goals and that sanctions cannot single-handedly achieve the more grandiose objectives of getting the target nation to retreat from aggression or change its system of government. In an anarchic and chaotic international environment, symbolic goals are important and may even be vital. Nations watch the behavior of other countries carefully for subtle clues about their intentions and resolve.

Sometimes the goals of sanctions will vary over time. When sanctions were first imposed against Iraq, they were ostensibly designed to compel Saddam Hussein to withdraw from Kuwait and impede the Iraqi army's readiness for war. After the war, the continuance of sanctions was justified as an incentive to make Iraq comply with UN resolutions ending the Gulf War, including those requiring destruction of weapons-manufacturing capabilities and allowing UN inspections of such facilities. The Bush administration then added that sanctions would not be removed until Hussein was ousted from power.

In reality, sanctions may have had little effect in achieving any of these goals. However, if events occurring early in the embargo are studied carefully, there is some evidence that George Bush had little faith that sanctions would compel Saddam to withdraw from Kuwait. By late September in 1990, not even two months after sanctions were imposed and certainly not long enough for them to have had a biting economic effect, George Bush privately became the biggest advocate in the administration for offensive military action to expel Saddam from Kuwait.[4] His stance was in contrast to that of his chief military advisor, Colin Powell, who wanted to give sanctions more time to work before resorting to war. Could the quick abandonment of sanctions by former President Bush, even before they had time to bite economically, suggest that he believed that sanctions alone could not achieve this ambitious goal? Did President Bush push for the adoption of multilateral sanctions merely to uphold the perception that he was exhausting all peaceful avenues, thus building international support for the war he believed was inevitable?

Factors Affecting Target Compliance:
The Rally-Around-the-Flag and Internal Opposition Effects[5]

The goals of using sanctions against Iraq to compel Saddam's withdrawal from Kuwait, to ensure compliance with UN resolutions, and to drive Hussein from power all involve target compliance, the most difficult objective to achieve with sanctions. Here, the most universally adopted, comprehensive sanctions in world history, which were enforced by a tight naval blockade and had a grinding economic effect on Iraq's economy, failed to achieve any of these goals. This result would seem to validate the pessimistic conclusions of Johan Galtung,[6] who said that sanctions with internal economic effects could still be rendered ineffective in achieving their stated goal by noneconomic factors. Galtung used the term rally-around-the-flag effect to argue that leaders in target nations could use the economic pain caused by foreign nations to rally their populations around their cause. Rather than creating disintegration in the target state, sanctions would invoke nationalism and political integration. It can be further argued that target regimes that tightly restrict all aspects of society, including the media and the ability of a political opposition to operate, can generate even larger rally-around-the-flag effects than democratic societies. This is especially true when sanctions have a severe economic effect and the target regime can blame all of its economic problems on foreigners with ill intent. Fidel Castro was apparently able to do this in the wake of the tightened U.S. sanctions against Cuba.

Galtung took the first step in showing that the degree of political success is not necessarily closely associated with the amount of economic damage caused by sanctions. A further step needs to be taken. If economically strong sanctions can be negated by the political rally-around-the-flag effect, can economically weak effects "succeed" politically? As noted before, without causing severe economic damage to the target nation, sanctions as symbols can demonstrate the sanctioning nation's resolve, deter further unacceptable behavior, isolate the target nation politically, and show support for allies or the political opposition in the target nation. Can sanctions that are mild in their economic effects also *contribute to* achieving ambitious compliance goals? Sanctions against South Africa prove this can happen.[7] The South African case is one of the few recent episodes of sanctions in which the measures played a positive role in pushing the target nation to comply with the wishes of the sanctioning nations. Although selective sanctions did not single-handedly cause the government to initiate reforms, the measures did contribute to this end through tremendous psychological pressure.

Little has been written on the actual mechanism by which sanctions succeed or fail. As noted above, Galtung was a pioneer in this area by identifying the rally-around-the-flag effect. If a military analogy can be used, severe comprehensive sanctions with grinding economic effects are the equivalent of war by attrition. That is, they are an attempt to win by materially crippling the opponent. More restrained, selective sanctions, with the all-important threat of future escalation can be compared with maneuver warfare, where the objective is to destroy, by well-timed attacks in key places, the opponent's will to fight. Instead of incurring heavy losses by grinding down the entire opposing army, shattering the opponent's confidence holds friendly casualties to a minimum and shocks the opponent into surrender. In war, and with economic sanctions, the goal should be not necessarily to decimate the opponent's society, but to affect the psyche of the opposing leader to induce the termination of unacceptable activities. In fact, trying to decimate the target society may have the opposite effect and cause the opponent to fight harder. The saturation bombing of Germany toward the end of World War II, to crush the German will to fight, may have actually strengthened the resolve of the German population. Galtung would probably agree that the psychology of warfare is similar to the psychology of economic sanctions.

The sanctions against South Africa, both by governments (national, state, and local) and private businesses and groups, on selected imports, exports, and financial transactions were the equivalent of maneuver warfare. They affected key sectors of the South African economy, lending and investment, thus creating the powerful effect of chilling business confidence and inducing a long-term drag on the South African economy. The measures isolated South Africa politically, making it an international pariah. Furthermore, South African Whites, who consider themselves European, were shunned by these countries. The noneconomic sanction of banning sports-crazy South Africa from international sporting events had a particularly potent negative effect on the psyche of South African Whites.

The relatively restrained set of sanctions imposed and the threat of future measures probably had greater effect than grinding, comprehensive sanctions imposed rapidly. Since the world has many buying and selling nations, at least some of which are usually unwilling to impose sanctions on the target nation, and since private parties and national governments have incentives to evade any sanctions imposed, harsh comprehensive measures are usually less effective economically than both the target and sanctioning nations' first estimate. Therefore, the fear of the unknown contained in the threat of future measures may have greater psychological effects on the target than the actual sanctions that turn out to have less drastic economic effects than anticipated. Furthermore, once comprehensive sanctions are imposed, no further threat exists and any future easing of sanctions is politically difficult because the sanctioning nation would appear to be "caving in" to the target nation.

The threat of future sanctions caused sectors of the South African society with international ties, i.e., the white business community (particularly the English-speaking sector), to oppose apartheid and exert powerful pressure on the Afrikaner-run government to initiate political reforms. When strong political opposition exists in the target nation, as it did in South Africa, the threat of future sanctions can strengthen the internal opposition. The selectively imposed sanctions gave South Africa a taste of the economic pain that comprehensive sanctions could have brought, but without inducing the severe rally-around-the-flag effect against "foreign meddling" that often accompanies grinding measures. Some rally-around-the-flag effect did occur as conservative Whites reacted to foreign pressure, but the absence of severe economic hardship mitigated this effect. Wrenching economic dislocation would have forced the business community into an alliance for survival with the South African government, in which business opposition would have been muted to ensure the use of the government's resources to evade sanctions and would have disproportionately hurt white and black opposition forces within the country. In most cases, a target government, with control of the organs of state power, can redirect the pain of severe sanctions from its supporters to its opponents. This redirection happened in Iraq when Saddam Hussein was able to rechannel the hardships of sanctions away from the security forces that keep him in power. In Haiti as well, the desperately poor were suffering greatly while the rich supporters of the government were only marginally affected by sanctions, and the military actually enriched itself by illegal smuggling.

In sum, economic sanctions will rarely compel the target nation into compliance unless a strong political opposition exists to ally with the sanctioning nation and put pressure on the target government. The internal opposition effect is strongest and the rally-around-the-flag effect weakest when partial sanctions are imposed and more are threatened. The political benefits of imposing graduated sanctions override their major disadvantage: allowing the target nation time to adjust its economy. This is good news for sanctioning nations because domestic economic costs often make the imposition of severe comprehensive sanctions unlikely. Furthermore, when comprehensive measures are imposed rapidly (the ideal case according to conventional wisdom in the sanctions literature) even the political opposition in the target nation may become allied with its government for economic survival, thus creating an insurmountable rally-around-the-flag effect.

The internal opposition effect is particularly strong when the political opposition includes sectors of society that generate significant amounts of gross domestic product, have significant political power, or both, as in the case of important sectors of the business community. Because the opposition to the Cedras government in Haiti in 1993–94 was so weak compared to the opposition in South Africa, sanctions had less chance of inducing an internal opposition effect and thus were less likely to compel the Haitian government to reach a political settlement with Aristide than they were in pushing the South African government to negotiate political reforms. Not only was political opposition weaker in Haiti, but the Haitian economic elite sided with the military government. In cases where the target government has absolute totalitarian control over society, especially over the media and the formation of political opposition, the rally-around-the-flag effect will dominate and no internal opposition effect will arise to pressure the government to comply with the sanctioning nation's wishes. Sanctions against ruthless dictatorships, such as Saddam's Iraq, should have symbolic goals only.

Other extraneous factors, such as an ongoing war, can mitigate the internal opposition effect and enhance the rally-around-the-flag effect. In Serbia, the war's drain on the economy, which has compounded the economic dislocation caused by severe sanctions, has had this effect. The war has allowed the Milosevic government to argue that the political opposition's cause is unpatriotic.

Other Factors Affecting Success

Sanctions imposed by a friendly nation—a nation with well-developed political, economic, and cultural relations with the target nation—will have a greater chance of inducing compliance than measures initiated by an adversary.[8] The target nation's cost of noncompliance, i.e., the disruption of those close ties, is greater when a friendly nation imposes sanctions. Western sanctions contributed to the South African government's movement toward political reform because that country conducted 80 percent of its trade and received all of its capital from six Western nations and had extensive political and cultural ties to them. The same close ties that make sanctions on friendly nations more likely to be effective, however, can also make them less likely to be imposed. Disrupting these ties with friendly nations has greater costs for the sanctioning nation than disrupting them with adversaries.

Sanctions do not need to be multilateral to have positive political effects. In 1933 the British government imposed import sanctions and successfully achieved the release of its citizens held in Russia. In 1989 India imposed sanctions on Nepal, a traditional buffer against its adversary China, because of a pro-China tilt in Nepal's foreign policy. The sanctions reversed the tilt. Multilaterally-imposed sanctions can have enhanced political effects over unilateral sanctions, but not solely because of grinding economic pressure put on the target nation. Despite the recent examples of multilateral sanctions against Iraq and Serbia, which are rarities, it is usually difficult to get many countries to agree to impose severe, comprehensive measures because of their economic interests. It is easier to win multilateral imposition of partial sanctions. As more nations impose partial sanctions on the target, the psychological threat of future measures and the *potential* economic damage caused by this threat are made more credible. The more nations that impose sanctions, the greater political legitimacy the effort has and the greater the international ostracism and isolation the target experiences.[9] Some care must be taken by nations wishing to make their sanctions multilateral. Failure to get adequate multilateral cooperation can send a message of weakness to the target, rather than the signal of resolve intended by the sanctioning nations. For example, in the wake of martial law in Poland in 1981, a dispute arose in the Western alliance over an embargo on equipment to be used in constructing a Soviet natural gas pipeline. The dispute made the alliance seem divided instead of sending an unambiguous signal of protest to Moscow about the crackdown.

Publicity Surrounding Sanctions

The conventional wisdom that publicity hurts the chances for "successful" sanctions is too simplistic. The effect of publicity is determined by what the sanctions are intended to accomplish. If severe comprehensive sanctions are being used to obtain target compliance, publicity will probably enhance the rally-around-the-flag effect and lead to target intransigence. The target government, with its domestic opinion inflamed by foreign economic "aggression," may have no choice but to resist. The target might be more likely to comply if news of the sanctions can be kept from its people. Yet, the more severe the economic effect of the sanctions, the more likely the population of the target country will be aware of it. Thus, one further advantage of selective sanctions is that the amount of publicity may be reduced.

Often if the sanctioning government does not publicize the sanctions, the target government will do so and add its own spin. Castro used comprehensive U.S. sanctions, when first imposed, to rally Cubans against the "aggressive, imperialist United States," thereby consolidating his weak hold on power. By 1993, he was using these sanctions as a scapegoat for his own economic mismanagement.

In some cases, the sanctioning nations might want to publicize severe measures even though it might impair efforts to induce target compliance. If sanctions are being used to set an example, that is, to punish a target to uphold international norms, publicity is vital. In the case of sanctions against Serbia, the extensive publicity surrounding the drastic measures may have undermined efforts to end Serbian aggression by rallying the Serbian people around their government, but it probably enhanced efforts by the world community to demonstrate punishment for heinous human rights violations. The severe public sanctions may have been appropriate punishment to uphold international norms against such outrageous conduct. Thus, publicity can enhance the ostracism and international isolation of the target.

Publicity can also enhance the delivery of a symbolic message of disapproval even when the goals are less lofty and the measures less damaging to the target nation's economy. In 1981 and 1982 the United States imposed restrictions on new credits, high technology exports, preferential trade status, and International Monetary Fund membership for Poland. It chose a very public form of protest when it imposed these sanctions against Poland to punish that nation for imposing martial law and suppressing the Solidarity trade union. Similarly, trade and financial sanctions against Libya in the 1980s were powerful symbols of U.S. displeasure with that nation's terrorist activities and practices of intervening in the affairs of neighboring states. Here, the sanctioning nation showed that it was willing to make economic sacrifices to send a political message that was stronger than a diplomatic protest. Publicity is also vital when moderate sanctions are imposed and more are threatened. The psychological impact of the future threat is enhanced when knowledge of it permeates the target society, as it did in South Africa. Any hint of future sanctions from the West was monitored very closely by the South African government, the business community, and the public. The South African example shows that publicity can enhance the power of international ostracism and the threat of future sanctions to generate an internal opposition effect within the target nation.

Publicity may be most important when using sanctions as symbols to deter nations from unacceptable behavior or to show political support for allies or opposition groups in target nations. Publicity probably enhanced President Carter's efforts to use sanctions to deter the Soviets from further aggression in the Near East in 1980. It also aided the Western nations' efforts to show support for South Africa's black opposition in its fight against apartheid. Some analysts say the latter show of support encouraged Blacks to take stronger stands against the South African government, thus creating more pressure for reform. U.S. sanctions against critical sectors of the Polish economy in 1981 and 1982 were a powerful symbol of U.S. support for the Solidarity movement in the face of communist repression.

Economic Effects of Selected Sanctions

Most often, the goal of sanctions should not be to destroy the target economy but to have the maximum political effect through inducing psychological pressure against its political leaders and populace. Sanctioning nations should hold no delusions that strangling the target nation's economy will improve its behavior by compelling compliance with their wishes.

Partial sanctions should be aimed at vulnerable sectors of the target's economy. If the target nation feels pain in these sectors, its political leaders may overestimate the effects of the additional measures that are being threatened either implicitly or explicitly. This will induce the maximum psychological pressure on the target and have *the greatest chance* of producing compliance. Even if the goal of sanctions is symbolic, selected sanctions should have a demonstrated economic effect in critical sectors to convey the symbolic message. Sanctions that are too weak will be dismissed by the target nation.

The type of economic effect for which the sanctioning state should aim is raising the cost of commerce for the target nation or slowing the growth of its economy. Unless a tight military blockade that completely seals all of the target nation's borders is instituted (despite a recent rash of peaceful blockades, they are rare historically), these limited economic goals are the most that sanctions can hope to achieve. Even the economic effects of comprehensive, multilateral sanctions can usually be eroded significantly by smugglers and nonsanctioning nations that want to profit from the new market opportunities. The main direct effects of sanctions are to raise the target nation's cost of doing business by increasing expenses of importing and transporting goods, developing new export markets, and raising capital (interest rates).

Indirect effects of sanctions can sometimes be more potent than direct effects. When partial sanctions are imposed and the threat of more looms, business confidence by foreign investors and lenders, and even domestic business interests, are chilled, causing a substantial drag on the economic growth of the target nation. In South Africa, foreign private and government sanctions on lending and investment in 1985 and 1986 contributed to slow economic growth in the late 1980s.

Sanctions can also create inefficiencies in the target economy. The target may have to develop new industries to become self-sufficient in embargoed items. The resources used could be better used elsewhere in the economy. For example, the multilateral oil and arms embargoes against South Africa caused that nation to make expensive and inefficient investments in the arms and synthetic fuel industries.

Import, Export, Financial, and Cultural Sanctions Compared

If the sanctioning nation decides that selective measures should be employed, the type of sanction used should reflect the economic goal. Import and export sanctions usually have their maximum effect in the short term when the target nation's trading patterns are disrupted, while dissipating in the long term as new trading partners are cultivated and illegal evasion takes its toll. In contrast, the effects of financial and cultural sanctions (for example, banning South Africa from international sporting activities) increase over time. Raising the cost of capital, thereby chilling investment and business confidence, will eventually take its toll in slower economic growth. The longer a target nation remains politically ostracized by cultural sanctions, the more psychologically exhausted it becomes.

When used together, partial import, export, and financial sanctions can reinforce each other. Embargoes on exports to the target nation raise the prices of its imports. When sanctions are imposed on financial flows to that nation and on imports of the target's hard currency-generating exports, they will reduce funds vitally needed by the target to pay these higher import bills. For example, a UN boycott of Iraq's exports (including oil, which constituted 95 percent of its revenues) and a freeze on new credit and its assets overseas severely impaired its ability to pay the higher prices for imports generated by the UN export embargo.

The sanctioning nation often has an easier time obtaining international cooperation when imposing a ban on imports from the target nation than when imposing an embargo on exports to that nation. Often third world target nations export products that are in surplus on world markets, such as primary and agricultural products, or widely produced manufactured items such as textiles, iron, and steel. Developed nations, which often seek protection for these same industries, will readily impose and enforce sanctions on imports from the target state. Import boycotts against goods in excess supply can also benefit from the reduced number of alternate markets available for the target to redirect its exports.

Market forces also frequently strengthen the effects of financial sanctions. Financial sanctions can have a chilling effect on the target economy. A ban on lending or investment or the threat of such measures against the target by one nation may cause public and private capital from other nations to dry up or be withdrawn. Banks are especially sensitive to the behavior of other international banks when assessing the risks of doing business in a particular nation. Banks are also reluctant to lend if multilateral lending organizations suspend loans. In effect, the international banks, centered in a few Western industrial nations, in some ways act as a cartel. When one bank refuses to lend to a country because sanctions are threatened or imposed, other banks might perceive increased risk and end their lending.

Conversely, abundant supply in many world markets and the concomitant competition for sales create an incentive for alternative suppliers in nonsanctioning nations to fill the vacuum left by suppliers from the sanctioning nation. So that they do not lose to such foreign competition, companies in the sanctioning nation may then have an incentive to illegally evade sanctions by laundering exports to the target nation through third countries. These companies may even be privately encouraged in their

TABLE 3.1 Factors Affecting the Success of Sanctions

	Factor	Factor Increases Chances for a Positive Outcome	Factor Reduces Chances for a Positive Outcome
Goals	Target Compliance w/ Goals of Sanctioning Nation		X
	Deterrence	X	
	Punish Target to Uphold Int'l. Norms	X	
	Support Target Opposition Groups	X	
Severity	Harsh, Comprehensive Sanctions		X
	Moderate Sanctions & Threat of More	X	
	Multilateral Sanctions	X	
Nature of Target	Friendly	X	
	Adversary		X
	Strong Political Opposition	X	
Publicity	Publicized Moderate Sanctions with Threat of More	X	
	Publicized Harsh, Comprehensive Sanctions		X

evasion efforts by the sanctioning government, which wants to gain politically from imposing the sanctions but cheats to avoid economic loss. For example, the governments of Arab oil-producing nations agreed to halt shipments of petroleum to South Africa, but then looked the other way when shipments found indirect routes to the target nation.

Conclusion

As noted in this chapter, every time policymakers in the sanctioning nation consider imposing sanctions, they should assess the nature of the target nation, what goals sanctions are most likely to achieve, how comprehensive the measures should be, and whether they should be well publicized or behind-the-scenes. Table 3.1 summarizes these factors.

A sanctions regime is not a surgical tool. Often they have collateral effects not foreseen by the sanctioning nation. It is also difficult to channel the pain of sanctions to particular population groups within the target nation, which is further exacerbated by the fact that target governments can redirect the pain of sanctions to their opponents, while sparing key supporters. To determine the likelihood of "success" for economic sanctions, each potential episode should be analyzed individually. Each episode is unique and there are no fixed rules to insure success. Yet, as this chapter has demonstrated, various factors generally contribute either positively or negatively to the outcome.

Notes

1. David Baldwin, *Economic Statecraft* (Princeton: Princeton Univ. Press, 1985), pp. 3–4.

2. James Barber, "Economic Sanctions as a Policy Instrument," *International Affairs*, Vol. 55, No. 3, July 1979, p. 374.

3. M.S. Daoudi and M.S. Dajani, *Economic Sanctions: Ideals and Experience* (Boston: Routledge and Kegan Paul, 1983), pp. 168–69.

4. Bob Woodward, *The Commanders* (New York: Simon and Shuster, 1991), pp. 298–301.

5. "Internal opposition effect" is similar to what Albert Hirschman referred to as the "fifth column effect." The editors' preference is to define this phenomena as an "internal opposition effect" to avoid negative connotations associated with the phrase "fifth column." See Albert Hirschman, *National Power and the Structure of Foreign Trade* (Berkeley: Univ. of California Press, 1945).

6. Johan Galtung, "On the Effects of International Economic Sanctions, with Examples from the Case of Rhodesia," *World Politics*, Vol. 19, No. 3, April 1967, pp. 26–28, 31, 47–48.

7. William H. Kaempfer and Anton D. Lowenberg, "The Theory of International Economic Sanctions: A Public Choice Approach," *American Economic Review*, Vol. 78, September 1988, p. 2. See also William H. Kaempfer and Anton

D. Lowenberg, "A Model of the Political Economy of International Investment Sanctions: The Case of South Africa," *Kyklos*, Vol. 39, No. 3, 1986, pp. 390–91, 394.

8. Gary Clyde Hufbauer, Jeffrey Schott, and Kimberly Ann Elliott, *Economic Sanctions Reconsidered*, 2d ed. (Washington, D.C.: Institute for International Economics, 1990), pp. 99–100.

9. Margaret Doxey, "International Sanctions: Trials of Strength or Tests of Weakness?" *Millennium*, No. 12, May 1983, p. 85.

4

A Review of Economic Sanctions: A Russian Perspective

*Alexander Konovalov, Sergey Oznobistchev
and Dmitry G. Evstafiev*

The increased use of international, political, and economic sanctions has provoked several complicated political and legal conflicts. First, the implementation of economic sanctions has the possibility of influencing the internal politics of different countries and threatening the absolute sovereignty of a nation. Secretary General Boutros Boutros-Ghali of the United Nations maintains that in the post–Cold War era, the UN may want to redefine national sovereignty, placing more limitations on what was once regarded as inviolable. This idea should be approached with some caution. Although the theory has been widely discussed as an advanced viewpoint, it bears a striking resemblance to the so-called Brezhnev Doctrine issued in the mid 1960s. Put in practice, that policy led to the invasion of Czechoslovakia in 1968. The idea of limited sovereignty can thus lead to a new imperialism. We need more sharply focused ideas about when sanctions should be used, how they should be enforced, and how decisions should be made to lift them. The most pressing task for the UN is to establish a proper legal basis for the employment of sanctions that would be according to the realpolitik principles of international politics accepted by the leading nations in the developed and developing world.

The second conflict is related to the first, namely the problem of a clear and unquestionable definition of the mandate for sanctions. During the Iraqi crisis many questions were raised about the extent to which the United States and its allies had the right to supersede that mandate in their attempt to influence the internal life of that country. In the future, the UN mandate and the legal basis for economic and political sanctions regimes should be precise and detailed. The limits of UN–related activity must also

43

be clearly defined. Sanctions cannot serve as the sole element of a UN–based international crisis response and management mechanism. Sanctions should be supplemented by other efforts, including effective international peacekeeping mechanisms and the use of positive rather than negative inducements.

Russia is likely to support international economic and political sanctions when there is a clear-cut understanding of their objectives. However, it will not always be possible for Russia to support the call of other nations to impose international sanctions. Russian objections to sanctions might stem from two sources. The first is that sanctions, both economic and political, always involve the use of force, although indirectly. The second is that the nature and geographic character of the conflicts in which sanctions are likely to be implemented in the future might involve situations that would obviously affect the security interests of Russia. Therefore, Russia cannot be expected to unequivocally transfer its decision-making rights to any regional or international body.[1] In this regard we must conclude that one of the most dangerous tendencies that can jeopardize the situation is the diversification of the number of bodies that can or do adopt practical decisions about the employment of sanctions. Another important problem for Russia is securing objectivity in using international sanctions. The sanctions regime should not be turned into a tool of "post–Cold War imperialism" in which any group of countries can punish a nation or nations with whom they do not agree.

In Iraq's case, the basic decision to employ sanctions was adopted by the UN Security Council, and several other international organizations followed suit. But when economic and political sanctions were employed against the former Yugoslavia, the leading role was played by the European Community (EC). Germany also put pressure on the United Nations and took the lead in formulating UN policy. In this situation, the EC countries were prepared to employ sanctions despite any decision the United Nations might have made. This tendency could lead to the imposition of economic and political sanctions by a regional or political organization in which Russia has little or no influence. Within the framework of the Security Council, Russia still possesses the right to exercise a veto; it can block activities that contradict its national interests. In other organizations and structures, however, there is no such possibility, even if the sanctions threaten the economic, political, or security interests of Russia. Additionally, participation in a regime of economic and political sanctions may involve the deployment of direct military force to enforce the sanctions. This involves serious and sensitive aspects of national security. The Russian government believes that any sanctions policy that involves military activity, including the deployment of Russian military forces as members of a peacekeeping force, involves serious and sensitive aspects of national security and should only be made by the state body of the Russian Federation, which has the power to declare war.

The Russian Federation needs to establish guidelines for the implementation of sanctions policy. Its legislature needs to consider the impact of a decision to participate in a sanctions regime on the internal political situation in Russia, and it must be prepared to defend and argue the case for that decision. When the Soviet Union participated in the initial introduction of economic and political sanctions against Iraq, that action produced neither political turmoil nor any outcry about unbearable economic losses. This was partly because of the nature of the conflict, i.e., unprovoked aggression by Iraq against a sovereign country, Kuwait. Participation was also facilitated because the Soviet Union articulated a clear explanation of its position. Not even the extreme communist opposition argued against the initial introduction of sanctions, although it harshly criticized the use of military force against Iraq and condemned the continuation of sanctions after Baghdad accepted the cease-fire.

On the other hand, the economic sanctions imposed against the two republics remaining in the Federal Republic of Yugoslavia, Serbia and Montenegro, produced internal political turmoil and highlighted the split in opinion among Russian leaders. Although it is popular in the West to attribute the depth of negative feelings about the sanctions imposed on Yugoslavia to procommunist groups or to the historical and religious ties between Russia and Serbia, it is a mistake to do so. While the Yeltsin administration may feel comfortable labeling the opposition procommunist and antidemocratic, in this case at least, that description is not accurate. It could have been partially true regarding former Vice President Alexander Rutskoi, who at the time of the debate was already shifting his allegiance to the opposition. But such an approach is completely incorrect regarding other political figures who expressed doubts about Russia's position regarding the sanctions against Yugoslavia. For example, one of Foreign Minister Andrei Kozyrev's fiercest critics was the chairman of the Committee on the Foreign Economic Relations of the former Russian Supreme Soviet (disbanded in September 1993), Evgeny Ambartsumov, who now is a participant in the Yabloko faction in the State Duma.[2]

The Russian Foreign Ministry has also been widely criticized by opposition groups for its participation in the continued regime of sanctions against Iraq. It should be noted, however, that the criticism is much weaker than that regarding Serbia and relates to the Russian role in the decision-making process. The focal point of political discussions has become the question of the authority of implementation. The U.S. Air Force bombing of the Iraqi air defense batteries in January 1993 produced turmoil among the Russian political and military elites. The reason for such a nervous reaction was not the bombing itself, (no one expressed doubts about the necessity for doing so) but two interrelated aspects of the problem. First, Russia was not consulted before the bombing, and the U.S. thereby demonstrated that it was ready to act independently. The Russian Ministry of Defense newspaper, *Krasnaya Zvezda*, in its initial response to the U.S. actions argued that the UN had not granted the U.S. and allied forces the right to use immediate military actions.[3] Second, the mandate for sanctions and related military arrangements (including the "no-fly zone") was poorly defined. From the Russian politicians' point of view, there was not a proper legal formula for the action that occurred. *Krasnaya Zvezda* published an editorial with the title, "Is the Legal Formula for Intervention Needed?" criticizing U.S. actions for their "selectivity" and the absence of legal grounds for action.[4]

The subject of sanctions is generally used in connection with the growing activity of influential conservative groups as a basis for challenging the course of the democratic government in the sphere of foreign policy. Among these groups are the Congress of Russian Communities, the Zemstvo Movement, and the Union of the Orthodox Christian Brotherhoods. This opposition is beyond the hysterical criticism of the procommunist and extreme nationalist political groups that reject the very foundations of Russian foreign policy. The question of Russian participation in the future of sanctions is becoming more of a domestic policy problem and less of a foreign policy issue. Certain changes in Russian policy toward sanctions in the former Yugoslavia, particularly the proposal to widen the scope of sanctions beyond Serbia, are the first steps toward a more conservative foreign policy approach that considers Russian ethnic and religious sympathies. Russia may again become a difficult partner in cooperative security matters. The domestic opposition stemming from Russia's participation in these controversial sanctions regimes is a result, at least in part, of mistakes made by the executive branch. Sanctions were adopted without a proper understanding and articulation of the Russian Federation's position in each conflict. Further, the policies were adopted without being discussed or approved in the legislative branch, and the conditions for the ending of the sanctions regimes were never outlined.

The adoption of sanctions against Yugoslavia, and to a lesser extent against Iraq, was perceived by many political elites, including some pro-Yeltsin figures, as conciliation to the policy of the West, without regard for independent Russian national interests.[5] The situation was aggravated when the Foreign Ministry refused to discuss the matter, while referring to the "interests of the world community"[6] and labeling its opponents "red-browns."[7] As a result, the policy not only gave ammunition to the procommunist opposition, it also radicalized moderates. Thus, Mr. Kozyrev was acting in isolation on these matters, supported only by Yeltsin himself and the Choice of Russia faction in the State Duma. At the same time, Russian foreign policymakers were trying to broaden support through the slogans of the national patriotic opposition. Russian political discourse has been rife with "great imperial" motives and appeals to the national interest of Russia.

If the Russian Federation is to prevent such negative domestic fallout in the future, it should adopt a special legislative procedure to address the issues raised when Russia participates in sanctions regimes. Such legislation should consider the following principles. First, the procedure for decision making should be clearly delineated. This should obviously include some means of reconciling any differences in the positions of the executive and legislative branches, and it should provide for open discussion of the issues with representatives of different political groups and parties. Second, Russian policy on sanctions should be specifically defined by legislation and regulation. The articulation of Russian policy should be independent of the position of the world community or of any international organization. Nonetheless, it is in the interests of Russia to further promote the consolidation of international decision making within the UN Security Council. This will prevent both fragmentation of the world community and an increase in political ambitions of newly appeared regional subsuperpowers. Additionally, this would prevent the possibility of unlawful use of sanctions to achieve the egoistic objectives of a particular country or group of countries. A process should be initiated within the UN Security Council framework to reconcile different national laws on sanctions, with the goal of developing a universally accepted and codified mechanism for economic and political sanctions.

Many remaining questions need to be answered regarding internationally imposed and enforced sanctions. Because of the long Cold War and the ineffectiveness of UN mechanisms, the international community lacks experience in the field of joint efforts to influence the foreign and domestic policies of other nations. Recent attempts to impose sanctions should be considered only the first steps toward the creation of a set of internationally recognized peacemaking mechanisms. In neither the case of Iraq nor Yugoslavia did the introduction of sanctions lead to the fulfillment of the goals articulated by the international community, though the sanctions did undermine vital areas of the target countries' economies. The indiscriminate introduction of sanctions may help consolidate or even strengthen the power of the targeted nation's leader. Additionally, an embargo on certain types of deliveries may help prevent the escalation of conflict. In the Yugoslavian case, the position of leader may have been solidified, but the sanctions did succeed in decreasing the intensity of the conflict.

A study of the present record of sanctions, with all its successes and failures, could yield extremely rich material for improving interstate cooperation in peacekeeping. Although more study and discussion of the record are necessary, some preliminary conclusions are possible. First, internationally imposed economic and political sanctions have proven to be a highly complex problem for all participants in the process; they can have unexpected effects on both international and domestic politics. Sanctions should not be regarded as an instrument of routine political interaction between nations, but as an extraordinary instrument to be adopted only after careful study of all the circumstances. Secondly, UN sanctions cannot be effective without regional cooperation. In practical terms, a military blockade can only be effectively introduced under conditions of regional consensus. For example, the inability of regional powers, the United States and its Western allies, to seal the Iraqi/ Jordanian border lessened the effectiveness of the sanctions regime in Iraq. If any other neighboring country had violated the sanctions in an open or tacit way, the whole regime would have become useless. Clearly the proper implementation of the sanctions regime demands active regional cooperation both political and economic.

Notes

1. Andrei Kozyrev, "The Lagging Partnership," in *Foreign Affairs*, Vol. 73, No. 3, May/June 1994, p. 61.

2. On numerous occasions, Mr. Ambartsumov expressed his dissatisfaction with Mr. Kozyrev's policy towards the former Yugoslavia. For the most severe criticism see his interview, "Evgeny Ambartsumov: Pragmatism is What We Need Now," *Krasnaya Zvezda*, (The Red Star), February 11, 1993.

3. *Krasnaya Zvezda*, January 15, 1993.

4. *Krasnaya Zvezda*, January 16, 1993.

5. In addition to Mr. Evgeny Ambartsumov, we could name Mr. Sergei Stankevitch, former political adviser for Yeltsin; Mr. Oleg Soskovets, First Vice-Premier; Mr. Sergei Glaziev, former minister for foreign economic relations; and other figures.

6. For the classic example of this approach see: Andrei Kozyrev, "Renewal of the Kafkian Metamorphoses," *Nezavisimaya Gazeta* (The Independent Newspaper), August 20, 1992. Also see his interview, Andrei Kozyrev, "There are More Internal Enemies than External Ones," in *Kuranti*, April 16, 1993.

7. The *de facto* alliance of hardline communists and fascist elements in post-Soviet Russian politics.

PART TWO

Assessing Sanctions

5

Factors Affecting the Success
of Sanctions

Kimberly Ann Elliott

After forty years in which it imposed economic sanctions only twice, the United Nations Security Council has approved mandatory economic sanctions on six occasions between 1989 and 1993. Sanctions in most of the post–World War II period had a distinctly unilateral flavor, often with a Cold War twist. Of 104 sanctions episodes from World War II through the UN embargo of Iraq, the United States was a key player in two-thirds. In 80 percent of U.S.–imposed sanctions, the policy was pursued with no more than minor cooperation from its allies or international organizations. Since 1990 the United States has imposed new unilateral sanctions in only one case (against Russia and India over a sale of missile technology), and expanded them in another (Cuba). If the trend toward multilateralism continues, this will mark a sharp reversal in the use of economic sanctions for foreign policy goals in the post–World War II period.

A Framework for Analyzing Economic Sanctions[1]

Senders usually have multiple goals and targets in mind when they impose sanctions, and coercion is not always at the top of the list. When selecting a sanction, a government or international organization should keep in mind the actual, as opposed to formal, primary target. A unilateral sanction may, in fact, be intended to coerce the government of the country against whom sanctions are imposed. Alternatively, there may be no expectation of successfully influencing the apparent target. Instead, the sanctions may be aimed at third countries that the sender hopes to deter from engaging in objectionable behavior; or they may be intended to enhance the sender's credibility among its allies. Finally, the sanctions may be a response to domestic political pressures.

Different types of sanctions, having greater or lesser economic impact, may be appropriate in different circumstances. Sanctions imposed for symbolic or signalling purposes should be just as carefully crafted as those designed for coercive purposes. Although sanctions may be the best or even the only option in some cases where it is necessary to *do something*, not just any sanction will do. Prudence argues that a nation carefully scrutinize unintended costs and consequences before choosing a particular measure. It makes sense to tailor sanctions carefully to the objective they are genuinely intended to achieve.

The possibility that the formal target may not be the real intended target raises problems for researchers trying to assess the effectiveness of sanctions. Some sanctions may be judged to be a failure even though they were never intended to succeed in the sense of producing a change in the target's behavior. Nevertheless, in what follows, "success" is judged on the basis of whether sanctions appeared to contribute to the achievement of stated foreign policy goals, including changes in the policies, capabilities, or government of the target country. This can be justified on several grounds. First, it is difficult, if not impossible, to know whether a sanction successfully deterred a third party from taking objectionable actions in most cases. Second, a sanction imposed in response to domestic political pressure is almost by definition a success. Even in those two cases, however, it could be argued that sanctions that fail to influence the formal target will also be unlikely to deter third countries or to satisfy outraged domestic political constituencies. Finally, the United Nations and other international organizations trying to enforce international law are interested not only in punishment of transgressors, but in compliance. In other words, they would usually like to see changes in the behavior of the target country.

The success of an economic sanctions episode, as viewed from the perspective of the sanctioning country, has two parts: the extent to which the foreign policy outcome sought by the sender country was, in fact, achieved; and the contribution made by the sanctions (as opposed to other factors, such as military action). The Hufbauer, Schott, Elliott methodology uses a simple index system to rank each of these elements on a scale from 1 (failed outcome; zero or negative sanctions contribution) to 4 (successful outcome; significant sanctions contribution). By multiplication, the two elements are combined into a "success score" that ranges in value from 1 to 16. We characterize a score of 9 or higher as a "successful" outcome. A score of 9 means that sanctions made a modest contribution to the goal sought by the sender country and that the goal was, in part, realized; a score of 16 means that sanctions made a significant contribution to a successful outcome. By contrast, a score of 1 indicates that the sender country clearly failed to achieve its goals and that sanctions may even have left it worse off than before. In some cases the sender may have achieved some or all of its objectives, but the case will still fall into the failed column if sanctions played only a minor role in the outcome. In fact, this occurred in all of the episodes we scored an 8 and in about a third of those scored a 6.

Since sanctions cannot coerce the surrender of territory as easily as they can free a political prisoner, the first step was to arrange the cases into five categories based on the objective sought: (1) modest, including settling expropriation disputes, improving human rights, and inhibiting nuclear proliferation; (2) destabilization of the target government; (3) disruption of relatively minor military adventures; (4) impairment of the military potential of an adversary; and (5) "other major goals," for example, ending apartheid in South Africa. In addition to the goal, several factors were identified that might be expected to affect the outcome of a sanctions effort. Information on six political and five economic variables was compiled for 115 episodes of foreign policy sanctions beginning with World War I and continuing through 1989.[2] Analysis of the cases indicates that sanctions are most effective when:

- the goal is relatively modest, thus lessening the importance of multilateral cooperation, which often is difficult to obtain, and reducing the chances a rival power will bother to step in with offsetting assistance. However, if significant international cooperation is achieved, as in the Iraq case, more difficult goals may move within a coalition's reach;
- the target is much smaller than the country imposing sanctions, and economically weak and politically unstable. In successful cases, the average sender's economy was 187 times larger than that of the average target;
- the sender and target are friendly toward one another and conduct substantial trade. The sender accounted for 28 percent of the average target's trade in success cases but only 19 percent in failures;
- the sanctions are imposed quickly and decisively to maximize impact. This allows the target no time to adjust and enhances the political credibility of the sender, signaling its commitment to the sanctioning. The average cost to the target as a percentage of GNP in success cases was 2.4 percent and 1 percent in failures, while successes averaged 2.9 years in duration and failures 8 years;
- the sender avoids high costs to itself.

Although sanctions overall were successful in 34 percent of the 115 cases studied, success has become increasingly elusive in recent years. If one splits the sample of cases roughly in half, into those initiated before 1973 and those begun after that date, a striking difference emerges. Of the sanctions episodes in the pre-1973 period, 44 percent ended successfully, whereas the success rate among cases begun after 1973 was just under 25 percent. Even more striking is the decline in the effectiveness of sanctions imposed in pursuit of modest goals, from 75 percent to 21 percent, most of which are accounted for by the United States.

Declining Hegemony and Declining Success

In the decades following World War II, the United States attempted to impose its will on a wider variety of targets and sought a broader array of objectives than did any other country, including the Soviet Union, which generally confined its use of sanctions to trying to keep rebellious allies in line. Reflecting its roles as economic hegemon and political and military superpower, the United States relied less on international cooperation and, on average, had more distant relations and weaker trade linkages with its targets than was observed with other users of sanctions. In the early 1970s the United States sharply increased its use of sanctions in pursuit of relatively modest goals. Détente with the Soviet Union briefly allowed the United States to turn its attention to other matters, such as human rights violations and nuclear proliferation. Because the targets of these policies were more likely to be found among the developing countries, they tended to be economically weaker and less stable than the average target in earlier years. Détente, together with economic problems at home, made the Soviet Union less and less willing and able to play "the white knight" and provide offsetting assistance to target countries.

All of these factors should have boded well for U.S. sanctions in the 1970s. All too often, however, resort to economic sanctions appears to have been part of an effort to conduct foreign policy "on-the-cheap." After the withdrawal of American troops from Vietnam, U.S. presidents faced strong congressional and public opposition to military intervention, as well as a variety of economic problems, including stagflation, fiscal constraints, and increasing trade deficits. Economic sanctions do not directly put one's own citizens lives at risk and, nearly as important, they are typically off-budget. But effective economic sanctions do not often come cheap. Repeated failure, moreover, erodes the credibility of the sanctioning country or institution, an effect that may have been compounded by the decreased credibility of the U.S. military threat after Vietnam. Equally important, the global economy had changed dramatically. Although U.S. goals were relatively more modest and the targets usually smaller and weaker than before, the United States found that it had less leverage.

In the early years after World War II, the U.S. economy was the reservoir for rebuilding war-devastated countries. It was also the major, if not sole, supplier of a variety of goods and services. Well into the 1960s, the U.S. remained the primary source of economic assistance for developing countries. Since then, however, trade and financial patterns have grown far more diversified, new technology has spread more quickly, and the U.S. foreign aid budget has virtually dried up for all but a few countries. Recovery in Europe and the emergence of Japan have created new, competitive economic superpowers, and economic development has reduced the pool of potentially vulnerable targets. These trends are starkly illustrated by the declining average trade linkage between the United States and its targets (from 24 percent prior to 1973 to only 17 percent since), the lower costs imposed on targets (1.7 percent of gross national product GNP v. 0.9 percent of GNP), and the fading utility of manipulating aid flows.[3] For example, the success rate for financial sanctions used alone (these are usually cases involving reductions of aid to developing countries) declined from nearly 80 percent before 1973 to less than 20 percent since then.[4]

The Soviet invasion of Afghanistan and the election of Ronald Reagan brought an intensification of the Cold War that restored an East/West flavor to sanctions campaigns. This change in emphasis manifested itself in several differences between the sanctions cases in the 1980s and those in the preceding decade. Only about half of the 1980s cases involved modest goals, down from three-quarters in the 1970s. The incidence of companion policies nearly tripled (although from a low level given the predominance of modest goals in the 1970s); and the average cost imposed on the target doubled. Perhaps in recognition of its declining leverage, the United States also tried to harness more international cooperation. Still, the costs imposed remained below pre-1970 levels, the average trade linkage remained low, the average cost borne by the U.S. economy (although still small) increased, and the overall effectiveness of sanctions continued to decline. In addition to a declining relative economic position, the type of goals pursued with sanctions affected the type of sanction chosen in ways that undermined effectiveness. In the antiterrorism and nuclear nonproliferation cases, denial of key hardware was typically as important as inducing a change in policy, and so selective export controls were the tool of choice. Since the goals were relatively modest in the overall scheme of U.S. foreign policy, broader and more costly sanctions would have seemed like overkill, or in conflict with other more important goals. But because alternative suppliers of the sanctioned goods were usually available, even the denial goal proved elusive.

The type of financial sanction used most frequently also changed. Economic aid was the dominant choice in the earlier period. Military assistance was prominent in the later period, especially in the human rights cases, where military governments were often the target. Again, in some cases, alternative sources of arms and financial assistance were available. Even more important, however, these governments perceived internal dissent to be a greater threat to their longevity than U.S. enmity and sanctions.

Unilateral Sanctions After the Cold War

The inevitable decline of American postwar hegemony has substantially reduced the utility of unilateral U.S. economic sanctions. The end of the Cold War raises two questions for the future of sanctions. Can the utility of unilateral U.S. sanctions be restored? And does the UN embargo of Iraq presage a new approach to international diplomacy, with multilateral sanctions playing an important role?

The collapse of the Soviet Union provides a geopolitical benefit that partially offsets the negative economic trends facing U.S. policymakers in this area. Evidence from the case studies of recent decades reveals that "offsetting assistance," i.e., compensating aid or trade flows provided by a third party to offset the effects of the sanctions on the target country, was an important factor undermining the effectiveness of some sanctions. Cases involving offsetting assistance most often were embroiled in Cold War politics, with one of the superpowers providing assistance to a target of its rival's sanctions. Perhaps the best example of the importance of offsetting assistance to a target country government is Fidel Castro's Cuba. Estimates of the value of the subsidies provided by the Soviet Union to Cuba over the thirty years of the U.S. embargo typically are in the billions of dollars.[5] In 1990 Soviet officials estimated that Soviet assistance to Cuba in recent years might have been as much as $2 billion to $3 billion annually.[6] The decline in superpower rivalry, combined with severe economic problems at home, means that the now former Soviet Union is far less likely to play "the white knight" to countries seeking assistance to offset the impact of U.S. sanctions. Although Libya and occasionally sympathetic neighbors (South Africa for Rhodesia and Saudi Arabia for Pakistan) have played this role, the resources and commitment of potential new "white knights" are certain to pale beside those of the former Soviet Union at the height of the Cold War.

While the provision of offsetting assistance, if generous enough, can cause a sanctions effort to fail, its absence does not guarantee success. Other factors, especially the difficulty of the goal and the political as well as economic vulnerability of the target, usually will be decisive. Even if "white knights" are fewer in the 1990s, changes in the international economy in recent decades have reduced the number of targets likely to succumb to unilateral economic coercion, even if "white knights" go the way of dragons. Many potential targets have developed strong and diversified economies that will never again be as vulnerable as they once were. And even relatively weak economies are less vulnerable today as a result of the growth in world trade and the rapid dispersion of technology, which means that most U.S. exports can be replaced at little cost and alternatives, even to the large U.S. import market, can usually be found.

Thus, one by-product of the evolution of the world economy since World War II has been a narrowing of the circumstances in which unilateral economic leverage may be effectively applied. A more interdependent global economy means that the effectiveness of unilateral sanctions increasingly depends on the subtlety, skill, and creativity with which they are imposed—a test the United States has frequently failed.

Multilateral Sanctions and the "New World Order"

For many, the reaction to Iraq's invasion of Kuwait provided a vision of a post–Cold War world in which the United Nations, without the superpower rivalries that have hamstrung it in the past, would finally play the dispute-settlement role originally intended for it. Unfortunately, the civil war in the former Yugoslav republics vividly illustrates the difficulties in organizing effective multilateral cooperation. The end of the Cold War opened the door for an unprecedented degree of international cooperation against Iraq; but the real source of that near unanimity was the threat to global prosperity and political stability posed by Saddam's aggression. Had the invasion of Kuwait not placed him in a position to control the second largest oil reserves in the world, with one-half of his million-man army poised on the Saudi Arabian border, it is unlikely that the world would have been so united in confronting Saddam Hussein.

Even though the formal UN sanctions against Serbia are quite similar to those imposed against Iraq, the embargo of Iraq remains unique among sanctions efforts in this century. The sanctions were imposed quickly, comprehensively, and with an unprecedented degree of support. The economic embargo was agreed to by the UN Security Council less than a week after the invasion of Kuwait. Within a month, it approved the use of naval forces to enforce the sanctions. Within two months, the UN had added an air embargo and authorized secondary boycotts of countries violating the resolutions. Finally, Iraq's economy, geographically isolated and skewed toward oil, is far more vulnerable to economic coercion than other targets of sanctions have been. Because 90 percent of its export revenues come from oil, which could be easily monitored and interdicted, smugglers would have had no incentive to evade the sanctions once Saddam had exhausted both his reserves and whatever he was able to plunder from Kuwait.

By contrast, it was two to three weeks after the outbreak of civil war in Croatia before the European Community and United States embargoed arms, and several months more before they suspended aid flows and trade preferences for Serbia. The greater diversity of the Serbian economy also lessened the economic impact relative to that in Iraq, while the geography of the Balkans makes enforcement much more difficult. Because the former Yugoslavia serves as a land route for Turkey to Eastern and Central Europe, and the Danube River an important transportation route for Eastern and Central Europe to open water, a major loophole in the sanctions allowed for continued transshipment of goods, including petroleum products, through Serbia. Finally, in November 1992, more than a year after the crisis erupted and five months after the sanctions had been mandated, the Security Council approved naval interdiction on the Adriatic Sea to enforce the sanctions, called on Serbia's neighbors to crack down on abuse of the transshipment allowance, and approved the placement of UN personnel on the ground in neighboring countries to monitor enforcement.

Although the sanctions against Serbia were never stringently enforced, even the tightest sanctions usually weaken over time, in part because the high costs to the sender countries themselves erode support for the coercive measures. To counter this tendency during the Middle East crisis, the U.S. and its allies went to extraordinary lengths to ameliorate the costs of removing Iraqi and Kuwaiti oil from the market, especially for the hardest hit. Saudi Arabia and other oil exporters capable of doing so boosted oil production to offset losses from Iraqi and Kuwaiti production. In addition, the United States took the lead in organizing an "economic action plan" to recycle the short-term windfall profits gained by the Saudis and other oil producers, and to encourage Japan, Germany, and others to provide grants and low-cost loans to developing countries hurt by higher oil prices, and lost trade and workers' remittances.[7] The International Monetary Fund and World Bank also provided concessional loans to developing countries suffering balance-of-payments stresses because of the sudden jump in oil prices. There is no provision in the Serbian case for secondary sanctions and no compensation scheme for countries severely injured by enforcing the sanctions. Perhaps if both had been in place it would have been easier to control abuse of the transshipment allowance on the Danube.

Conclusions

Although modest sanctions may achieve modest goals, collective security goals are typically ambitious, and the key to success in these cases is the commitment of the sanctioning country or group. The comparison of the Iraq and Yugoslav cases supports the general conclusion that, especially when the goal is ambitious, sanctions should be imposed quickly and comprehensively. To maximize the chances for a successful outcome, the leaders of the sanctioning coalition should also try to even out the distribution of the costs, providing assistance to the hardest hit. They must also be prepared to extend sanctions to member countries that fail to enforce the measures agreed.

The degree of commitment achieved during the Middle East crisis was extraordinary. What a lack of commitment produces is tragically evident in Yugoslavia, where the imposition of comprehensive trade and financial sanctions was too little and, more important, too late. While a credible threat of military action underscored the coalition's determination to enforce the sanctions and ultimately to reverse Iraq's invasion of Kuwait, obvious reluctance to use force weakened the credibility of the coalition in enforcing the sanctions against Yugoslavia. Lack of credibility weakens a sanctions effort in two ways. It encourages greater intransigence on the part of the target country because the target believes the sanctioning coalition cannot hold for long; and it contributes to the perception in third countries that there will be no consequence as a result of breaking the sanctions.

The end of the Cold War removed an important obstacle to the use of economic sanctions as a tool of collective security, but it did not erase all the economic and political interests that divide countries. Nor did it make difficult objectives easy, or strong and stable targets more susceptible to economic pressure. And while increased economic interdependence has reduced potential vulnerability to unilateral sanctions in many cases, it is also a double-edged sword for multilateral sanctions. It may increase the power of broad economic sanctions, because countries are more dependent on trade and financial flows. It also means more countries will need to be involved in a sanctions effort to make it effective, and that there may be more countries capable of undermining the effect of a sanctions effort should they choose to do so.

Notes

1. The methodology, examples, and conclusions about economic sanctions generally are based on Gary Clyde Hufbauer, Jeffrey J. Schott, and Kimberly Ann Elliott, *Economic Sanctions Reconsidered*, 2d ed. (Washington, D.C.: Institute for International Economics, 1990).

2. The UN embargo of Iraq is not included in the database because it was still ongoing at the time the book went to press.

3. Hufbauer, Schott, and Elliott, *Economic Sanctions Reconsidered*, pp. 91–113.

4. Ibid.

5. Gary Clyde Hufbauer, Jeffrey J. Schott, Kimberly Elliott, *Economic Sanctions Reconsidered: Supplemental Case Histories*, 2d ed. (Washington, D.C.: Institute for International Economics, 1990), pp. 200–201.

6. Ibid.

7. Hufbauer, Schott, Elliott, *Economic Sanctions Reconsidered*, pp. 288–9.

6

The Problems and Promise
of Sanctions

William H. Kaempfer and Anton D. Lowenberg

Economic sanctions constitute a less costly method of international pressure than outright hostilities and have gained wide approval as a tool for unilateral and bilateral foreign policy in a variety of situations. They have been most often applied in cases of foreign policy disputes (e.g., Iraqi aggression in Kuwait) or human rights issues (e.g., antiapartheid sanctions against South Africa) and occasionally as an adjunct to commercial policies, such as retaliation against countries accused of unduly restricting foreign access to their domestic markets or of engaging in dumping practices. Recent examples of the latter include U.S. trade restrictions imposed against Brazil for its refusal to allow the importation of U.S. computer products, similar restrictions on European Community agricultural exports in reprisal for European prohibitions on American hormone-fed beef exports, and threatened U.S. tariffs on European white wine exports in retaliation for European soybean subsidies. Sanctions have even been contemplated or applied in disputes involving environmental issues and cross-border externalities. For instance, under pressure from conservation groups, the U.S. recently threatened sanctions against Japan for its commercial uses of almost extinct sea turtles.

But much controversy surrounds the use of sanctions. How are sanctions designed to cause policy change in target countries? Are sanctions used too frequently (or infrequently) as a policy option, or are they imposed for the wrong reasons? Why do sanctions so often lack significant economic impact? To address these questions, we will compare the traditional method of analysis of sanctions with an endogenous policy model of sanctions use and effectiveness based on the principles of public choice economics, which explores state behavior from the perspective of

61

rational, individual decision making by participants. The insights of the public choice approach should help to explain some peculiarities surrounding the use of sanctions and some reasons why a sanctions regime may be a viable policy tool for changing the objectionable policies of foreign governments.

Problems for Effective Sanctions

Popular wisdom about economic sanctions is that they are relatively ineffective. The traditional method by which sanctions are presumed to work is for the sanctioning country, in response to some objectionable policy in the target country, to impose economic damage on the target country, which will (supposedly) produce a change in the objectionable policy. This instrumental approach to sanctions relies on massive economic pressure being applied and suggests that only the most imposing economic bullies will have much of a chance at being successful sanctioners. Most economists believe that sanctions are ineffective because they do not impose significant economic damage upon the target nation. Economists are fond of pointing out that sanctions often do not have the damaging impact on the target economy that they are intended to have. Without the full cooperation of all existing or potential trading partners, boycotts of a target's exports or embargoes on its imports are difficult to achieve, because a competitive world market provides many sources of supply and alternate buyers. Willett and Jalalighajar point out that:

> . . . except in unusual situations, alternate sources of supply and the transshipment of goods will nullify most of the intended effects of economic restrictions. A single country [imposing sanctions] seldom has sufficient control over the market of an important good for a boycott or embargo to have any major impact.[1]

To make trade sanctions effective in reducing the wealth of the target country, it is necessary that the sanctions be comprehensive in coverage (i.e., include most trade flows between the target and the rest of the world), and that the opportunities for redirecting trade be minimized. This latter condition, in turn, requires that the sanctioning countries account for almost the entire world market in the traded goods, or, failing this, that the cooperation of other countries be secured. In light of the strong incentives for an individual buyer or seller to renege on a collusive cartel agreement, this latter condition is seldom met.

The economic injury caused by trade sanctions can best be measured by a price effect felt in the target.[2] When a target has sanctions enforced against it, its terms of trade worsen as the restricted number of import sources causes import prices to rise, while export prices fall due to a decrease in the number of export customers. This price effect mechanism demonstrates the incentives for nations (or individuals) to cheat against the sanctions or not join a multilateral sanctions effort. Any country that does not abide by the sanctions setup against a target has the opportunity to profiteer by exporting sanctioned goods to the target and importing the target's restricted exports at sanctions-distorted prices. The more severe the economic impact of the sanctions, the greater the opportunity for gain to any one willing to maintain trade with the target. This, incidentally, helps to explain why the bitter enemies of a target nation often are so willing to be sanctions busters. The conclusion is that the economic impact of sanctions is unlikely to cripple a target because of the availability of alternate sources and markets and the possibility of transshipment of goods.

A further, and more serious problem for the instrumental approach to sanctions relates to how the economic damage of sanctions is transformed into policy change in the target. The exact channel of transmission is obscure, but what is clear is that all too often the policy change desired by the sanctioning countries is not forthcoming in spite of sanctions that impose extensive economic damage. Consider, for instance, the continuing resistance by Iraq and by Serbian authorities in the former Yugoslavia to intense foreign sanctions pressures. Causing changes in objectionable policies in target countries is not simply a function of the intensity of economic damage from sanctions.

The Public Choice Approach

Public choice economics explores state behavior from the perspective of rational, individual decision making by participants. This branch of economic analysis suggests that many government policies, including international economic sanctions, can be viewed as endogenous policies that are the outcome of domestic political decisions in which the redistribution of domestic wealth plays a major factor.[3] Thus, trade sanctions that restrict imports from target countries create benefits for producers of import substitutes in the sanctioning countries, at the expense of consumers of those goods.[4] The interests that benefit from such policies or sanctions are sure to support them through the political process for their own ends. Some interest groups lobby for sanctions, not to obtain pecuniary gains, but to enhance the psychic welfare of their members. Thus, antiapartheid activists in the U.S. and other Western countries often sought sanctions against South Africa to assuage their members' dislike for the South African government's policies. On occasion groups with a pecuniary interest in sanctions will join forces with other groups seeking sanctions for largely nonpecuniary gains. For instance, U.S. sugar producers might join anti-Castro interests in lobbying for a boycott of Cuban sugar imports to the U.S. Kaempfer and Lowenberg argue that many antiapartheid sanctions imposed by the U.S. and European Community in the late 1980s also served protectionist interests in those countries.[5]

Despite the motives of the groups lobbying for sanctions, any such restrictions on trade inevitably result in substantial costs for others in terms of higher prices and foregone trading opportunities. Given these costs of sanctions accruing to individuals and groups in the sanctioning countries, it is hardly surprising that sanctioners often deliberately apply sanctions that have weak economic impacts on the target countries. Elementary trade theory suggests that a sanctions regime that has a severe economic effect on one trading partner is likely also to impose substantial pain on the other partner. Therefore, governments in sanctioning countries will often attempt to meet the demands of interest groups pressuring them to apply sanctions by choosing fairly innocuous sanctions, usually on imports or exports which comprise small shares of the sanctioner's total market, thereby avoiding some wrath of other groups who might be hurt by more severe sanctions. This helps to explain why, for example, the U.S. Comprehensive Antiapartheid Act of 1986 included sanctions against South African textiles, steel, and agricultural goods, none of which represented a significant share of the U.S. market, but exempted various strategic metals of which South Africa is a major world supplier. Politicians like to be seen to be "doing something" about a foreign government's violation of moral or ideological values, thereby satisfying interest groups lobbying for sanctions without simultaneously incurring any substantial costs that could raise the ire of other influential interest groups within the sanctioning polity.[6]

This interest-group analysis implies that the forms and severity of sanctions applied depend on several factors, including the relative influences of various interest groups within the polity of a sanctioning country, the ability of policymakers to act independently of interest-group pressures, and the amount of information possessed by individuals and groups within the sanctioning country regarding the objectionable policy of the target country. Thus, for example, the greater the awareness of injustices practiced by a target government, the greater the momentum of the sanctioning campaign. It follows that sanctions are often imposed not so much to initiate political changes in a target nation, but as a *response* to events that are already unfolding there. Resistance against the policies of the target government by its own citizens, for example, raises the profile of their struggle in the minds of sympathetic individuals abroad, and this enhanced consciousness of the problem leads to increased pressure on the sanctioning country's government to do something.[7]

The Impact of Sanctions

Just as the pressure for sanctions in sanctioning countries is a function of interest-group politics, so the effects of the sanctions in the target country also depend on interest-group politics in that country. Consider a simple interest-group model of the domestic polity of the target country,[8] in which there are two domestic interest groups, X and Y, and a redistribution policy, A, which is viewed as objectionable by some foreigners and therefore attracts foreign sanctions. The objectionable policy might be aggression toward a neighboring country, human rights abuses, or destruction of some scarce natural resource. Suppose that members of group X benefit from policy A, which is a net transfer to members of X, whereas members of group Y are harmed by A because they are taxed to pay for the transfer to group X. Politicians decide the level of A by weighing the relative influences of group X and group Y. The presumption here is that politicians seek only to maximize their political support, by choosing policies in accordance with the relative influences of interest groups.[9]

The more resources a group is willing or able to allocate to political activity, the more effective it is in exerting political influence, and therefore the greater the relative weight which politicians attach to that group. Group X's preference for policy A is revealed in a downward sloping demand curve. The height of this curve at any given value of A is group X's marginal willingness to pay for policy A. This willingness to pay can be interpreted as a willingness to allocate resources to lobbying and political pressure to persuade the government to supply more A. Similarly, group Y reveals a downward sloping demand curve for *reduced* levels of A, or alternatively, an upward sloping "supply" curve for increased levels of A. Members of group Y are willing to allocate increasingly large amounts of resources at the margin to prevent A from increasing. Thus the height of their willingness-to-pay curve represents the "supply price" which politicians must incur, in terms of increased opposition from group Y, as a consequence of allowing A to increase.

As shown in Figure 6.1, the political equilibrium occurs at the intersection of these demand and supply curves. Support-maximizing politicians will supply A up to the point where X's marginal willingness to pay for an increase in A is equal to Y's marginal willingness to pay for a decrease in A.[10] An increase in either group's political effectiveness will cause an upward shift of its willingness-to-pay curve. Thus, for example, an increase in X's effectiveness relative to Y's effectiveness will cause X's demand curve to shift up relative to Y's, and the equilibrium value of A will increase.

The preceding analysis implies that any exogenous event that increases X's political effectiveness by more than it increases Y's effectiveness, *ceteris*

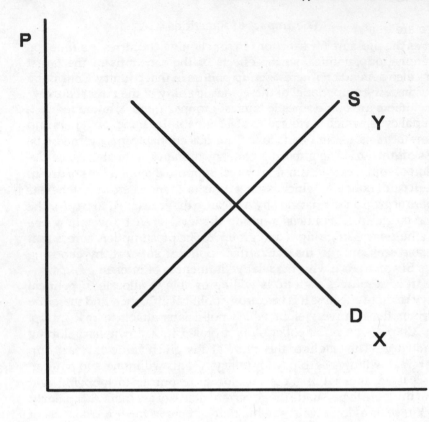

FIGURE 6.1

paribus will cause an increase in the equilibrium level of A. Such an event, which shocks the domestic political system and alters the policy equilibrium, could emanate from outside the domestic polity. Examples include international sanctions, other foreign policy initiatives, lobbying activities of foreign interest groups, revolutions, or uprisings in neighboring countries. With sanctions, an embargo that reduces the incomes of both groups by the same amount will cause reductions of equal magnitude in the political effectiveness of both groups, and the equilibrium level of the objectionable policy A will not change. Only if the sanctions reduce the income of one group by more than that of the other will the equilibrium level of A change.[11] Trade embargoes and financial sanctions, however, normally have widespread impacts on all groups in the target country. It is difficult to design sanctions to have selective economic impacts on different groups, especially due to the haphazard way that sanctions policies are generated out of interest-group politics in the sanctioning countries.[12]

Sanctions affect political processes in the target country not only through their income effects but, perhaps more significantly, through their impacts on each interest groups' effectiveness in organizing the collective action of its members. For example, a sanction that threatens to impose substantial costs on the supporters of the regime (group X), and perhaps threatens to escalate those costs in the future if the objectionable policy is not altered, might cause members of group X to become discouraged in their support for the group. This enhances free riding among X's members and reduces the group's political effectiveness. The equilibrium level of A falls. Alternatively, the sanctions might increase the ability of group X to organize collective action among its members, perhaps due to a rally-around-the-flag effect induced by unwelcome foreign intervention.[13] The sanctions also can change the political effectiveness of the opposition group Y. Since sanctions are typically aimed against the ruling regime's policies, it is conceivable that the imposition of sanctions could be interpreted by members of group Y as foreign support for their struggle against X and its policy A. Members of group Y also might perceive that the sanctions have diminished the capacity of the existing government to retain power, which enhances the private return to individuals from opposing the government. In either case, members of Y might be willing to allocate more resources to political opposition, thereby diminishing free riding within Y and enhancing Y's political effectiveness. The result is a fall in equilibrium A.

Kaempfer and Lowenberg explore in greater detail the mechanisms linking sanctions with changes in political influences of interest groups in a target nation. Their analysis is based on a rational-choice model of collective action in which individuals are assumed to obtain utility from conforming with certain beliefs, even if conformity requires a sacrifice of income or other goods.[14] For example, Higgs argues that an individual's utility depends not only on a basket of goods consumed, but also on "the degree to which one's self-perceived identity corresponds with the standards of one's chosen (or merely accepted) reference group, that is, with the tenets of the ideology one has embraced."[15] Groups, in essence, reward their supporters with selective incentives, such as the right to share in a feeling of group identity or "political presence."[16] Individuals obtain "reputational utility" from supporting the policy of a group, and this utility rises with the size of the group or the number of its supporters.[17] The rationale for this assumption is that individuals "fortify their reputation(s) as supporter(s) of a given cause by rewarding other supporters and by withdrawing favors from opponents."[18] People wishing to draw attention to their decision to support a group do so partly by complimenting and rewarding other supporters, because this carries more weight than a mere verbal declaration. Therefore, the individual obtains greater utility from joining in with a large group of peers than a smaller group, because the larger group creates a greater sense of group identity. Interest groups or political parties can foster greater support if they can convince individuals that their platforms are already popular. This helps to explain why a great deal of effort is often expended by the leaders of groups or parties in trying to convince people that their policies command the support of a considerable portion of the public.[19]

There are three distinct methods by which the leadership of an interest group can propagate public support for its policies:

1. The group might succeed in lowering private thresholds for collective action, perhaps by saturating the public with information or publicity designed to alter private preferences in favor of the group's objective;
2. The group could increase reputational rewards available to individuals contributing to the group's cause, which might be achieved by convincing potential contributors that the group has a good chance of success in attaining political influence or power to make appointments in government; and
3. The group could try to convince individuals that a critical mass of citizens already supports its policies.

All three cases can initiate a bandwagon process that raises support to a higher level in the population.

Pressures of foreign interest groups or events in foreign countries can serve as catalysts for all of the above mechanisms. First, individuals might revise their private beliefs and preferences when they discover that foreigners publicly profess belief in some policy objective. An individual's private preferences are shaped by his private beliefs, which, in turn, are partly dependent on the beliefs expressed publicly by other people. The greater the number of people who appear to hold an opinion, the greater the extent to which private beliefs and preferences will be altered to accord more closely with that opinion. Sanctions imposed against a target country can provide information to individuals in the target country that produces a change in private preferences regarding the objectionable policy pursued by the target's government.[20]

Second, foreign pressures might produce an increase in reputational utility awarded to individuals who support certain domestic interest groups, by increasing the effectiveness of those groups in rewarding their contributors with selective incentives. Thus, a signal of foreign support for the policies of a domestic group could be perceived as raising the probability of eventually achieving the goal sought by the group, which in turn might encourage activists in that group to work harder and devote more effort to organizing collective action. Third, sanctions, or foreign interest-group lobbying, might produce an increase in collective sentiment for the policies advocated by a domestic interest group. Such foreign pressures create the perception among individual citizens of the target nation that the policy pursued by their government is generally viewed as reprehensible by many people outside. This may also hold true for many individuals within the target country, implying that a large proportion of the population is strongly opposed to the policy and is willing to take action against it. In all three of the above cases, pressures, policies or events emanating from abroad serve to enhance the political effectiveness of certain domestic interest groups and reduce the effectiveness of others. These changes in the relative influences of competing interest groups can cause changes in public policy outcomes.

Conclusion

From the perspective of both the instrumental approach and the public choice approach, sanctions face many difficulties in being a successful element of a nation's foreign policy portfolio. On the one hand, the traditional, instrumental view of sanctions must face the fact that damaging economic sanctions will be difficult to apply in most situations and even more difficult to maintain. Public choice analysis suggests that damaging sanctions will be infrequently used because of the costs associated with them to sanctioning countries. Furthermore, when sanctions are used they can be expected to be distorted toward the ends of influential special interests, rather than being fine-tuned toward the goal of the sanctions.

On the other hand, the public choice approach does give some insight into exactly how sanctions might be expected to work in resolving international disputes. Objectionable policies in target countries are the result of the political processes of those countries and the decisions reached in those political systems. Sanctions can be effective by realigning the various interests at work in the political process. By strengthening the political effectiveness of internal interests seeking to change the objectionable policies of the target regime, sanctions can help to foster that change.

Notes

1. Thomas D. Willett and Mehrdad Jalalighajar, "U.S. Trade Policy and National Security," *CATO Journal*, Vol. 3, Winter 1983/84, p. 723.

2. William H. Kaempfer and Anton D. Lowenberg, *International Economic Sanctions: A Public Choice Perspective* (Boulder, Colo.: Westview Press, 1992).

3. The classics in the economic theory of regulation are George J. Stigler, "The Theory of Economic Regulation," *Bell Journal of Economics and Management Science*, Vol. 2, Spring 1971, pp. 3–21; and Sam Peltzman, "Toward a More General Theory of Regulation," *Journal of Law and Economics*, Vol. 19, August 1976, pp. 211–40.

4. William H. Kaempfer and Anton D. Lowenberg, "Sanctioning South Africa: The Politics Behind the Policies," *CATO Journal*, Vol. 8, Winter 1989, pp. 713–27.

5. Ibid.

6. For more details on this process, see Kaempfer and Lowenberg, "Sanctioning South Africa," pp. 713–27. See also Kaempfer and Lowenberg, *International Economic Sanctions*.

7. Thus, the Soweto riots in South Africa, the Tiananmen repression in China, and the reported rape and pillage of Bosnians by Serbs, all led to increased pressure on the U.S. government to impose economic and other sanctions against the offending nations.

8. This model is in the tradition of Peltzman, "Theory of Regulation," pp. 211–40; and Gary S. Becker, "A Theory of Competition Among Pressure Groups for Political Influence," *Quarterly Journal of Economics*, Vol. 98, August 1983, pp. 371–400. See also Gary S. Becker, "Public Policies, Pressure Groups, and Dead Weight Costs," *Journal of Public Economics*, Vol. 28, December 1985, pp. 329–47.

9. According to this conception of the political process, the government acts as a more or less impartial broker of interest group pressures. See Becker, "Theory of Competition," pp. 371–400; and Becker, "Public Policies," pp. 329–47. See also William H. Kaempfer and Anton D. Lowenberg, "The Theory of International Economic Sanctions: A Public Choice Approach," *American Economic Review*, Vol. 78, September 1988, pp. 786–93. Typically, interest groups deliver support to politicians in the form of votes or in the form of funds which can be used to finance campaigns, etc. In this stylized interest-group model, however, other forms of political expression, such as demonstrations and insurrection, are also effective ways of pressuring politicians or imposing costs associated with specific policies.

10. Peltzman, "Theory of Regulation," pp. 211–40.

11. We are assuming here that sanctions are, in general, income-reducing for both groups X and Y. It is possible, of course, the members of one group might actually receive net pecuniary gains as a consequence of sanctions.

12. Barry E. Carter, *International Economic Sanctions: Improving the Haphazard U.S. Legal Regime* (Cambridge: Cambridge Univ. Press, 1988).

13. Kaempfer and Lowenberg, "The Theory of International Economic Sanctions," pp. 786–93.

14. William H. Kaempfer and Anton D. Lowenberg, "Using Threshold Models to Explain International Relations," *Public Choice*, Vol. 73, June 1992, pp. 419–43.

15. Robert Higgs, *Crisis and Leviathan: Critical Episodes in the Growth of American Government* (New York: Oxford Univ. Press, 1987), p. 43.

16. Carole Jean Uhlaner, "'Relational Goods' and Participation: Incorporating Sociability into a Theory of Rational Action," *Public Choice*, Vol. 62, September 1989, pp. 253–85.

17. Timur Kuran, "Chameleon Voters and Public Choice," *Public Choice*, Vol. 53, No. 1, 1987, pp. 53–78.

18. Timur Kuran, "Preference Falsification, Policy Continuity and Collective Conservatism," *Economic Journal*, Vol. 97, September 1987, p. 645.

19. Kuran, "Chameleon Voters," p. 72; and Uhlaner, "'Relational Goods'," p. 272.

20. Kuran, "Preference Falsification," p. 655.

7

Sanctions and International Law

Christopher C. Joyner

The United Nations' increased reliance on international sanctions raises interest in how political consensus can be fashioned through international legal channels to make sanctions more effective instruments. This is made more difficult when one considers the decentralized nature of the international legal system, which is not endowed with sophisticated lawmaking and law enforcing procedures like those associated with domestic sanctions within states. Other issues are raised as well: What systems and institutions must be fortified to increase the chances that sanctions will be effective? How can the political will of sanctioning countries be maintained to enforce a sanctions regime over time?

The Efficacy of Sanctions

It is important to note at the outset that the notion of efficacy is not necessarily synonymous with that of "success." It is entirely possible that sanctions could be effective in terms of breaking commercial relations, imposing economic costs, and fulfilling a punitive role, yet ultimately not be successful in achieving their stated political objectives.[1] When considering efficacy, we must consider the goals and objectives of a sanctions operation. If sanctions are used simply as a signal by the imposers that a particular course of action is unacceptable, then it may be unnecessary to examine the actual economic impact of the measures on the target state since the objective has been achieved. If, however, sanctions also seek to bring about an actual policy shift by the target state, such as the withdrawal of troops or the cessation of hostilities, then it becomes vital to consider whether the economic penalties will be sufficient to cause this result.

Several of the following conditions may increase the likelihood of an effective sanctions operation. First, sanctions measures should be imposed quickly, and should be sweeping in scope. Second, international support for the measures must be strong, despite costs inflicted on the sanctioning nations. Third, the sanctioning nations must maintain their determination to achieve their goal over time. Fourth, it must be determined that the target state is actually vulnerable to sanctions. This means that the deviant state must be reliant upon international trade and has little chance of developing self-sufficiency for embargoed goods or successfully undertaking evasion strategies, e.g., by encouraging cheating by sanctioning states.

Efficacy can also be adversely affected by certain unintended events that could occur in the target state. It is possible that sanctions might actually create a stronger sense of internal solidarity in the target state by generating a rally-around-the-flag effect. The extent to which that population is willing to accept lower standards of living will directly influence how much economic punishment is required to produce a successful sanctions effort.[2]

The Rationale for Sanctions

As instruments of self-help in international law, sanctions can serve several objectives and goals. Sometimes they may be preventive, by seeking to preclude the commission of an illegal act or deny a violator from achieving its objective after committing an illegal act.[3] More often, though, sanctions assume a punitive nature by representing the "penalty attached to transgression and breach of international law" in the form of "punitive actions initiated . . . against one or more states for violating a universally approved charter, as inducements to follow, or refrain from following, that particular course of conduct and conform with international law."[4] Thus, punishment is often coupled with the intent of a sanctioning state to inflict sufficient economic harm to compel a change in the behavior of the target state.

While the instrumental objective is implicit in most instances of sanctions, other objectives may also come into play. Perhaps most significant among these is to send a clear signal to the target state that its behavior is unacceptable to the international community. In this manner, notice is served that further illegal action or a continuation of the present illegal action may lead to more serious measures.

Economic sanctions supply a useful function by providing a means to demonstrate disapproval that is stronger than diplomatic protest, but falls short of resort to armed force. In a broader sense, sanctions aim to isolate the target from the rest of the international community and thereby deprive it of the benefits of international intercourse. This function may also satisfy domestic pressures in a sanctioning state, where the population has demanded some action by the leadership.[5]

The imposition of sanctions is not without costs to sanctioning states, however. Lost trading opportunities, suspended contracts, and elaborate implementation mechanisms can impose significant costs that vary according to a sanctioning state's size and relationship to the target state. The fact that governments are aware of these costs, yet implement sanctions in spite of them, underscores the political determination and will of sanctioning states to show disapproval of an offending state's actions.[6]

Components of a Sanctions Operation

The array of economic measures available to the United Nations Security Council for enhancing the political efficacy of a sanctions operation is impressive.[7] First, a boycott can be put into effect against a target state's commerce. A complete prohibition on the import of all commodities and products originating in the target state can be imposed by Security Council resolution,[8] or such action could be directed only at halting sales of critical commodities whose trade is needed by the target state to secure foreign exchange earnings. The political efficacy of a sanctions operation can also be reinforced by the imposition of an embargo against all the exports of goods or services to the target state. Although an embargo should be total in scope, provisions can allow for the possibility of exceptions for humanitarian aid or medical supplies, approved by the appropriate sanctions committee in consultation with the Security Council.

UN sanctions against a deviant state might also include financial restrictions. To intensify economic isolation, a complete ban could be imposed on all financial transactions and transfers of funds to the target government or to any other entity in that state.[9] Another means for enhancing the political efficacy of international sanctions involves the imposition of contract restrictions on presanctions commercial arrangements with the target state. Such obligations may undermine the sanctions regime. An order by the UN Security Council could stipulate that its provisions must be upheld by all states irrespective of any contract entered into or license granted before sanctions were implemented.[10]

Imposition of a multinational naval interdiction, if needed, should be approved by the Security Council to carry out the sanctions operation. In an effort to tighten the enforcement of the sanctions, cargoes and destinations must be verified to ensure strict compliance with sanctions provisions contained in the appropriate Security Council resolution.[11] Authorization can also be given for the detention of vessels belonging to the target state implicated in violations of the sanctions order, but which have entered foreign ports.[12] To complement the naval interdiction, an air embargo might also be imposed. Under the terms of a sanctions order, states should be prohibited from permitting the takeoff of any aircraft from their territory that might carry cargo to or from the target state, unless it is a specially designated shipment approved as part of authorized humanitarian or medical efforts. States should also deny overflight permission to any aircraft bound for the target state, unless inspection of its cargo at a designated airfield determines that such cargo does not violate sanctions prohibitions. Supervision of the air embargo should be entrusted to the Sanctions Committee, which would be authorized to receive reports of implementation measures taken by participating states.[13]

Still another facet of enhancing the political efficacy of a sanctions operation involves travel restrictions. As a matter of course, travel restrictions to and from the target state should be imposed on an individual basis by governments in support of the broader aims of the sanctions program. Notable exceptions might be made in the cases of diplomatic initiatives and evacuations of third-country nationals.

Imposition and strict enforcement of an embargo on arms remains critical to any international sanctions effort. The appropriate embargo provision on commodities and products should include weapons or any other military equipment as prohibited items.[14] Depending on the special circumstances of the target state, this dimension of the operation might be expanded to include a more detailed listing of prohibited items, including conventional arms, weapons of mass destruction, ballistic missiles, and services related to technical support and training.

International Enforcement

The Sanctions Committee. The political efficacy of a UN sanctions regime is activated by the Security Council's creation of a special committee on sanctions, the composition of which includes all members of the Security Council. Its mandate should include review of the responses from states concerning measures taken in support of the sanctions resolution and acquisition of further information about the implementation process as required.[15] Observations and recommendations based on the Sanctions Committee's findings can then be conveyed to the Security Council. The scope of activity of the Sanctions Committee can be broadened in subsequent resolutions to include regular briefings by the Secretary General on matters related to humanitarian assistance.[16] Authority can also be granted to the committee to examine and recommend appropriate action regarding requests made by states under Article 50,[17] and responsibility can be assigned for monitoring and approving flights by aircraft to or from the target state.[18] The committee might also be charged with the responsibility of approving exceptions to sanctions in cases of humanitarian assistance.[19] The work of a sanctions committee in facilitating implementation by states is made effective largely through the reporting requirement[20] and the possibility of inflicting negative publicity on states whose efforts fall short of the requirements.

Military Staff Committee. The Military Staff Committee (MSC) is a body created by the UN Charter to advise the Security Council on military matters, with special attention to the command and deployment of military forces under council control. Article 47(2) specifies that the committee is comprised of the chiefs of staff of the five permanent members of the Security Council, or their representatives. Chairmanship is to rotate monthly. Paralysis of the Security Council during the Cold War decades and failure to develop the military arm of the council as envisaged in Articles 43–48 of the charter has rendered the Military Staff Committee (MSC) moribund since its creation. It meets only occasionally without any pressing mandate, and its personnel are at the junior level. The recent UN sanctions operations have prompted agreement by the United States and Russia to re-examine the MSC considering the military-related provisions of Security Council resolutions.[21] Yet no new sanctions role has been assigned to the MSC and its precise usefulness for UN sanctions efforts remains undefined.

The Sanctions Committee and the Military Staff Committee are both intended as mechanisms to coordinate and facilitate the implementation of sanctions measures by states in the hope of achieving a more unified response. As with any international body, however, the power of the Sanctions and Military Staff Committees lies solely in the political willingness of governments to delegate authority to them and thereby to accept their decisions and guidance. As one might have expected, that power has been noticeably limited in recent UN sanctions efforts, as national governments have preferred to retain control of sanctions operations through their own domestic laws and regulations.

National Enforcement. The measures described previously consist largely of decisions taken by the United Nations Security Council under the mandate and authority of relevant sections of the UN Charter. These measures are binding upon members and carry the full force of law. Their effects, however, cannot be appreciated without noting that actual implementation of such measures must take place at the national level. It is at the national level that enforcement and decisions of compliance become critical considerations.

Each national government has developed its own particular means for implementing international sanctions. As a leading advocate in recent years for imposing sanctions against deviant states, the United States government finds its legislative basis for taking implementing actions in four principal acts: the International Emergency Economic Powers Act (IEEPA), the National Emergencies Act (NEA), the United Nations Participation Act (UNPA), and the Trading With the Enemy Act (TWEA). The International Emergency Economic Powers Act[22] authorizes the president to investigate, regulate, or prohibit transactions with a particular country if a situation exists which threatens American national interests. To invoke these powers, a national emergency must be declared through the issuance of an executive order in accordance with the National Emergencies Act.[23] Authorization to impose sanctions in accordance with a mandatory decision by the UN Security Council is also granted to the president by virtue of the United Nations Participation Act.[24] Although not invoked during recent UN sanctions episodes, additional basis for the regulation of economic relations is provided by the Trading with the Enemy Act,[25] which is operable only after a formal declaration of war by the Congress.

While each state retains the sovereign right to implement international sanctions however it sees fit, the fact remains that participating governments must legislate the means to enforce sanctions regulations. Whether by executive decree or legislative fiat, this facet of an international sanctions operations remains critical for ensuring its enforcement. The importance of international coordination should not be undervalued. Administration and oversight remain pivotal to the effectiveness of the sanctions regime, especially in light of inherent differences in existing national legislation, individual legislative processes, and bureaucratic capabilities to adjust to complex implementation measures.

Factors Enhancing the Political Efficacy of Sanctions

Having set forth the scope, authority, and implementation of international sanctions, it is useful to consider how political efficacy and enforcement work. Why do governments comply with a Security Council order for sanctions against a certain state? What combination of political, legal, and economic factors can enhance the political efficacy for an international sanctions mandate, and how might those factors be translated into viable policy preferences in the future?

Several factors must be weighed by a government in its calculus to decide whether to support international legal principles or to seek greater benefit by ignoring or violating such principles. These include:

1. Knowledge of both the norm in question and the penalty for violation;
2. The status of the authority in terms of legitimacy;
3. The status of the norm;

4. The motivation and competence of the authority to detect violation of the norm, to apply sanctions, and to effectively enforce the sanctions;
5. The estimated impact of the sanctions on the state; and
6. The value of the nonconforming conduct.[26]

Several factors help to explain why compliance is most often the preferred choice. These factors become salient considerations of political efficacy.

Self-Interest. Independent sovereign states would have little incentive to accept obligations to a system of international law unless certain tangible benefits were perceived as derived in the process. Perhaps chief among the benefits of complying is that of the predictability of relations that adherence to international legal rules conveys. International law establishes a framework for conducting orderly relations with other states that facilitates important activities such as trade, diplomatic exchanges, and travel. This creates expectations by states that others will comply with international norms as well. Economic concerns weigh heavily upon a state's compliance decision. In most cases, the growing interdependence of the world economy creates a common desire among states for friendly and cooperative relations to foster productive economic intercourse. In contemporary UN sanctions, self-interest plays a preeminent role. Governments perceive that a fundamental norm of international order, namely Article 2(4) of the UN Charter, has been violated and a legal remedy is required. Some states may be concerned about becoming the target of punitive measures themselves, and are thus persuaded to uphold the sanctions, thereby validating the legal rules involved.

Peer Pressure and Public Opinion. The political efficacy of sanctions may also be enhanced because of peer pressure and public opinion at both the domestic and international levels. States are concerned with national honor and prestige, and may be afraid of opposing world public opinion. Thus, they often opt to take the particular course of action perceived as best benefiting their standing in the world community. Public opinion on the domestic level may demand a response by the nation's leadership to a brutal or repulsive international act, resulting in sanctions measures. Fear of opposing world public opinion may also produce a similar effect. As a prime example, the international effort against Saddam Hussein gained considerable momentum when prisoners of war were paraded before television cameras as the world watched in horror and outrage.

Ethics and Morality. While it remains difficult to speak of a single international code of ethics, there nonetheless exists some notion of international standards widely accepted by states as a guide to their international actions. In a real sense, these standards are linked to world public opinion, which is said to reflect the conscience of mankind. These values—peaceful relations, nonintervention, human rights, peaceful settlement of disputes, respect for national sovereignty, and so forth—are embodied in international law in treaties, customs, and general principles of law. In this context, the brutal invasion of a tiny state by an aggressive neighbor led by a man portrayed as a murderous dictator became a real factor in fostering international compliance with the sanctions effort against Iraq. Similarly, widespread reports of murder, torture, rape, mass executions, and other brutalities by Serbians against Bosnian Muslims during 1992 persuaded governments to use the Security Council to enact international sanctions against Serbia.

Legitimacy of Authority. Sanctions have often been employed as a tool of foreign policy by an individual state seeking to achieve its own ends. A marked distinction must be drawn between such cases, which fall under techniques of economic warfare, and mandatory enforcement actions taken by the Security Council according to the UN Charter. The latter claims an authoritative basis in a multilateral treaty that is binding upon most of the world community, and thereby conveys an extraordinary degree of legitimacy in the international system. This concept is associated with *pacta sunt servanda,* that is, the principle that treaties agreed to in good faith are legally binding on the parties.[27] When weighing the question of compliance with sanctions, governments clearly are mindful of the duty under international law to uphold their treaty obligations, lest their national credibility is damaged regarding the fulfillment of other obligations. The Security Council reminds states of this principle in each sanctions resolution, which calls for the participation of all member states in the sanctions effort and specifically implies that violators could be subjected to Security Council action.

The variety of self-interest factors, the pressure of peers, domestic and world public opinion, the notion of international "justice," and the lawful basis of authority all combine to enhance the political efficacy of sanctions.

Intimidation Through Enforcement Means. The actual means by which international sanctions can be enforced by sanctioning states take a variety of forms. At the international level, perhaps the most visible means of enforcement will be the naval interdiction. Comprised of warships from various governments, naval forces should be authorized to use the minimum force necessary to halt any shipments of cargo that violate the UN resolutions. Signals would first be given by radio, loudspeaker, flags, or other means, including warning shots across the bow. Suspicious ships could then be boarded to inspect the cargo.[28] Vessels found violating the sanctions can either be turned away or impounded. An international sanctions effort can also be assisted by reconnaissance technology. Observation aircraft and satellites can be used to monitor aircraft, ships, and vehicles attempting to break the embargo. By publicly announcing suspected violations, enforcing states aim to embarrass a derelict government so it will enact tighter national enforcement measures.

There are instances when a government might conclude, based upon its appraisal of the cost/benefit question, that violation of international law produces greater advantage than does compliance. Factors that may particularly appeal to a decision not to comply include excessive economic costs, lack of political will, lack of clarity of norms allegedly violated and insufficient commitment among those comprising the international consensus to impose sanctions. The cost dimension is a particularly salient consideration. It is not unusual for international sanctions to impose very high costs on sanctioning states, which can exact weighty repercussions on their national economies.

Furthermore, if costs are high, and the sanctions effort continues over a prolonged period, the likelihood increases that a sanctioning state's resolve will weaken. Such a situation also may occur if the burden of sanctions is distributed disproportionately among the sanctioning states.[29]

The importance of the cost consideration is addressed by Article 50 of the UN Charter, which allows states to request assistance if they are adversely affected by mandatory enforcement measures. Such requests are reviewed by the appropriate sanctions committee,[30] and liability for damages is likely to be assessed against the target state. The Security Council is also likely to create a compensation fund and establish procedures for lodging claims.[31] Other measures taken by states to lessen costs to enjoining states include increased economic opportunities to offset displaced goods and low-cost lending by the International Monetary Fund and the World Bank.[32]

A second factor that may induce violation concerns the political will of a particular government. Even if a state has the necessary implementation mechanisms in place in its domestic law, the degree to which such measures are enforced depends mainly on the earnest commitment of the leaders of that government. Reluctance to enforce regulations might not be expressed in public statements supporting the sanctions, but can become evident by a government's lengthy delays in implementing sanctions regulations.[33] A third factor, sometimes problematic for political efficacy, relates to the strength of international consensus supporting the goals, objectives, and means of the sanctions effort. The absence of clearly defined intentions in any of these areas may weaken the effort by creating a situation in which states are asked to expend great time and expense in support of an ill-conceived enforcement action.

The Balance Sheet

Analysis of contemporary UN sanctions operations points out particular lessons from those episodes and general trends for the broader notions of security regimes and compliance enforcement.

1. States are more likely to mobilize in response to a call for sanctions when an offense explicitly violates international norms. Iraq's invasion of Kuwait, for instance, was widely viewed as a flagrant violation of the territory of a sovereign state. Conversely, an action that involves complex or convoluted legal questions, or possibly even a legitimate dispute, may not produce a strong international consensus. Sanctions appear to enjoy greater prospects for implementation when the action in question clearly violates international norms and standards and shocks the "conscience of mankind."

2. To make sanctions effective, a consensus to act must develop promptly. If delays in implementing sanctions occur, target states could develop alliances with undecided states or prepare more readily for subsequent enforcement action.

3. Political efficacy can be improved when sanctions are comprehensive in scope and universal in application, thereby maximizing factors that induce compliance and minimizing those which induce violation. The Iraqi sanctions were unique in that they affected virtually every aspect of economic relations and were applied simultaneously. This episode shows that the efficacy of enforcement can be heightened when sanctions are comprehensive and universal. It remains too early to determine how this lesson has measured up for either the case of Libya or Serbia.

4. Public opinion can furnish vital support for the force of international law because it plays a role in the policymaking process of states. When domestic and world public opinion mobilize in support of sanctions to enforce compliance, the chances for international success are enhanced.

5. The United Nations lacks an effective mechanism for determining either rule violations or penalties. The failure of the United Nations Military Staff Committee to play a significant part in the coordination of enforcement activities reveals that national sovereignty remains paramount and that prospects for a supranational enforcement body remain distant. Governments of states decide individually whether, what, and how sanctions measures will be implemented and enforced. This tendency seems likely to persist. Enforcement measures will continue to be implemented and coordinated principally by individual states, rather than be subjected to a supranational authority.

6. Recent UN sanctions episodes also suggest that international adoption of sanctions must be backed by an international commitment to supply the necessary resources to effectively set up and enforce sanctions. The development of a multinational coalition that can supply ships, troops, and various types of support will give meaningful clout to a sanctions operation and help fill the void left by the lack of a Security Council military arm. Without such an international commitment, especially in terms of a strict program of naval interdiction, enforcement of sanctions measures will be difficult.

7. Opportunities for international compliance with sanctions are enhanced when enforcement measures are derived from the legitimate exercise of the Security Council's authority and carry the full force of international law. This approach provides the highest degree of legitimacy possible in the international system. If governments choose to violate the measures, they perforce violate the UN Charter, thereby abrogating their duty under *pacta sunt servanda* and jeopardizing their general reputation for upholding treaty obligations.

8. In a system comprised of sovereign states, a government is likely to support enforcement of sanctions when its interests are adversely affected by the illegal action. Economic issues are particularly vital. The conquest of Kuwait by Iraq undoubtedly created apprehension about an oil-rich Middle East being conquered by a ruthless and uncooperative dictator. This caused serious economic concern throughout the international community. When vital international economic interests are threatened by some situation, participation in a sanctions operation aimed at mitigating that situation appears less burdensome to a government.

9. Opportunities to effectively implement sanctions may improve when a major power takes the lead in mobilizing international action and can minimize the possibility of interference by rival powers. The United States was the "architect" of contemporary UN sanctions operations against Iraq, Libya, and Serbia, and Great Britain assumed a similar role in the UN sanctions effort against Rhodesia during the late 1960s.

10. The political effect of international sanctions is strengthened when economic coercion is carried out by governments experienced in sanctions enforcement and which possess the required infrastructure and mechanisms to implement sanctions, provided that these countries have sufficient political will to enforce such measures. To this end, the suggestion has been made to establish an international draft law that would give effect to Security Council resolutions and thereby harmonize international implementation efforts.[34]

11. Regional organizations can also play a part in UN sanctions. During the Iraqi operation, a useful role was played by regional organizations such as the European Community and the Western European Union. These organizations became vehicles for implementing European sanctions and proved their worth in providing valuable support to universal enforcement actions. When maximum involvement by regional organizations in a sanctions operation occurs, members' responses can be harmonized in a form that is more acceptable to each state and less threatening to its sovereignty.

12. As a final observation, commitment by the international community must include giving support to states that are adversely affected by economic repercussions from a sanctions program, but still opt to comply with it. The UN Sanctions Committee is entrusted with the task of examining requests from states made under Article 50. Funds to assist such states, however, must originate from members of the international community. Stronger international compliance can be won if resolute remedial action and genuine concern by wealthier states is forthcoming for those other countries that experience extreme economic hardships from sanctions enforcement actions.

Conclusion

Sanctions approved by the United Nations have not, in and of themselves, been successful in radically altering the domestic conduct or foreign policy behavior of target states. The pressure imposed has been insufficient, and the will asserted and the means adopted by the UN membership to repress a target state have been less than steadfast. Sanctions by the United Nations must therefore be viewed as achieving only halfhearted success. Sanctions might make life more difficult for a target state by extracting a cost for its deviant behavior, but often that cost is not high enough to convince that state to change its policies. UN sanctions thus remain much like a primitive tax on a state for its illicit conduct, rather than a compelling measure to coerce compliance with international norms.

Nonetheless, no state is impervious to the effects of economic sanctions, although those effects may only be minimal. All states depend on foreign trade for securing foreign exchange, obtaining needed imports, acquiring markets for exports, and attracting foreign investment. To the extent that sanctions imposed by the United Nations successfully disrupt those activities, the impact will be felt by a target state. In the end, the political efficacy of sanctions imposed by the United Nations will be only as strong as member states permit. That is the essence of political effectiveness:

States must work together to make sanctions work well. Members of the United Nations must exercise sufficient political will, national determination, and sometimes economic sacrifice to make international sanctions work. Otherwise, they will remain more symbol than substance—a failure that will undoubtedly long delay attainment of anything approaching a just New World Order governed by the rule of law.

Notes

1. Christopher Joyner, "The Transnational Boycott as Economic Coercion in International Law: Policy, Place, and Practice," *Vanderbilt Journal of Transnational Law*, Vol. 17, 1984, pp. 205, 225–27.

2. Maarten Smeets, "Economic Sanctions Against Iraq: The Ideal Case?" *Journal of World Trade*, Vol. 24, Dec. 1990, p. 115.

3. Royal Institute of International Affairs, *International Sanctions* (London: Oxford University Press, 1938) p. 14.

4. M.S. Daoudi and M.S. Dajani, *Economic Sanctions: Ideals and Experience* (Boston: Routledge and Kegan Paul, 1983), p. 8.

5. When used to satisfy domestic pressures, there is a danger that the national government may present overinflated goals to the population. In doing so, the domestic situation may be worsened if the sanctions measures are unable to achieve such goals. David Leyton-Brown, ed., *The Utility of International Economic Sanctions* (New York: St. Martin's Press, 1987), p. 306.

6. Robin Renwick, *Economic Sanctions* (Cambridge: Harvard Univ. Center for International Affairs, 1981), p. 86; and Leyton-Brown, *Utility of Economic Sanctions*, p. 305.

7. See James Ngobi's chapter in the present volume.

8. See e.g., Security Council Resolution 661, paragraph 3(a) (1990) for the case of Iraq. In the case of Libya, Security Council Resolution 748 (1992) aims mainly to deny permission to Libyan aircraft to take off from, land in or overfly states' territory, as well as prohibit the supply and servicing of aircraft and components to Libya (Security Council Resolution 748, paragraph 4). For Serbia, air restrictions are contained in Security Council Resolution 757, paragraph 4.

9. As, for example, the measures authorized against Iraq in Security Council Resolution 661, paragraph 4.

10. This was done in the case of Iraq by Security Council Resolution 661, paragraph 5 and for Serbia in Security Council Resolution 757, paragraph 11.

11. This was accomplished in the case of Iraq by UN Security Council Resolution 665 (1990), paragraph 1. For Serbia, see Security Council Resolution 757, paragraph 12.

12. In the case of Iraq, see UN Security Council Resolution 670 (1990). For Serbia, see Security Council Resolution 787, paragraphs 12 and 13.

13. In the case of Iraq, an air embargo was imposed by UN Security Council Resolution 670. Similarly, such an air embargo entails the main sanction directed in Security Council Resolution 748 against Libya and by Security Council Resolution 757, paragraph 7(a) against Serbia.

14. For Iraq, an arms embargo is mandated by Security Council Resolution 661, in paragraph 3. For Libya, an arms embargo is affirmed in Security Council Resolution 748, paragraph 5. For the Federal Republic of Yugoslavia (Serbia), an arms embargo is mandated by Security Council Resolution 713, paragraph 6.

15. Separate Sanctions Committees have been formed to deal with each particular sanctions operation. For Iraq, see Security Council Resolution 661, paragraph 6. For Libya, see Security Council Resolution 748, paragraph 9. For Serbia, see Security Council Resolutions 724, paragraph 5(b) and 757, paragraph 13.

16. For example, this was done for Iraq through UN Security Council Resolution 666 (1990), paragraph 3.

17. See UN Security Council Resolution 669 (1990), Preamble paragraph 5.

18. For Iraq, see UN Security Council Resolution 670 (1990), paragraph 3; for Serbia, see Security Council Resolution 757, paragraph 13.

19. As exemplified against Iraq by UN Security Council Resolution 687 (1990), paragraphs 20 and 23 and against Serbia by Security Council Resolution 757, paragraph 13.

20. For Iraq, see Resolution 687, paragraph 6; for Libya, see Resolution 748, paragraphs 8 and 9. For Serbia, see Resolution 757, paragraphs 12 and 13.

21. Paul Lewis, "Soviets Seek Meeting of UN Military Panel," *New York Times*, October 11, 1990, sec. A, p. 19; and Paul Lewis, "U.S. Seeks to Revive Panel that Enforces UN Decrees," *New York Times*, September 19, 1990, sec. A, p. 11.

22. 50 United States Code (U.S.C.) Sections 1701–06 (1982).

23. 50 U.S.C. Sections 1601–51.

24. 22 U.S.C. Sections 287–287(e).

25. 50 U.S.C. App. 6(b) (1982).

26. Margaret Doxey, "International Sanctions: A Framework for Analysis with Special Reference to the UN and Southern Africa," *International Organization*, Vol. 26, 1972, pp. 532–35.

27. This is also related to the "law abiding habit" of nations. A. Pearce Higgins, *The Binding Force of International Law* (Cambridge: Cambridge University Press, 1910), p. 36; and Oran Young, *Compliance and Public Authority: A Theory with International Applications* (Baltimore: Johns Hopkins Univ. Press, 1979), p. 24.

28. Michael R. Gordon, "Navy Begins Blockade Enforcing Iraq Embargo," *New York Times*, August 17, 1990, sec. A, p. 10.

29. These negative costs were apparent in Romania's response to the Iraqi sanctions. Although Romania did in fact join the sanctions effort, its government, in detailing national implementation measures to the Sanctions Committee, stressed the extreme difficulties caused by the UN enforcement action to its economic reform program. In particular, Romania cited losses and expenses of $2.9 billion, broken down as follows:

$1.7 million -- Iraqi debt to Romania, to have been paid by the oil shipments;

$46.1 million -- Goods specially designed for Iraq and Kuwait with no other export market;

$142.6 million -- Value of interrupted construction projects and technical assistance in Iraq;

$64.7 million -- Value of abandoned equipment and material in Iraq;

$200.6 million — Bank guarantees and blocked assets;

$746 million -- Increased price of crude oil from August to December 1990 as compared to pre-crisis level.

Given these costs, government officials forecast a negative impact of 14 percent on the GNP of Romania. Clearly, when states face costs of this magnitude, the decision to comply will be far more problematic. See "Security Council Committee Established by Resolution 661 (1990) Concerning the Situation Between Iraq and Kuwait, UN Doc S/AC.25/53 (1990)," (reply of the Romanian Government to a Security Council questionnaire concerning the implementation of Security Council Resolution 661).

30. "Remarks of Gilberto Schlittler," in American Society of International Law 85th Annual *Proceedings* (Washington, D.C.: American Society of International Law, 1991), pp. 175–81.

31. Security Council Resolution 687, paragraphs 18 and 19.

32. Ved Nanda, "The Iraqi Invasion of Kuwait: The UN Response," *Southern Illinois University Law Journal*, Vol. 15, 1991, p. 431. Also see Yossef M. Ibrahim, "OPEC to Increase Oil Output to Offset Losses from Iraq," *New York Times*, August 30, 1990, sec. A, p. 1.

33. Examples of this situation in the case of Iraq were the actions of Jordan and Germany. Jordan, a border state and major trading partner of Iraq, found itself in a difficult position due to its economic ties and the intense domestic pressures from its large Palestinian community which favored Iraq. The result was a delay in implementing Resolution 661 in order to "study" it more closely. Joseph B. Treaster, "Goods Reach Iraq Through Jordanian 'Back Door,'" *New York Times*, August 15, 1991, sec. A, p. 19.

Germany, on the other hand, was accused of permitting its nationals through lax enforcement to conduct trade with Iraq after the imposition of sanctions. Press reports claimed that at least 12 firms had broken the embargo, but that the German government's resolve was not sufficient to tighten enforcement of the restrictions. Miriam Widman, "German Business Groups Calling for Tighter Controls on Exports," *Journal of Commerce and Commercial*, January 30, 1991, p. 5A.

Recent reports indicate that Iran may be importing oil from Iraq in violation of the sanctions regulations. R. Jeffery Smith, "Iraq Shipped Oil to Iran, U.S. Alleges," *Washington Post*, March 31, 1993, sec. A, p. 1.

34. "Statement of Jeremy Carver," in American Society of International Law 85th Annual *Proceedings* (Washington, D.C.: American Society of International Law, 1991), pp. 181–83.

8

The Political and Moral Appropriateness of Sanctions

Jack T. Patterson

The American Friends Service Committee (AFSC) has both supported and opposed the implementation of sanctions, at times with clear strength of conviction and, at other times, with doubts and apprehensions. AFSC supported economic and cultural sanctions against apartheid in South Africa since 1976. It supported the prewar sanctions against Iraq after it invaded Kuwait, but has opposed their continuation since the end of the war. It supports sanctions against the former Yugoslavia and against the military government of Haiti. It has opposed sanctions against Vietnam, Cuba, Nicaragua, Libya, the former Soviet Union and other nations. Challenged by its experience with sanctions in the 1991 Gulf War and recognizing the seeming contradiction with the earlier positive experience in South Africa, the AFSC Board appointed a working group early in 1992 to clarify issues surrounding the use of economic sanctions. The product of the deliberations was the publication: *Dollars or Bombs: The Search for Justice Through International Economic Sanctions.*[1] This chapter will highlight the moral issues addressed in that document and address some outstanding questions which require further clarification.

Concerns and Dilemmas

The AFSC's experience with Iraq before and after the Gulf War illustrates the many dilemmas the organization faces regarding both the efficacy and the morality of sanctions. The Service Committee favored sanctions following Iraq's invasion of Kuwait because it opposed the aggression and wanted to reverse its consequences, and because it wanted the world community to address, without force of arms, the problems that the invasion created. Simultaneously, along with many other peace, justice, and religious organizations and agencies of the UN, the AFSC sought to respond to the needs of the civilian population of Iraq, which was threatened both by sanctions and by war.

The committee quickly confronted contradictions that challenged its optimism about sanctions as a humane alternative to war. First, rather than functioning as an "alternative" to war, sanctions were used by the Bush administration and its supporters in the UN to co-opt the broad support that arose for sanctions. The White House argued that time had run out, sanctions had been tried and failed, and stronger military action was therefore required and justified. Economic sanctions and the UN Charter, rather than serving as the "threshold for peace," became a "trap door to war."

Second, the AFSC discovered that sanctions were being used somewhat "opportunistically," to quote Richard Falk.[2] That is, the rationale for their use seemed to shift with changing circumstances that led to jarring contradictions. Why, for example, if economic sanctions were said to have failed in the lead-in to war, were they so important to continue at war's end? We began to see that economic sanctions are sometimes used (as in Iraq) as a stage or prelude to military action, and in others (as in the U.S. response to the situation in the former Yugoslavia) as an excuse to avoid taking stronger military or nonmilitary action—a justification, really, for inaction. Third, the AFSC quickly observed in Iraq that economic sanctions were not a humane alternative to war, but had many of the same effects of increasing human suffering of the civilian population as smart bombs dropped from the air.

The AFSC came to the conclusion that if economic sanctions are to be rescued as an alternative to war and an acceptable vehicle for social change, it would be necessary to reconsider the extent and limits of their usefulness and our responsibility to insure, as best we can, that sanctions themselves do not become part of the problem. We lay more on economic sanctions than they can bear if we do not also create, develop, and support a broad mix of nonmilitary alternatives to accompany sanctions.

Areas of Clarity and Conviction

The working group reached several conclusions regarding the morality of using a sanctions regime. First, the decision on when and how to apply sanctions is always "contextual," although some conditions are "constant and absolute." This goes beyond mere questions of "efficacy." The AFSC has supported sanctions when it knew they would not work and opposed them at other times when it thought they would work but were unjustifiable in their human consequences. Whether supporting or opposing, we need to be as clear as possible about motives. The goals for sanctions that are most frequently cited are: (1) to punish, (2) to enforce compliance, (3) to withdraw either symbolically or in reality from evil, and (4) to assist or promote social change.

A lack of clarity (or honesty) about motives leads to co-option and the inevitable conflict among goals. The evaluation of success clearly depends on which motives guide the action. It was difficult, for example, to expect the Iraqi government and Saddam Hussein to engage in serious diplomatic efforts aimed at securing compliance with UN directives when those generating the momentum towards military confrontation wanted to see Baghdad's leadership overthrown. Economic sanctions became another element of the confrontation rather than an instrument for problem solving.

Second, the AFSC concluded that sanctions are coercive and impose real suffering. When enforcing a sanctions regime, the sanctioning body must insure that suffering is proportional to the severity of the situation. Sanctions themselves must not violate fundamental human rights. That is, while economic sanctions involve hardships, even suffering, they should not and cannot be justified when they threaten or lead to the loss of life itself. The principle of proportionality demands limits. A line must be drawn when deaths are knowingly inflicted. Extreme sanctions in the form of blockades on food, medicine, and the basic requirements for shelter and health must not only be exempted from sanctions, but assurance must be provided that basic needs are being met.

Third, close monitoring is needed to fulfill the moral obligation of maintaining proportionality and insuring that basic human survival needs are met, or at least not jeopardized by the sanctions themselves. There is an urgent need for those imposing and supporting sanctions regimes to carefully monitor their effects. Obviously, sanctioning parties have an interest in knowing whether and how sanctions are affecting the target country and achieving the goals set for them. As indicated in the AFSC Guidelines and also in the proposed SANCTIONS[3] draft, developing a capacity for monitoring might rely on some existing agencies (e.g., UNICEF, WHO, World Food Program) and credible NGOs with experience evaluating human health needs. The AFSC also recognizes and acknowledges that adequate monitoring in some situations, especially in closed societies hostile to any outside intervention, may pose formidable obstacles. That challenge must be met with innovative approaches.

Guidelines for monitoring also must insure that monitors on the ground, where permitted, are not co-opted for political purposes. This is a particular problem where both political and humanitarian motives are involved in a contradictory tension. When the UN itself is the originating agency for sanctions, independent and credible alternative means of monitoring may be needed to avoid politicizing the situation. Monitoring needs to provide information about conditions in the target society that would allow sanctioning parties to maintain proportionality and avoid lethal consequences. Monitors must distinguish between levels of "hardship," "suffering," and "lethality." When the latter level is reached, one may say that sanctions themselves violate basic human rights enshrined in UN conventions. The members of the UN, as well as the UN itself, must be held to their own standards when acting against individual states, even when the target country is in gross violation of those same human rights.

Fourth, the credibility and authority of sanctioning parties must be established. The AFSC struggled with the question of what constitutes credible or legitimate authority for the imposition of sanctions. The committee was deeply suspicious and concerned that the current structure of the UN Security Council and the absence of real accountability by member states allows the Security Council to be manipulated by its most powerful members. This weakens the moral authority of the sanctions and of the UN itself, making it easier for others to justify evasion and noncompliance. In general, the AFSC has tended to oppose harsh sanctions unilaterally imposed by powerful nations on weaker ones, as in the cases of U.S. sanctions against Cuba, Nicaragua, Vietnam, Cambodia, and Libya. To be effective and genuinely claim moral authority, sanctioning parties should seek a consensus so broad and deep that no nation will want to break the sanctions. The credibility of sanctioning bodies can only be enhanced when they demonstrate that their actions enjoy broad and voluntary support. To this end, the AFSC wants to enhance the moral authority of sanctioning bodies by encouraging them to promote power sharing in decision making. Efforts by one or more superpowers to bribe or coerce support (as in the lead-in to the Gulf War) diminish the authority of both the sanctions and the sponsoring body.

Fifth, the AFSC working group easily concluded that an important moral criterion for supporting or opposing sanctions should be whether there is significant support for sanctions within the target country. This support should be evident especially among people with a record of support for human rights and democracy or among the victims of injustice. Such groups are inevitably among those who will be on the receiving end of sanctions and, often, are best positioned to help monitor the effects of sanctions on the most vulnerable. They are often powerless to affect or change their own government's policies, yet often bear the brunt of actions taken against that government. Determining the views of indigenous groups is also a moral responsibility of sanctioning parties because in some instances significant portions of the people are, in effect, "double-victims," i.e., victims of externally imposed sanctions *and* of sanctions imposed upon them by their own government. Meeting this criterion is easier to do when, as in South Africa, Haiti, or Burma, there were significant popular opposition movements with credible authority to speak on behalf of those who may be hurt most. The situation is more difficult and morally problematic when such movements either do not exist, or have been driven underground, or when they oppose the imposition of sanctions. Both Iraq and Serbia represent situations in which mixed signals are given by indigenous groups. Judgments must be made about how much weight to give to different voices. In the AFSC's experience this is easier when the organization has a history of work in an area in question, and more difficult when it lacks that experiential connection.

Sixth, the working group concluded that sanctioning nations must recognize the importance of universal human rights as a standard when judging the morality of a sanctions regime. The group recognized the importance and value of establishing global norms or "world order values" for evaluating whether and how to impose sanctions. It found these values encoded in the UN Charter, the Geneva Conventions and in the growing number of universal declarations on individual and group rights (such as the Universal Declaration of Human Rights and the Convention on the Rights of Children). Together, these documents embody widely accepted values and principles of international governance against which the decision to impose sanctions can be measured and justified. The AFSC recognized that established global norms on national sovereignty are eroding and that this invites interventions into what until recently would have been considered "internal affairs." However, this erosion is not occurring equally, with the North generally giving up much less sovereignty than the South. It is still difficult to imagine that sanctions, even if justified by universal law or conventions, could be imposed against the U.S., Europe, or Japan.

Seventh, working group members agreed that, unless one is considering completely blockading the entry of critical goods into a target country unable to supply its own essential needs, sanctions require time to work. But how long? Is there a need for proportionality here as well? If so, how would it work? In the Gulf War, Americans were told that sanctions had "failed" and that "time had run out" after six months. Gross human rights violations in Kuwait required immediate military action to reverse the aggressive invasion.

Policymakers and scholars often refuse to accept that sanctions usually take time for their effects to be felt and for targeted governments to take remedial actions to lift them. When extreme or complete sanctions are avoided, the time it will take for sanctions to become effective is further extended. In such situations, sanctions must be a coordinated part of a "package" of approaches designed to alleviate the grossest aspects of a situation while allowing time for sanctions to "bite," and for a political process to move forward toward resolution. John Paul Lederach of Eastern Mennonite College suggests that we need to "reconceptualize time." He argues that, as in Iraq, the argument that sanctions and negotiations "buy time" for tyrants is based on "a shaky assumption that war is a more direct and time-effective way of resolving conflict. In fact, the reverse is generally true. Wars, and their aftermath, inevitably take more time and resources than initially projected."[5] While sanctions and negotiated approaches demand patience, they may be viewed as an investment in the future when they translate into "cost- and time-effective long-term solutions."[5]

Other Issues Needing Clarification

Several issues related to sanctions are still in need of clarification and study. First, very little is known about the actual effects of sanctions. Most people have to acknowledge that their hopes for the effectiveness of sanctions as an alternative to war and agent for change have outdistanced the way sanctions actually work on the ground. Both the U.S. General Accounting Office's 1992 study of economic sanctions and the work of peace researcher George Tsebelis seriously question the effectiveness of sanctions to achieve many of the announced goals. The GAO study found sanctions more effective in achieving less ambitious goals like upholding international norms and deterring future objectionable actions than in making target countries change more serious behavior. They also found the threat of future sanctions more effective in changing behavior than currently imposed sanctions.[6] George Tsebelis, in his study of 83 cases in the twentieth century, found a low rate of success [33 out of 83 (39.8 percent)]. The problem, he found, is that sanctioning countries are unable to select appropriate cases. They often use sanctions in situations in which the chance of success is low.[7] Developing the capacity to evaluate the effectiveness of sanctions will be an important, even crucial, part of maintaining proportionality and avoiding lethal consequences. Thus far sanctions have been used as a blunt instrument. Scholars are far from discovering what combination of elements works to pinpoint pressure on those who have the power and responsibility to change policies.

Second, how can sanctioning bodies develop sanctions as an alternative to armed conflict and diminish their use as a precursor to war? To succeed in building a wall, a "firebreak," between the use of economic sanctions as an alternative to war and their use as an "amber light" on the path to war, scholars and policymakers will need to open themselves and others to the fullest possible range of strategies for utilizing sanctions in combination with other approaches. Sanctions may include not only economic components, but also noneconomic measures that bring pressure to bear or signal displeasure, including the suspension of diplomatic recognition, sporting and entertainment boycotts, and the banning of flights and communication. In addition to punitive sanctions, positive incentives need to be presented to strengthen the impact of negative sanctions and to offer an alternative through which to resolve problems. Based on his research of negative sanctions and positive inducements in U.S./Soviet relations, Louis Kriesberg of Syracuse University argues that inducements tend to elicit counterproposals with concessions from other negotiators, while threats generally yield counterproposals with no concessions.[8] This carrot-and-stick approach, with the emphasis on carrots, was being demonstrated, or at least tested, by the U.S. and South Korea from 1992 to 1993 in efforts to persuade North Korea to end its suspected nuclear weapons program, to stop its missile sales abroad, and to move towards unification with the South.

To be moral and effective, sanctions need to be part of a coherent vision of a "rightly ordered world." However much one may wish that economic sanctions alone could end civil wars or reverse aggression, it is unlikely that they will do so. Their fullest effectiveness will likely come in combination with a larger package that contains either military threats or nonmilitary alternatives. The problem is that while military approaches often do not work, they exist, while most nonmilitary alternatives remain underused and underdeveloped. Boutros Boutros-Ghali drew particular attention to the latter prospect in his important report, *An Agenda for Peace*, which called for the strengthening of the UN's capacity for "preventive diplomacy" and "peacemaking" as well as "peacekeeping." Dr. John Burton, a pioneer in the field of analytical, problem-solving conflict resolution, argues:

> It is time to shift our emphasis from conflict resolution to conflict prevention, i.e., to eliminating the sources and removing the causes of conflict, to promoting the conditions that eliminate an environment of conflict.[9]

Scholars and peace activists have not focused on the prevention of undesired events. Instead they have largely emphasized remedial measures based on applying force, including sanctions, against symptoms of a problem rather than pursuing a process of prevention which could deal with the sources of the problem. Burton claims that there is no word for what he is talking about, so he uses the term "provention" to make the point that the scholarly community needs to focus on causes, and not symptoms, of conflict.

All of this is to suggest a need to reserve some of the best energy for the work that precedes sanctions, for early intercession in conflicts while "option formation" is useful and possible. Indeed, early intercession in problem solving is a moral responsibility if one is to avoid some of the worst consequences of economic sanctions. When economic sanctions are placed in the context of "war prevention," the question can then be asked: Will economic sanctions help prevent war in this situation? Will they build support for war prevention policies and structures? Will they slow escalation until better options are developed? Fifty years after the ending of World War II and the beginning of the United Nations, the world community has a moral responsibility and a unique opportunity to make war impossible. Whether confronting war in Bosnia, illegitimate authority in Haiti, or violence in South Africa, scholars, activists, and world leaders need to identify and remove the elements that give rise to war and injustice.

Notes

1. Examples and conclusions about the moral issues presented here generally are based on *Dollars or Bombs: The Search for Justice Through International Economic Sanctions* (Philadelphia: American Friends Service Committee, 1993).

2. Ibid., pp. 13, 14.

3. Marc Hardy, "Sanctions Assessment of Non-Compliance and Cooperation Through Information and Observations from Non-Governmental Sources." Paper presented at the conference, Economic Sanctions and International Relations, Notre Dame, Ind., April 4, 1993.

4. John Paul Lederach, "From War to Peace," *Mennonite Central Committee U.S. Peace Section Conciliation Quarterly Newsletter*, Vol. 10, No. 1, Winter 1991, p. 15.

5. Ibid.

6. U.S. General Accounting Office, *Economic Sanctions: Effectiveness as Tools of Foreign Policy*, GAO/NSIAD-92-106, February 1992, p. 2.

7. George Tsebelis, "Are Sanctions Effective?: A Game Theoretical Analysis," *The Journal of Conflict Resolution*, Vol. 34, No. 1, March 1990.

8. Louis Kreisberg, "Positive Inducements in U.S./Soviet Relations," *The Syracuse University Program on the Analysis and Resolution of Conflict (PARC) Newsletter*, Vol. 2, No. 3, March 1988, p. 2.

9. John Burton, *Conflict: Resolution and Provention* (New York: St. Martin's Press, 1990), pp. 5–7.

9

Economic Sanctions and the Just-War Doctrine

Drew Christiansen, S.J., and Gerard F. Powers

Economic coercion is nothing new, nor is the debate over the morality of coercive diplomacy. Woodrow Wilson tried to sell Americans on the League of Nations by arguing eloquently for sanctions as an alternative to war:

> A nation boycotted is a nation that is in sight of surrender. Apply this economic, peaceful, silent, deadly remedy and there will be no need for force. It is a terrible remedy. It does not cost a life outside the nation boycotted, but it brings pressure upon the nation that, in my judgment, no modern nation could resist.[1]

At about the same time, in a report by the U.S. Committee on Economic Sanctions issued after World War I, John Foster Dulles opposed such boycotts on the moral grounds that they tended to harm innocents, not the rulers responsible for aggression. He proposed confining sanctions to arms embargoes and other specific steps that would embarrass the target state without imposing undue hardships and inequities.[2] Others have argued that all forms of economic coercion are inherently immoral and illegal. The Serbian Orthodox Synod is not alone in decrying the kind of sanctions imposed on Serbia as "immoral and inhumane."[3]

Unlike their first cousin war, sanctions have largely escaped serious moral analysis. Yet as the early debate between Wilson and Dulles indicates, key ethical issues are at stake:

1. Should economic sanctions be evaluated solely by standards of efficacy or are there other morally justifiable grounds to employ them?

2. What are we to learn from the customary rejection by just-war theorists of sieges and blockades in wartime? To be more exact, is the just-war criterion of civilian immunity a useful moral guide when employing sanctions as an alternative to the use of force?
3. Are sanctions a morally superior and effective alternative to the use of force? If they are, how can we respond to Dulles' objections that they are counterproductive and tend to harm the innocent and vulnerable most?
4. What protections are there against the unjust use of sanctions, especially by powerful states against small, weak ones?

The premise of this chapter is that comprehensive economic sanctions may be legitimate if they satisfy several conditions: (a) they are a response to a grave evil; (b) they are pursued as one part of a concerted diplomatic effort to avoid war and find a just resolution to the problem; (c) the sanctions avoid irreversible, grave harm to the civilian population of the target country; (d) less coercive means are pursued first; (e) the harmful effects of sanctions are proportionate to the good ends likely to be achieved; and (f) sanctions are imposed by a multilateral entity. We will first examine the relevance of both consequentialist and deontological considerations in a moral analysis of sanctions. We will then consider the extent to which sanctions may be considered an alternative to war that requires a moral framework different from a just-war analysis. Finally, we will elaborate on criteria for evaluating the morality of a particular sanctions regime.

Consequentialism, Deontology, and the Political Function of Sanctions

It is useful for purposes of moral analysis to distinguish five broad purposes of sanctions: (1) to induce or compel a country to change its domestic polices or even its government, (2) to defend against or prevent illegal or aggressive action, (3) to renounce complicity in illegal or immoral actions, (4) to punish a country, and (5) to symbolically signal disapproval with a country's policies.[4] Much of the commentary on economic sanctions evaluates sanctions solely in terms of how effective they are in achieving the first two objectives. Such commentary represents a purely consequentialist or utilitarian approach to the moral problem of sanctions. The ethical analysis of sanctions cannot be reduced to consequentialist assessments of effectiveness, but effectiveness is a major component of the moral analysis. As we shall see, while the immunity of all persons in their basic rights is a not-to-be-compromised threshold from an ethical perspective, calculations of consequences are still relevant at many points in the design, implementation, revision or discontinuance of a sanctions regime. They are relevant, for example, in making judgments of probable success, that is, in determining not only whether sanctions will attain their end but also whether people will be made to suffer uselessly when sanctions fail to influence an offending government. Consequences matter in assessing whether a particular sanctions regime has been counterproductive in strengthening the hold of outlaw governments on power while victimized populations are made to suffer all the more. Thus, while the moral analysis of economic sanctions ought not be reduced to questions of effectiveness, such treatment will frequently intersect with political appraisals where consequential judgments are salient, as they are when sanctions are imposed to achieve specific changes in government or policy.

Because the last three objectives of sanctions—noncomplicity in evil, punishment of an offending nation, and symbolic disapproval for violation of international standards—are less directly intended to effect specific behaviors of the target country, they raise a set of questions that differentiate the moral from the political arguments about sanctions. If forcing a change in policy or deterring aggression are objectives concerned with efficacy, these latter three seek integrity. If the first two objectives call for standard forms of political argument about consequences, the latter three objectives involve primarily deontological justifications, that is, stands based on moral principle with less regard to actual or potential consequences. To be sure, contemporary schools of ethics, both secular and religious, differ over whether at least some ethical principles are unconditioned and, therefore, are immune from the casuistry of consequential analysis. There are nonetheless significant schools of thought that adhere to deontology. In practice, moreover, individual activists and social movements engaged in influencing social and public policy, groups which political analysis should not overlook, are inclined to be purists who will initiate proposals for deontological reasons and will oppose compromise in attaining solutions.[5] In this chapter it is not possible to present a full-scale treatment of what appears to be deontological attitudes and behavior by religious, human rights and other activists as they relate to economic sanctions; but we can identify several ways in which *acting on principle* is dominant in the latter three objectives of sanctions.

The third objective uses sanctions to avoid complicity in immoral policies. Characteristically public ethics deals with the morality of acts or policies (e.g., apartheid, massacres, genocide, exploitation), but both ethical theory and common practice also concern themselves with moral agency. When the results are grave enough, states, like people, are held accountable for the indirect consequences of their actions. One traditional moral category is that of complicity or material cooperation—the notion that, even when one is not immediately responsible for a grave moral offense, one is forbidden from cooperating in an act that aids and abets that evil. For example, the denial of Most-Favored-Nation trading status to China as a response to the use of slave labor may be justified on the grounds of noncomplicity in an immoral practice. The deontological concern for renouncing complicity in evil is closely aligned with the use of sanctions to give expression to moral censure for grave and pervasive moral and legal offenses by governments. Campaigns to bring about corporate disengagement from South Africa, in the face of objections that sanctions would be ineffective, may be viewed as moral protests of this sort. They constituted a form of social conduct that demonstrated public condemnation of apartheid.

In the case of punishment, we meet a form of deontological reasoning where acting-on-principle is not exclusively symbolic, as consequentialist critics tend to allege, but also possesses a practical dimension. When used to punish an egregious offense against international order and common morality, sanctions may express international revulsion for certain classes of crimes. On a deontological analysis, for example, some would justify sanctions against Serbia as a punitive expression of international repugnance for ethnic cleansing without regard to its role in reducing the conflict or bringing about a political settlement.[6] Thus, when sanctions are imposed wholly or in part because strong action is regarded as an appropriate response to a grave moral offense—one so abhorrent that it must be punished as a matter of natural justice—the motive (and justification) inclines to the side of acting-on-principle. It is done because it is the morally required response (Greek: *deon*, "it is necessary") in the situation. In other words, some acts (e.g., systematic rape) are simply so abhorrent that they must be punished as a matter of natural justice. A strictly moral (i.e., duty-based) function of sanctions involves a principled concern for the character of a people, namely, to assert a people's human dignity and rights in the face of unjust policies. Gandhi's protest of the salt tax and boycott of British textiles would fall in this category. The Organization of American States' sanctions against Haiti may be regarded as a reaction of the democratic states of the hemisphere against a government imposed by military coup. The sanctions were a collective expression under the Santiago Agreement of the governments' common commitment to democracy.

Even the first two objectives (influencing policy or deterring aggression) may have a deontological dimension. Outside parties may join in rejection of a policy by indigenous groups out of reasons of solidarity, that is, to lend support to groups struggling against some form of injustice.[7] Boycotts, whether of domestic lettuce and grapes or of Salvadorian coffee, are conducted out of motives of solidarity. Effectiveness may or may not be relevant to such protests. Even without results, identification with a just cause may satisfy the protesting party. Solidarity, of course, is more frequently a motive of activist social groups, and less frequently among governments. When interest groups are strong enough, solidaristic commitments can become government policy as well. Pressures brought on the former Soviet Union for the emigration of Jews may be seen as an instance of a solidaristic use of coercive diplomacy at the international level.

In politics, deontologically motivated and justified policies are seldom found in their pure form. Policies undertaken without regard to consequences may prove to have desirable consequences. In democratic political practice, policy design and implementation will inevitably entail doing business with those who have purely consequentialist outlooks. Indeed many activists will themselves have a mixture of deontological and consequentialist ways of thinking.[8] Just-war theory, with its mixture of hard principles and consequentialist reasoning, is one example of this practical complexity. The operative distinction between basic human rights and other less-basic rights, or in UN practice, that between rights of bodily integrity and human rights generally, is another. In the same way, the practical demands of implementing a just-sanctions regime will require moving back and forth between deontological and consequential considerations. The ethical analysis of sanctions must include both a deontological view of public policy choices and consequentialist assessments of effectiveness.

Sanctions: Alternative to War or Alternate Form of War?

Scholars often treat economic sanctions as analogous with acts of war. At times, international law has regarded sanctions as a *casus belli*, and moralists and legal scholars sometimes treat them, along with blockades and sieges, as acts of war. Indeed they do constitute a form of coercive diplomacy, sometimes undertaken as part of a war effort or a prelude to war and other times as an alternative to war. While many of the ethical issues which sanctions raise parallel those found in contemporary just-war analyses, it would be misleading to apply the criteria of just war, without qualification, to the sanctions question. Especially in the cases of concern here—comprehensive sanctions imposed by the United Nations or regional institutions as an alternative to the use of military force— ethicists and policy analysts should be prepared to examine the moral issues of this new phenomenon on their own terms, and be cautious about applying the pre-existing schema used to evaluate wartime blockades. They need to be alert to the limits of analogy and the unique and emergent features of sanctions as a moral phenomenon.

Sanctions as War: Sieges and Blockades

Most contemporary cases use economic embargoes as an alternative to war, but some do not. The widespread use of siege tactics in Bosnia-Herzegovina is evidence of the continued relevance of a just-war analysis when economic coercion is a means of war. The just-war tradition, including the international law of armed combat, is an effort to establish restraints on the use of force and prevent the downward spiral of conflict into "total war." A primary way in which restraint has been established in the conduct of war has been the principle of noncombatant or civilian immunity. In wartime, only military personnel are liable to direct attack because only they bear arms. Civilians and other noncombatants, because they are considered innocent and threaten no one, are immune from direct attack. Just-war analysts generally extend the immunity of civilians in wartime to cases of economic coercion in which the lives of civilians are placed at risk. When wartime blockades are employed, just-war theorists tend to presume that they constitute a long step on the road to total war because they intensify the conflict by making noncombatants, who have no possibility of escape, the victims of attack. As Michael Walzer argues, these blockades, like saturation bombing, may be aimed at the political and military authorities, but they are aimed through the civilian population.[9] From a moral point of view, Walzer contends, the besieger "can risk incidental deaths, but he cannot kill civilians simply because he finds them between himself and his enemies." According to Walzer, noncombatants must be afforded free exit or another form of protection from the indiscriminate effects of sieges and blockades. Such humanitarian provision is, in fact, required by international laws of war.[10]

Sanctions Without War

A plausible case can be made for extending the prohibition on wartime blockades to the kinds of sanctions imposed by the international community against Iraq, Serbia, and Haiti.[11] After all, comprehensive sanctions, in or out of war, can do what just-war theory regards as immoral: inflict serious harm on an entire population to affect political and military authorities. To the extent that sanctions do in fact try to effect change in the policies of a government by inflicting suffering on its people, our moral analysis shares with just-war reasoning a strong presumption against economic coercion unless adequate humanitarian provision is made for the civilian population. Nonetheless, while the analysis of wartime blockades provides a helpful point of departure for thinking about sanctions, dissimilarities in the two cases make it an ultimately inadequate paradigm for moral analysis of comprehensive sanctions. The siege-and-blockade model is even an impediment to evaluating sanctions imposed in a nonwar context. The international community, following Woodrow Wilson, persists in seeing sanctions as different from wartime sieges and blockades.

Let us be clear, the search for an alternative model is not a convenient way to clear the obstacles to a policy we may want, in any case, to carry out. An alternative model is necessary for an explicitly moral reason: for the international community to correct a grave evil in a way that will be less destructive than war. We might then conceptualize economic sanctions in a way that enables us to reason about them as a potentially moral policy option by acknowledging that, while military force, sieges, economic sanctions, and diplomatic pressure are all forms of coercive diplomacy, the differences between these types of coercion are at least as important as the similarities.

We start, then, by considering three characteristics of sanctions that distinguish them from wartime blockades: (1) unlike wartime blockades, these sanctions are not imposed as a form of war but as an alternative to war; (2) some harms caused by sanctions may be justified, either because the affected population has consented to sanctions, or because it shares responsibility with its government for the injustices which warrant sanctions; and (3) with appropriate humanitarian provisos, the harm inflicted by sanctions is not as grievous as the harm of war. We then consider the problem of effectiveness: do sanctions offer a realistic prospect for avoiding war?

Sanctions as an Alternative to War. It helps to think of economic sanctions as a policy option independent of active hostility between states or between the international community and an offending state. In this 'pure' form, sanctions possess three defensible goals, all of which have foundation in international law and the practice of states: (1) to affirm international standards of conduct; (2) to deter, correct, or punish a grave infraction of the international order;[12] and (3) to do so without recourse to armed force.

In this revised model, what distinguishes economic sanctions from sieges and blockades in wartime is the intention to avoid the use of armed force, as opposed to an intention to multiply the effects of war. Economic sanctions allow for more deliberation and negotiation while avoiding the abrupt lethal and maiming effects of warfare. The availability of sanctions, therefore, increases the nonmilitary options policymakers have at hand, and so raises the threshold for resort to force, thereby strengthening the just-war standard of "last resort." As we discuss below, it is necessary to assess whether, in fact, sanctions do less harm than armed conflict and whether they are effective in achieving their objectives. Nonetheless, the intention to avoid the use of force is, morally speaking, a desirable one. It distinguishes sanctions from wartime blockades, where there is no such intention.

In light of increasing doubts about the efficacy, political viability, and morality of war, the intention to avoid force gains added importance. Military analysts themselves sometimes question the utility of force in contemporary international affairs. If, as some commentators claim, military force is no more than dubiously effective in attaining political ends, then the uncertainty of the nonviolent coercion would be more tolerable morally than the destructiveness of ineffective armed conflict. Moreover, as U.S. military doctrine of overwhelming and decisive force makes the use of force at once less available as a policy tool and morally problematic in terms of the strategies this doctrine justifies, sanctions become not only a moral tool for the conduct of foreign policy, but a practicable one as well. Finally, though the contention is much debated, religious leaders and moralists question the morality of modern warfare on grounds of the disproportionate harm it often entails. Thus, the development of economic sanctions as a tool for the enforcement of international policy in matters of fundamental human importance seems not only desirable, but necessary.

Economic Sanctions and the Suffering of Innocents. Sanctions may be intended and conceived as an alternative to war, but if the harm they cause is like that caused by war, are they, in fact, morally superior to war? And even if the harm caused does not compare with that caused by war, how can one justify imposing even a lesser harm on the civilian population? Skepticism about its effectiveness may be the major policy hurdle for justifying sanctions, but the harm sanctions inflict on the civilian population may be the major moral hurdle to legitimizing sanctions. Writing of the Gulf crisis, James Turner Johnson argues, the more "effective" sanctions were, "the greater their inherent impact on those persons most remote from the wrongdoing of their nation's leaders and least able to bring about change: the poor, the aged, children, the infirm. These are exactly the people who, in war, are regarded most clearly as noncombatants."[13] The case of Iraq, of course, is muddled by the interweaving of sanctions with the use of military force, but Johnson's point is valid in situations short of war as well. If sanctions impose the greatest harm on the most vulnerable in society and those most remote from the wrongdoing, something is wrong. A morally just sanctions regime must take account of the suffering it inflicts on these "innocents." As we shall argue, it can do so in two ways: (1) considering whether the population has assented to sanctions; (2) in the case of comprehensive sanctions, making effective humanitarian provision for the affected population; and (3) adopting a preference for using selective sanctions aimed at governing elites and others complicit in an offending policy.

The impact of sanctions on the civilian population varies in each case, depending upon several conditions: the type of sanctions imposed, the extent to which sanctions are being enforced, the degree to which the target country is self-sufficient in the production of basic commodities, whether adequate humanitarian exemptions are in place, whether the target government uses available resources to mitigate the suffering of its population, and whether the economy is strong.

A September 1992 study claimed that in Iraq, the combination of Desert Storm, civil strife, and trade sanctions caused a threefold increase in infant mortality between January and August 1991.[14] Even if comprehensive sanctions were not the principal cause of deaths and epidemics in Iraq, sanctions clearly involved a dramatic decrease in the standard of living. According to one study, in cases where sanctions were successful, the average decline in GNP was about 2.5%, a decline comparable to a serious recession, if not a depression. In Iraq, by comparison, sanctions reduced the living standard by about one-third. Sanctions against former Yugoslavia and Haiti have caused similar economic deprivation.

Innocence and assent. The impact of comprehensive sanctions on the civilian population raises the question of what protections are owed the population at large and especially vulnerable groups within it. There are many ways to approach the question of innocence. Technically, the term simply means a population is immune from attack because it is nonthreatening. In the wartime context, this protection is a means to restrain the use of force. In war, such immunity makes sense as the way to narrow the legitimate targets of military action because they do not threaten the enemy. Clearly, if such immunity were to transfer without qualification to nonwar situations, the international community would retain little leverage on offending states, because the military or government is often only indirectly harmed by the sanctions. At the same time, a weapon which affects the most vulnerable (and usually the least responsible) in the target country most severely appears morally objectionable. Is there an escape from this elenchus? If we follow James Turner Johnson, in situations short of war, the idea of innocence may be applied to vulnerable groups and the population at large on the grounds of distance from political decision making. Two aspects of assent, however, may mitigate concerns about the suffering imposed on those who, in war, would be considered immune from attack.

The first form of assent, which is not ordinarily a consideration in just-war analyses, is the willingness of a population to endure suffering under sanctions for the sake of removing an offending policy or government. Where economic sanctions are concerned, popular will is a plausible warrant, on the one hand, for imposing suffering where we should otherwise be very hesitant to do so or for prolonging it beyond the point where outside observers might judge it to be prudent. On the other hand, loss of assent by the affected population may require ending sanctions when outside agents would choose to prosecute sanctions to a decisive outcome. Without arguing the details, we would simply note that sanctions against South Africa and more recently against Haiti may in part be justified by the will of subject populations to endure greater suffering for paramount political ends. *Prima facie*, then, popular acceptance of sanctions, though inevitably a contested judgment, makes the imposition of conditions of suffering morally tolerable and lifts some of the burden of responsibility on the sanctioning side. At the same time, this does not relieve the sanctioning party of responsibility for judgments of proportion about when to alter or end a sanctions regime because too much harm is being done to no-good end, whether to the country under embargo or to the international system. Nor does it relieve the sanctioning party of the responsibility, as discussed below, to provide for humanitarian relief, even when the target country is unresponsive to the suffering of its own people.[15]

A second and different form of assent applies when the civilian population has not assented to sanctions but rather may be considered to have assented to the aggressive or unjust policies that justify imposing sanctions. In these cases, the civilian population becomes a legitimate target of sanctions because it shares responsibility for the actions of its government and thus may be pressured to remove that government from power or, at least, to force it to change its policies.[16] This argument presumes that the population approves or contributes, at least implicitly, to its government's actions and thus cannot enjoy the immunity otherwise afforded civilians. Such an argument can be plausibly made in cases like the former Rhodesia, South Africa, or Israel because a significant part of the population in those countries functioned democratically and supported offending policies, and because the more vulnerable populations (Rhodesian and South African Blacks and Palestinians) were disposed to call for the imposition of sanctions in support of their respective causes. A case can also be made for linkage between a population at large and an offending government concerning Serbia, where there is widespread popular support ("a general will") for the basic objectives pursued by Serb leaders. Because in such situations, as Michael Walzer suggests, the polity coheres through protecting a particular community's way of life, one can argue that citizens at large are justifiably liable to international economic pressure to correct their nation's offenses.[17]

The case is more difficult to make with authoritarian regimes where dissent is penalized, there are no independent centers of power, and there is little popular support for the actions of the government. Iraq would be an especially glaring instance of the disconnection between the population at large and the state apparatus. There the government shows not the slightest concern for the welfare of its own people, simultaneously making war on Kurds and Marsh Arabs and refusing to relieve the impact of sanctions on the rest of the population. Iraq illustrates the problems with imputing responsibility to an entire population when there is no way to express lack of assent short of emigration and rebellion. In such circumstances, the presumption for selective sanctions against ruling elites over comprehensive embargoes is strengthened, and responsibility of the international community for humanitarian provision to vulnerable groups in the target country increases.

Innocence and the basic rights distinction. Another model for thinking about sanctions may be found in the distinction between basic rights and lesser rights and enjoyments. This may prove more useful than the just-war principle of civilian immunity as a paradigm for economic sanctions. As long as the survival of the population is not put at risk and its health is not severely impaired, aspects of daily life might temporarily be degraded for the sake of restoring the rights of others. While one ought never deprive anyone of fundamental rights, it may be permissible, particularly when the basic rights of others are in jeopardy, to deny a population lesser rights and enjoyments. For example, it could be morally permissible to impose an embargo which would lead to a widespread, but short-term, loss of jobs. As long as the survival of the population was not put at risk and its health was not severely impaired, other aspects of daily life might be degraded, temporarily, for the sake of restoring the rights of others.[18] To use a domestic legal analogy, whereas military action or wartime blockades are akin to the imposition of the death penalty, sanctions are more like a court's attaching of assets. Sanctions, like attaching assets, may eventually place a population in crisis, but, whereas war's impact is speedy and frequently lethal, the impact of sanctions grows over time and allows more easily for mitigation of these harmful effects and for a negotiated solution than acts of war. In fact, comprehensive sanctions imposed as an alternative to war, with appropriate humanitarian provisions, are far less likely to lead to death and similar irreversible and grave harm to basic rights than wartime blockades. The British blockade of Germany during World War I, which Walzer rightly finds objectionable, led to some half million civilian deaths. If contemporary sanctions regimes were to cause even a fraction of this kind of harm, they would be morally objectionable. But sanctions that are properly designed need not cause such harm. If they do, they should be revised or lifted.

In cases where grave harm is due to the refusal of the targeted government to use resources at hand to ensure its population's basic needs are met, the international community may only stand aside for so long. From a moral point of view, at least, a government which fails to provide for its own people under such conditions rules illegitimately. Therefore, the responsibility for protection of the civilian population reverts to other legitimate authorities, particularly the sanctioning parties. In such cases, the sanctioning authority must look for alternate means to provide for innocents, and if it fails to provide for them, other tools, including the use of force, should be used to compel a decision without further loss of innocent civilian life. Thus, a basic rights approach means that, when imposing sanctions, the international community has a responsibility to alleviate the suffering of the most vulnerable in society. Humanitarian provision for sustaining basic needs of the population through sales or aid, therefore, will be a necessary provision of a just-sanctions regime.

Targeted sanctions. If humanitarian provisions are incapable of avoiding harm to basic rights, then sanctions that are more directly targeted at the nation's leaders should be pursued. There is a widespread belief that comprehensive sanctions that hit the economy hard and fast are preferable. Ivan Eland makes a persuasive case, however, that more restrained, selective sanctions (e.g., freezing assets, denying travel visas, imposing strict arms embargoes) are often more effective.[19] According to Eland, proponents of comprehensive sanctions wrongly assume that a destroyed economy will lead to desirable policy changes when, in fact, economic disintegration often leads to political cohesion, the so-called rally around the flag effect that we have seen in Serbia. For that reason, Eland contends, targeted sanctions are more likely to have the desired political effect. Targeted sanctions are less susceptible to this rally around the flag effect and are more likely to strengthen the political opposition to the existing government. Moreover, they can have a powerful psychological effect because political leaders will tend to overestimate the impact that still tougher sanctions might have in the event the sanctioning party should choose to escalate its enforcement measures. Even if comprehensive sanctions prove to be more effective than selective ones, the marginal benefits of less discriminatory sanctions must be weighed against the moral benefits of targeting sanctions more precisely at those most responsible for the policies in question.

We have argued in this section that in analyzing economic sanctions we must be cautious about using analyses too tightly tethered to pre-existing schemes of evaluation. The just-war analysis of sieges and blockades should not be applied, without qualification, to sanctions imposed as an alternative to war. The intention of sanctions is different: to avoid war and the harm it brings by raising the threshold of resort to force. The harm imposed by sanctions may sometimes be justified because the population has assented to suffer under sanctions to change its government or its policies, or because the general population has assented to the unjust actions of its government. As in wartime, civilian immunity applies to sanctions insofar as they threaten basic rights; sanctions, therefore, must have adequate humanitarian provisos or should be targeted to avoid grave harm to the civilian population.

Do Sanctions Avoid War? Even if one accepts that sanctions may be considered as different from wartime blockades and that at least some of the harm they impose on the civilian population may be justified, one still is faced with the question of the efficacy of sanctions. The efficacy of sanctions is morally relevant for two reasons. First, we cannot justify imposing harm on others if there is no prospect for achieving a legitimate objective; and, second, we cannot hold out sanctions as an alternative to war if they offer little possibility of achieving results short of war.

A senior State Department official recently summed up what is the most frequent critique of sanctions. "You cannot show one government that has changed due to sanctions.... When the government, the elite and the black marketeers are one and the same, the ones that we really want to hurt do well and the common people get hurt."[20] Sanctions, according to this argument, often prove the law of unintended consequences: Not only do sanctions have the least impact on the elites, they reinforce the power of the very people they were meant to undermine.

Former Yugoslavia serves as an example of this problem. Some analysts contend that Western sanctions against Yugoslavia have increased the possibility that the war will continue and spread. Sanctions, according to this view, are based on the false assumption that economic coercion will convince Serbian President Slobodan Milosevic to sue for peace, when, in fact, his political life may depend on a continuation of war. Rather than generate popular opposition to Milosevic's rule, sanctions appear to have isolated and undermined nascent democratic movements in Serbia and encouraged an exodus of those most likely to provide a democratic alternative to the existing regime. Meanwhile, they have enriched the elites and criminal elements who control the black market, and increased the power of political leaders who control rationing and the distribution of humanitarian aid and who use sanctions as an excuse for imposing emergency measures. Finally, according to this view, sanctions have strengthened, rather than weakened, militant nationalists by reinforcing the Serb sense of siege and victimization.[21]

The relationship between economic pressure and changes in political or military behavior is rarely direct. Sanctions have had a positive impact on Serb political leaders. Sanctions alone have not stopped the war in Bosnia-Herzegovina, but they have been an important factor in obtaining Belgrade's commitment to end its support for Bosnian Serbs and endorse a peace settlement they have rejected. Moreover, sanctions have made the creation of a Greater Serbia economically infeasible.[22]

In other places, it is too early to draw firm conclusions about the efficacy of sanctions; the results to date have been mixed. The recalcitrance of Iraq even after Desert Storm suggests the limited impact of sanctions, yet sanctions played a role in gaining compliance with the UN's cease-fire resolution and some experts contend that sanctions could have worked against Iraq given enough time.[23] The continuance of sanctions may not have improved the situation for the Kurds, but it probably forced Baghdad to comply with weapons inspections in 1993.

In Haiti, the imposition of UN sanctions was a major factor in the Governors Island Accord, but sanctions did not help implement the accord or work quickly to dislodge the military government. In South Africa, Nelson Mandela and others have credited sanctions with ending apartheid, despite the gradual, halfhearted and selective way they were imposed, the lack of international consensus in support of sanctions, and the relatively minor impact they had on the South African economy.[24]

The empirical evidence regarding the effectiveness of sanctions as cited in the 1990 study by Hufbauer, Schott, and Elliott should be troubling to moralists.[25] The low success rates in reversing aggression or achieving major policy changes suggest that a sanctions regime may not prove to be the long-desired alternative to war in a case when war is the most likely alternative. Sanctions seem to work best where there is a degree of democracy or at least social and organizational pluralism in a target country. The intransigence of "rogue regimes" such as North Korea and Haiti, which lack accountability or concern for their own people, strengthens the argument for pursuing means other than sanctions in these cases.

The State Department official's dismissal of sanctions as always ineffective is, however, too harsh a judgment. Sanctions do work at times. They are less effective in reversing aggression, but they have succeeded in discouraging some military adventures. Even if the chance of success is low, as in Yugoslavia or Haiti, sanctions might be morally preferable if the only alternative is a war that would likely cause disproportionate harm and offers little prospect for success. In general, as war becomes less feasible as an instrument of policy and as the moral problems with modern warfare become more apparent, the case for sanctions as an alternative grows proportionately. Moreover, as noted previously, evaluations of the effectiveness of sanctions usually are limited to only two of the goals of sanctions: compelling a change in policies and defending against illegal or aggressive acts. Sanctions might not succeed in achieving these goals, but might still be worth imposing for symbolic (deontological) or other less instrumental reasons. Sanctions might fail to reverse aggression or protect human rights but succeed in avoiding complicity in evil, in expressing moral revulsion and upholding international norms, and in showing solidarity with suffering people.

In sum, the historical record suggests that sanctions must be evaluated on a case-by-case basis, with attention to the particular political, economic, diplomatic, and military context. Sanctions are sometimes successful in changing behavior, but success also must be measured in terms of other, less instrumental goals. We should not presume that comprehensive sanctions are always more effective than targeted sanctions. The experience with sanctions does not provide a conclusive judgment about their effectiveness, but may provide the basis for countervailing presumptions about when sanctions are likely to be effective and when they are not.

Ensuring a Just-Sanctions Regime

Acknowledging the moral dilemmas posed by sanctions, we have argued that comprehensive sanctions may be considered as an alternative to war in terms of their intent, the nature of the harm they cause, and their effectiveness, although limited, in resolving problems without recourse to force. This is not to suggest, however, that sanctions may be given blanket moral approval. Far from it. We would propose that a morally legitimate sanctions regime should clearly meet several criteria.

First, imposing sanctions should be a response to a grave injustice committed. Because a comprehensive sanctions regime is a blunt and potent instrument of coercion, it should be imposed only in response to aggression or grave and ongoing injustice. Fundamental international norms must be at stake to warrant resort to this level of coercion. The violation need not be as serious as that necessary to justify the use of military force, but it must meet a high threshold.

Second, parties imposing sanctions should have a commitment to and reasonable prospects for reaching a political settlement. We have argued that the moral legitimacy of a sanctions regime depends, in part, on whether it is used as an alternative to war. That, in turn, requires that it be intended and pursued as an alternative to war; that it has a reasonable prospect of achieving legitimate objectives, instrumental or symbolic; and that it does not cause the grave or irremediable harm of the kind caused by war. It is imperative that any sanctions regime be tied to an abiding commitment to and a feasible strategy for finding a political solution to the problem that justified the imposition of sanctions. As Vatican Secretary of State Cardinal Angelo Sodano has said, "Sanctions—whether in the former Yugoslavia, Haiti, or Iraq—must also be accompanied by an international commitment to negotiations in order to be legitimate."[26] Without the requisite political will and reasonable prospects for a political solution, sanctions lose much of their moral attractiveness. Sanctions then fail to serve as a tool of international diplomacy and become more like a war of attrition or an excuse for inaction or indifference. The requirement that sanctions be part of a feasible political strategy means that a sanctions regime should have clear and reasonable conditions set for their removal. If it becomes clear that existing sanctions have no reasonable prospect of achieving their objectives and are causing unacceptable harm, they should be lifted.

Third, sanctions should only be imposed when less coercive means have failed. The international community should impose sanctions only if less coercive measures have been tried or are not likely to succeed. If war is the last resort, comprehensive economic sanctions are the penultimate resort. Generally, therefore, sanctions should be pursued as an alternative to and before the use of military force. But sometimes, as in Somalia and Rwanda, the urgency of the situation and the likelihood that sanctions would not work could justify the limited use of military force without first applying economic sanctions. With respect to less coercive measures, this condition also places a twofold burden on the international community. In the short term, it must look to international monitoring, diplomacy, political sanctions, arms embargoes, and similar measures to deal with particular crises before it moves toward imposing economic sanctions. In the long term, the international community has an obligation to develop and strengthen the full range of its collective security mechanisms, so that it can better prevent conflicts and injustices before they arise, and better deal with those that do through means less onerous than sanctions.

Fourth, parties imposing sanctions should make provision for basic human needs. As noted earlier, a basic-rights approach to sanctions necessarily entails a humanitarian proviso. Humanitarian provision can be made by exempting basic commodities and providing humanitarian relief. Protection for the basic rights of citizens in offending countries remains a continuing responsibility of international authorities and other sanctioning parties. When humanitarian exemptions have proven insufficient to prevent the death by starvation or disease of citizens of the targeted country, sanctioning authorities are duty bound to redesign mechanisms for humanitarian provision to make them effective. Further failure to provide for the basic needs of the target-country population would require additional decisions, either to fall back on selected sanctions, to discontinue comprehensive sanctions as morally unworkable, or ultimately to resort to the use of force. Humanitarian exemptions should be defined broadly enough that there can be no threat to human health or life. Broader exemptions than those permitted under existing sanctions regimes could make the enforcement of sanctions more difficult and might diminish the effectiveness of sanctions, but due care for civilian populations seems to require that these added difficulties be accepted if adequate provision is to be made for civilians.

Fifth, sanctions must be proportionate. Another criterion is proportionality. Is the overall harm caused by sanctions outweighed by the good to be achieved by them? This criterion ensures that there always be a relationship between the objectives of sanctions and the kinds of sanctions imposed. The imposition of comprehensive sanctions arguably is a proportionate response to Iraqi aggression against Kuwait or genocide in Bosnia-Herzegovina. Continuance of comprehensive sanctions (as opposed to lesser ones) against Iraq, however, long after Kuwait has been freed, to gain compliance with the few remaining unmet conditions of the cease-fire resolution seems disproportionate. As in war, this condition is inherently difficult to assess. Nevertheless, the proportionality principle, which is firmly rooted in both moral and legal frameworks, places an important limit on what can be done in the name of sanctions. It forces us to look beyond the prospects for achieving our objectives and to assess carefully the harm sanctions are causing. Because the harm caused by sanctions tends to increase and become irreversible the longer sanctions remain in place, proportionality provides a check against imposing sanctions for interminable periods of time.

Finally, the imposition of multilateral sanctions is usually preferable to unilateral sanctions. That economic coercion has been used most effectively and historically by big powers to impose their will on weaker states should give any moralist pause. Our framework might well respond to the moral problem of means: ensuring that the blunt instrument of economic sanctions conforms to moral norms. But sanctions could be imposed in a moral way, yet still be subject to the worst kinds of abuse by unscrupulous states or misguided multilateral organizations. It is not at all surprising that the most vulnerable countries of the developing world have frequently sought international condemnation of boycotts and other forms of "economic warfare" in the name of principles of nonintervention, nondiscrimination, self-determination, and solidarity.[27] As notions of sovereignty, nonintervention and other fundamental principles of international order are redefined and developed, the political and legal limits of sanctions should become clearer. Usually imposing sanctions multilaterally, especially within the collective security framework of the United Nations, tends to reduce the risk that sanctions will be used for unjust purposes. The more sanctions are employed by international institutions rather than individual states, the more there will be a procedural brake on any temptation to misuse sanctions to serve narrow interests of the powerful (as opposed to the interests of justice). That is not to say that multilateralism is a panacea. As David Hendrickson points out, the need to seek international legitimation can serve as an excuse for not acting when action is justified. It can also serve as a fig leaf for the interests of an uncompromising hegemonic power.[28] Multilateralism for its own sake is not the answer. But multilateralism combined with a commitment to the principles of collective security could at least lower the risk that sanctions could be used by the powerful to bully the vulnerable.

Conclusion: Sanctions and Moral Legitimacy

It should be clear from this analysis that, as with most matters of public policy, moral analysis does not provide easy or clear answers to the question, Should we impose sanctions? Morality cannot escape the same dilemmas and uncertainties that muddy the economic and political analyses of sanctions. What it can do is help ensure that we ask the right questions.

By way of summary and conclusion, we begin to answer these questions in the form of three primary theses and a set of six ethical conditions which must be satisfied before resorting to comprehensive economic sanctions:

Thesis 1. Sanctions cannot be evaluated solely by standards of efficacy. Nor can they be endorsed or rejected in principle, without reference to their likely consequences. Rather, sanctions must be evaluated morally on a case-by-case basis, keeping in mind the full range of consequentialist and deontological considerations.

Thesis 2. The just-war analysis of wartime sieges and blockades is not adequate to evaluate most contemporary cases of comprehensive sanctions because (1) these sanctions are not imposed as a form of war but as an alternative to war; (2) the affected population may have assented to sanctions; and, (3) with appropriate humanitarian provisos, the harm inflicted by sanctions is not as immediate or as grievous as the harm of war.

Thesis 3. Even when an alternative to war, the limited effectiveness of sanctions and the harm they cause to innocent populations create a presumption that a regime of comprehensive economic sanctions is morally problematic, and targeted sanctions are morally preferable. As the U.S. Catholic Bishops said recently, these concerns "counsel that this blunt instrument be used sparingly and with restraint."[29]

In assessing whether this presumption against the use of comprehensive economic sanctions may be overridden, the following six criteria should be considered:

1. *Grave injustice:* Sanctions could be imposed if the target country has committed a grave injustice.
2. *A commitment to and prospects for a political solution:* Sanctions should be pursued as an alternative to war, not as another form of war. They must be part of an abiding commitment to and a feasible strategy for finding a political solution to the problem that justified the imposition of sanctions in the first place.
3. *Humanitarian proviso:* Civilians should be immune from grave and irreversible harm from sanctions, though lesser harms may be imposed on the civilian population. Provision must be made to ensure that fundamental human rights, such as the right to food, medicine, and shelter, are not violated.

4. *Penultimate resort:* Less-coercive means should be used, whenever feasible, before resort to comprehensive economic sanctions.
5. *Proportionality:* The harm caused by sanctions must be proportionate to the good likely to be achieved.
6. *Legitimacy:* Multilateral sanctions are preferable as a procedural protection against the potential misuse of sanctions by the strong against the weak, and as a means of strengthening international mechanisms for collective security and the peaceful settlement of disputes.

A morally legitimate sanctions regime will be both less idealistic and draconian than Woodrow Wilson's vision and more assertive than that of John Foster Dulles. But with Wilson, we believe that as war becomes less feasible as an instrument of policy, as there is wider appreciation of the moral problems with warfare, and as international institutions develop as they were intended, the moral legitimacy and efficacy of sanctions should grow proportionally.

Notes

1. Quoted in Barry E. Carter, *International Economic Sanctions: Improving the Haphazard U.S. Legal Regime* (Cambridge: Cambridge Univ. Press, 1988), p. 9.

2. Patrick Clawson, "Sanctions as Punishment, Enforcement, and Prelude to Further Action," *Ethics and International Affairs*, Vol. 7, 1993, p. 20.

3. Holy Assembly of Bishops of the Serbian Orthodox Church, "An Appeal for Humanity to the Security Council of the United Nations," November 3, 1993.

4. Analysts of sanctions define the basic policy objectives in different ways. See, e.g., Carter, *International Economic Sanctions*, pp. 12–13; to influence policy; to punish; to symbolically oppose policies. O.Y. Elagab, *The Legality of Non-Forcible Counter-Measures in International Law* (Oxford: Clarendon Press, 1988), pp. 44–46; purposes of counter-measures: self-protection, reciprocity, settlement of disputes, revenge. Gary Clyde Hufbauer, Jeffrey J. Schott, and Kimberly Ann Elliott, *Economic Sanctions Reconsidered*, 2d ed. (Washington, D.C.: Institute for International Economics, 1990), pp. 11–12; demonstration of resolve, deterrence, change policies and capabilities. Michael P. Malloy, *Economic Sanctions and U.S. Trade* (Boston: Little, Brown & Company, 1990), pp. 19–22; directive; defensive; communicative.

5. Boycotts, corporate disengagement, and denial of credit often begin in the private voluntary sector with churches, investors, humanitarian aid groups, and human rights activists. They are a matter of popular political action and occasionally corporate decision rather than governmental initiative. The emergence of social action groups, especially in Europe and North America, raises issues of the accountability of popular organizations to which political theorists and moralists have given scant attention. The just-war test of legitimate authority, not to mention, geopolitical assumptions about the state-system, shed little, if any, light

on the authenticity of morally motivated actions by nongovernmental groups. Neither do they illuminate the limits of popular initiatives in the international arena.

6. Vatican Secretary of State Cardinal Angelo Sodano argues that punishment is not a justification for sanctions. Interview with Vatican Radio, April 7, 1994, quoted in Catholic News Service, April 7, 1994, p. 1. Sodano raises in the context of sanctions a disputed question of the just-war tradition. While much of the tradition permitted war to punish aggression, recent papal teaching has limited just cause for use of force to defense against ongoing aggression.

7. Solidarity is a significant motive in recent Roman Catholic social teaching on global justice. Paul VI, "Populorum Progressio," and John Paul II, "Sollicitudo Rei Socialis," in Catholic Social Teaching: The Documentary Heritage, ed. David J. O'Brien and Thomas Shannon, (Maryknoll, N.Y.: Orbis Books, 1992). While Western social activists tend to employ solidarity as a motive for intervention in developing societies, third world elites sometimes use the concept to reinforce traditional norms of nonintervention.

8. On the heterogeneity of moral reasoning, see Charles E. Larmore, Patterns of Moral Complexity (Cambridge: Cambridge University Press, 1987).

9. Michael Walzer, Just and Unjust Wars: A Moral Argument with Historical Illustrations (New York: Basic Books, Inc., 1977), pp. 170–75.

10. The Fourth Geneva Convention (article 23) requires free passage of medical supplies intended only for civilians and for foodstuffs for children under 15, expectant mothers and maternity cases. The First Geneva Protocol (1977) (articles 69–71) requires that essential humanitarian supplies be provided civilians in non-occupied territory if the civilian population is threatened in its survival. For a discussion of the Geneva Conventions and Protocols, see Frits Kalshoven, Constraints on the Waging of War (Geneva: International Committee of the Red Cross, 1987), pp. 52, 121–22.

11. In the case of Iraq, at least, a strong case may be made that the prohibition directly applies for two reasons. First, it appears that the prewar sanctions were never seriously attempted as an alternative to war in conjunction with a serious diplomatic effort to resolve the conflict short of combat. Prewar sanctions were a way to buy time while assembling the military coalition for Desert Storm. Secondly, war planners are reported to have deliberately aimed at destruction of civilian infrastructure as a means of intensifying the pressure on Saddam Hussein under the sanctions regime which remained after the cessation of hostilities.

12. As noted earlier, whether sanctions may be imposed as punishment is a disputed point. See, infra, f.n. 4.

13. James Turner Johnson, "Just-War Tradition and the War in the Gulf," The Christian Century, February 6–13, 1991, p. 134.

14. Alberto Ascherio, et al., "Effect of the Gulf War on Infant and Child Mortality in Iraq," New England Journal of Medicine, Vol. 327, No. 13, September 24, 1992, p. 931. See also Clawson, "Sanctions as Punishment," pp. 24–27; what deaths occurred in Iraq were mainly due to the war, civil strife, and the Iraqi government's noncooperation with humanitarian efforts.

15. National Conference of Catholic Bishops, The Harvest of Justice is Sown in Peace (Washington, D.C.: U.S. Catholic Conference, 1993), p. 15.

16. Clawson, "Sanctions as Punishment," pp. 20–21.

17. On the sovereign polity (statehood) as a means to preserve a distinctive way of life, see Walzer, *Just and Unjust*, pp. 53–55.

18. This distinction is similar to Damrosch's approach, which finds reductions in the standard of living morally tolerable so long as sanctions do not cause "a significant segment of society to fall below the subsistence level." We do not agree, however, with her argument that this condition may be violated to meet other objectives of sanctions, namely, containing the conflict. Lori Fisler Damrosch, "The Civilian Impact of Economic Sanctions," in *Enforcing Restraint: Collective Intervention in Internal Conflicts*, ed. Lori Fisler Damrosch (New York: Council on Foreign Relations, 1993), pp. 281–84.

19. Ivan Eland, "Sanctions: Think Small," *The Bulletin of the Atomic Scientists*, November, 1993, pp. 36–40.

20. Stuart Auerbach, "Are Sanctions More Harmful than Helpful?" *The Washington Post*, March 28, 1993, sec. H, pp. 1, 4.

21. Susan L. Woodward, "Yugoslavia: Divide and Fail," *The Bulletin of the Atomic Scientists*, Vol. 49, No. 9, November 1993, pp. 24–27. Peter Maas, "Serbian People, Politicians Scoff at West's Threats to Sanctions," *The Washington Post*, March 31, 1993, sec. A, p. 25.

22. James Rupert, "Yugoslavia's Inflation Ebbs, but Stability Remains Precarious," *The Washington Post*, February 19, 1994, sec. A, p. 22.

23. "Remarks by Kimberly Elliott," in American Society of International Law 85th Annual *Proceedings* (Washington, D.C.: American Society of International Law, April 18, 1991), pp. 173–74. See also Howard S. Brembeck, "A Nonviolent Solution to the Persian Gulf Crisis," in *Inforum* (Goshen, Ind.: Fourth Freedom Forum) No. 7, January 1991, pp. 1–2.

24. Hufbauer, Schott, and Elliott, *Economic Sanctions Reconsidered*, pp. 113–14.

25. Ibid, p. 93.

26. Cardinal Angelo Sodano, Vatican Secretary of State, quoted in *Catholic News Service*, April 7, 1994, p. 1.

27. Stephen C. Neff, "Boycott and the Law of Nations: Economic Warfare and Modern International Law in Historical Perspective," in *The British Yearbook of International Law 1988*, ed. I. Brownlie and D.W. Bowett (Oxford: Oxford Univ. Press, 1989), pp. 135–45.

28. David C. Hendrickson, "The Ethics of Collective Security," *Ethics and International Affairs*, Vol. 7, 1993, pp. 10–15.

29. National Conference of Catholic Bishops, *Harvest of Justice*, p. 15.

PART THREE

Case Studies

10

UN Sanctions Against Iraq

David E. Reuther[1]

The UN Security Council's response to the Iraqi invasion of Kuwait was a unique, post–Cold War event.[2] This brief essay will explore the narrow theme that, in turning to economic sanctions, the UN Security Council addressed both its humanitarian concerns and the political goal of seeking Iraqi compliance with the requirements of various Security Council resolutions. Responding to Iraq's invasion of Kuwait, the United Nations Security Council (UNSC) voted in August 1990 to impose economic sanctions.[3] In the first weeks the sanctions were symbols of international unanimity designed to encourage Baghdad to release its prize. Years later, economic sanctions sought Iraqi compliance with specific criteria embedded in UN Security Council resolutions, primarily UNSC Resolution 687, which Iraq had accepted as the terms of the Gulf War cease-fire. Economic sanctions against Iraq were not unlimited. UNSC resolutions never embargoed medicines or health supplies and the ban on importation of foodstuffs was lifted with the cease-fire. In the summer of 1991 the Security Council went even further and designed an exemption to the embargo on the sale of Iraqi oil, if Iraq used the proceeds to purchase humanitarian supplies and if they were equitably distributed under UN monitoring. To date Baghdad steadfastly refuses to implement this exemption.

After four years the embargo remains, raising questions about the efficacy of economic sanctions, particularly because Iraq was seen as uniquely dependent on a single export. Nevertheless, the Baghdad government has fairly successfully avoided compliance in detail with UN resolutions, shunned humanitarian assistance, shifted the burden of sanctions to that sector of the population which rose in revolt in spring 1991, and, through administrative and monetary policies, maintained its supporters. In the face of a ruthless, tenacious Iraqi leadership, economic sanctions have achieved only marginal success and left the world community with a moral, as well as political, dilemma.

Chronology of Events

The day Iraq invaded Kuwait, the UN Security Council unanimously passed Resolution 600[4] calling for Iraq to withdraw and for negotiations between the parties. This was the first of 27 resolutions seeking Iraqi compliance with international norms.[5] With Resolution 661, passed on August 6, 1990, the Security Council imposed economic sanctions on Iraq "to secure [the] compliance of Iraq . . . and restore the authority of the legitimate government of Kuwait." The imposition of sanctions in the beginning was primarily an indication of the international community's collective outrage at the Iraqi invasion and a harbinger of future penalties Iraq would suffer if it did not change its course. Resolution 661 called for the international community to bar all exports from Iraq and Kuwait, any activities which would promote such exports, and all trade in arms. The UN specifically exempted "supplies intended strictly for medical purposes, and, in humanitarian circumstances, foodstuffs . . . ." Paragraph 6 established the UN Sanctions Committee, the membership of which was synonymous with UN Security Council membership. Operating by consensus, the committee approved suppliers' applications for humanitarian supplies other than food and medical supplies. As an illustration of the items which came before the Sanctions Committee—and were routinely approved—in the last quarter of 1992, the committee approved 421 separate applications ranging from baby powder to 117 metric tons of raw materials for the production of medicine, or 4.5 tons of ball bearings for combine harvesters.

Resolution 665, passed on August 25, 1990, called for a maritime interception force to enforce UNSC Resolution 661 sanctions. Resolution 666, passed September 13, 1990, called for the Secretary General to study the humanitarian situation in Kuwait and Iraq. Resolution 666 set forth the principle that foodstuffs provided to Kuwait and Iraq "should be provided through the United Nations in cooperation with the International Committee of the Red Cross or other appropriate humanitarian agencies and distributed by them or under their supervision to ensure that they reach the intended beneficiaries." International aid agencies had reported that the Iraqi government had diverted humanitarian supplies. The Security Council's reaction was to insist that Iraq's performance be monitored and verified. Resolution 670, passed September 25, 1990, confirmed that the embargo strictures of Resolution 661 also applied to aviation and shipping. More resolutions followed until the Gulf War ended with Iraq's defeat and acceptance of the cease-fire resolution.

UN Security Council Resolution 687

Resolution 687, the cease-fire resolution, summed the bulk of the UN Security Council's requirements of Iraq. These requirements were designed to redress Baghdad's assault on the international system and forestall Iraqi destabilization of the Persian Gulf in the future. Resolution 687 was adopted on April 3, 1991, by 12 votes in favor (Austria, Belgium, China, Côte d'Ivoire, France, India, Romania, USSR, UK, US, Zaire and Zimbabwe), one against (Cuba) and 2 abstentions (Ecuador and Yemen).[6] The Resolution:

- Demanded that Iraq and Kuwait respect the border which the council would guarantee and called on the Secretary General to demarcate the existing border;
- Established a demilitarized zone along the border and a UN border surveillance unit;
- Ordered the destruction, under international supervision, of Iraq's weapons of mass destruction programs, and missiles with a range greater than 150 kilometers;
- Requested the return of all Kuwaiti property;
- Noted Iraq's liability for reparations; and called on the Secretary General to establish a compensation commission to pay private, corporate, and national claims;
- Lifted the ban on the sale of foodstuffs;
- Authorized a continued arms embargo on Iraq;
- Called for the return of missing Kuwaiti and third country nationals; and
- Required Iraq to eschew terrorism.

The Resolution required that the Security Council review Iraqi compliance every 120 days.

A Humanitarian Exemption to UN Sanctions

Six months after the end of the Gulf War, it became clear that Iraqi policy did not include compliance in detail with the terms of the cease-fire resolution. Iraq, defeated in battle but defiant, resisted compliance with each of Resolution 687's requirements. It refused to account for missing Kuwaiti citizens, return looted property, or recognize the border. Iraqi security agencies harassed the UN teams inspecting Iraqi's chemical, biological, and nuclear weapons programs. Initial Iraqi defiance suggested that compliance would come later rather than sooner.

If so, the Security Council would have to maintain the international consensus against Iraq. With Iraqi overseas assets blocked and sanctions forbidding the sale of oil, there was concern that Iraq would not have the financial resources to purchase approvable humanitarian provisions. Therefore, on August 15, 1991, the Security Council passed Resolution 706 which would allow states to import a total of $1.6 billion worth of Iraqi oil for a six-month period.[7] The resolution would also allow substantial deductions from that $1.6 billion total to (1) operate UN humanitarian programs in Iraq, (2) contribute to the UN Compensation Fund which would pay victims of Iraq's aggression, (3) pay the costs of eliminating Iraq's weapons of mass destruction, (4) cover the full costs of facilitating the return of all Kuwaiti property seized by Iraq, and (5) fund the Iraqi half of the costs of the UN Boundary Commission. The remainder, estimated at approximately $993 million, would be available for the purchase of humanitarian supplies. The resolutions required that the Secretary General submit a report to the Security Council on the modalities of implementing the resolution's program. The resolution noted the Council's desire that humanitarian relief be equitably distributed "to all segments of the Iraqi civilian population through effective monitoring and transparency." It also reminded Iraq of its responsibility under Resolution 688 to allow "unhindered access by international humanitarian organizations to all those in need of assistance in all parts of Iraq . . . ." The Security Council felt this admonition necessary because Iraq's physical intimidation of NGO and UN workers, especially in the South, was beginning to reach the point where there were concerns for the aid workers' safety.

Resolution 712, passed September 18, 1991, accepted a report from the Secretary General, created an escrow account for the expected oil revenues, established a subaccount for voluntary contributions to purchase humanitarian assistance for Iraq, and reiterated the requirement that distribution of assistance be equitable. The Secretary General's report outlined the specifics of a plan which called for Iraqi export of oil using the pipeline through Turkey. The report went into considerable detail about the mechanics of monitoring the sale of Iraqi oil, assuring the deposit of the resulting revenue in the escrow account, and guaranteeing that supplies would be equitably distributed. In the intervening months Iraq held discussions with the UN Secretariat from time to time on the modalities of the oil-for-food plan but ultimately refused to implement Resolutions 706 and 712. Baghdad objected to the requirement for UN monitoring.[8] Baghdad was also opposed because acceptance would have required it to lift its embargo against the 3.1 million people, primarily Kurds, who live in its three northern governates.

The Enforcement of Sanctions on Iraq

Iraq's invasion of Kuwait stimulated an unprecedented international consensus to hold Baghdad accountable and to cooperate in the broad application of sanctions. Sanctions have contributed significantly to preventing Iraq from rebuilding its war industries and replacing the material losses to its military machine. The economic costs to Iraq have been substantial. The suddenness of Iraq's invasion of Kuwait left much of Iraq's aviation and marine fleets outside the country, where they have remained. There are Iraqi-flagged commercial aircraft in Tunisia and Jordan, and ships in Yemen, Jordan, Mauritania, Egypt, Germany, Kuwait, Singapore, and Greece.

Each UN member has the responsibility to uphold the sanctions on Iraq. The United States has played a leading role in sharing information with other countries on possible sanctions violations by their nationals. U.S. policy on exports to Iraq has been more strict than the policies of some other countries. Overseeing U.S. suppliers' adherence to the sanctions has been the responsibility of the Treasury Department's Office of Foreign Assets Control (OFAC). U.S. policy has been to issue Treasury licenses when the commodity is purchased by or donated to a UN agency or reputable humanitarian NGO which will oversee the equitable distribution of the commodity.

Part of the international community's enforcement of the embargo has been through the provision of naval vessels to the Multinational Intercept Force (MIF) stationed in the upper reaches of the Red Sea and the Persian Gulf (although the Iran/Iraq war-damaged Gulf ports are beyond use). The MIF has the responsibility of inspecting all vessels for cargo consigned to Iraq, most of which passes through the Jordanian port of Aqaba. The MIF applied stringent rules concerning documentation of cargo. Ships were diverted if MIF vessels could not gain access to the cargo. The MIF in the Red Sea was dissolved in August 1994 and moved on land.

Major land transportation lines to Iraq are via Jordan and Turkey, both of which have an extra responsibility to enforce sanctions. There has been a steady volume of traffic over these borders since Iraq's invasion of Kuwait. The vast bulk of this traffic has been supplies approved by the Sanctions Committee. In fulfilling their responsibilities to enforce sanctions, local authorities have uncovered fraud and other circumvention schemes. Airtight sanctions have been elusive and their effectiveness has been influenced by several variables, including the resolve of sanctioning nations to maintain superior monitoring and enforcement capabilities. This task is all the more difficult because a country under sanctions can be expected to use its full authority and resources to resist those sanctions. As Hufbauer, Elliott, and Schott point out in their study, behavior modification comes slowly, if at all.[9]

Iraq's Adjustments to Sanctions

From the beginning the Iraqi leadership decided that it would, only minimally, if at all, comply with UN Security Council resolutions, and wait out the international community's enforcement of sanctions. The leadership's desire to stay in power has translated into the propitiation of the Iraqi security, intelligence, military, and party circles which insulate it from the Iraqi population. After the spring 1991 uprisings in the North and South were repressed, the Iraqi leadership rewarded outstanding cadres with gifts and various financial awards, some consisting of loot from Kuwait. To restore a sense of normalcy, the government quickly repaired Gulf War–damaged structures, but only in the Baghdad area. This was easily accomplished with the materials at hand. Restoration of power and other facilities was accomplished by cannibalizing equipment. Each completed project was inaugurated with fanfare and propaganda. Repairs were not undertaken in those areas of the country which experienced the spring uprisings. All water treatment facilities in the Baghdad area and the facility connected to the phosphate plant in Western Iraq were repaired and functioning before the first water treatment plant was repaired in the South. Only in recent months has Baghdad restored power and telecommunications to Basra in the South.

By late 1991, commodity shortages began to appear. Cannibalized equipment was breaking down. Inflation began in earnest. The appearance of counterfeit Iraqi and U.S. currency accelerated the pace of inflation. To counter the effects of inflation on regime supporters, the government initiated bonuses and other financial rewards, but only for the bureaucracies which kept it in power. A year and a half into the sanctions, the Iraqi government resorted to administrative means to overcome economic shortages. In a move to conserve stocks on hand, the government announced in April 1992 a long list of materials which could not be taken out of the country. In July 1992 the government accused 42 merchants of hoarding goods and then executed them. In November 1992, Baghdad announced a ban on the sale of 146 luxury items, ranging from cheese and perfume to videos and personal computers. Merchants had to dispose of their stocks and were ordered to use their capital to import foodstuffs. Administrative detentions and harassment followed.

The Iraqi economy has suffered severely from the impact of sanctions. Economic decisions have been made which may have long-term detrimental effects. For example, the government reportedly has ordered a level of oil production sufficient to maintain domestic consumption of gasoline. After refining the gasoline, the stock is pumped back into the underground oil field. All measures of economic activity have significantly declined, while inflation has soared. In 1993, the unofficial inflation rate was running about 4,000 percent over prices in August 1990. Iraqi society has also paid a heavy price as crime, black marketing, and corruption have eaten away at personal ties, public confidence, and societal allegiances.[10] There have been rumors of coup plots. Apparently Saddam can no longer even trust his clansmen.[11]

To conserve food supplies, reduce financial expenses, and punish the Kurds for their post–Gulf War insurrection, Baghdad pulled all government personnel, including health workers and teachers, out of the three governates of northern Iraq in October 1991. In contrast to the UN embargo, which allowed humanitarian supplies into Iraq, Baghdad applied an airtight embargo north of the military's security lines. The 3.1 million people of the North were severed from the Iraqi economy.[12] The international community now feeds these people. Since Operation Provide Comfort in 1991,[13] the U.S. alone has spent $250 million to feed the Kurds.[14]

The Baghdad government has followed similar policies in the southern part of the country, including cutting off all food, medicine, and fuel,[15] while draining the ecologically sensitive marshes.[16]

Iraq's Noncompliance

Four years of stern economic sanctions on Iraq have only had mixed results in terms of Iraqi compliance with UN resolutions. A more in-depth study would show that Iraqi compliance with the individual requirements of Resolution 687 alone has been grudging and halfhearted. Iraq has refused UN arrangements to organize reparations payments for the thousands of East and South Asian workers whose jobs evaporated with Iraq's invasion. It is not Iraqi policy to accept the offer in Resolutions 706/ 712 to feed the Iraqi people. In fact, Iraq deliberately withheld humanitarian supplies from the populations of the North and South to create the impression that international sanctions were imperilling these people. Most looted Kuwaiti military equipment has been smashed beyond repair just before its return. Iraq did not offer the required guarantees concerning the UN–guaranteed border with Kuwait until October 1994. Its security forces have kidnapped foreigners from the Kuwait side of the border, and Baghdad has sent civilian demonstrators across it.[17]

Iraqi intransigence caused the Security Council to pass an additional post-cease-fire resolution reiterating Baghdad's responsibility to respect the border. Other post-cease-fire resolutions were also passed restating Baghdad's responsibility to cooperate in the elimination of its weapons of mass destruction programs (see below). These additional resolutions were part of a dialogue with Iraq in which the Security Council outlined its requirements of Iraq, and Baghdad took the position that the UN resolutions, such as 687, conferred no obligation on Baghdad. Then Baghdad would offer to comply with some part of a resolution if other obligations were waved. This diplomacy was designed to break the international consensus, or at minimum, make the UN pay twice for the same results. This Iraqi diplomatic strategy strikes at the very authority of the Security Council.

The point to be made is that in accepting the cease-fire resolution, Iraq accepted the border with Kuwait. An obligation was created. Four years later, in October 1994, Iraq made a military feint toward the border as though it had no obligation, i.e., as though the previous UN resolutions had no authority. The Russians became tangled into negotiating Iraqi acceptance of an obligation Baghdad incurred in 1991. Iraq has been maneuvering the world community into paying twice for its adherence to its obligations, and undermining the UN in the process.

About the only area where, after four years, progress has been made in obtaining Iraqi compliance with Resolution 687 and other resolutions is the success of the UN Special Commission (UNSCOM) and International Atomic Energy Association Weapons Inspections Teams in destroying Iraq's weapons of mass destruction. However, starting with the very first declarations and inspections, it became evident that Iraq was not acting in good faith, would use every possible pretext to reinterpret UNSCOM's inspection rights and occasionally use harassment tactics to make inspections as difficult as possible.[18] In September 1991 Iraqi officials detained the sixth nuclear inspection team in a parking lot for four days. In July 1992 Iraqi officials blocked access to a Ministry of Agriculture building which reportedly held part of the archives for one of Iraq's weapons of mass destruction programs.[19] Iraqi recalcitrance led the Security Council to pass Resolutions 707 (August 15, 1991) and 715 (October 11, 1991).[20] Both resolutions reiterated UNSCOM duties, listed Iraq's responsibilities, and admonished Baghdad for obstructing UNSCOM's work. In November 1993 Baghdad officially informed the Security Council that it accepted the requirements of Resolution 715.[21] After four years, the economic sanctions, repeated demonstration of international solidarity communicated via additional resolutions, and the "the threat of resumed hostilities by the coalition"[22] have moved Iraq to a discernible measure of compliance with the requirement that it divest itself of weapons of mass destruction.[23]

An additional factor encouraging Iraqi compliance with the disarmament section of Resolution 687 may be its paragraph 22:

> 22. Decides that . . . upon (Security) Council agreement that Iraq has completed all actions contemplated in paragraphs 8, 9, 10, 11, 12, and 13 (note: destruction and long-term monitoring of weapons of mass destruction) above, the prohibitions against the importation of commodities and products originating in Iraq and the prohibitions against financial transactions related thereto contained in Resolution 661 (1990) shall have no further force or effect.

Unwilling to fulfill the terms of the cease-fire resolution, Iraq may be looking for a shortcut. A successful noncompliance policy, however, requires that the international consensus on the totality of Iraqi responsibilities must be broken.

Factors Affecting the Effectiveness of Sanctions Against Iraq

The ability of economic sanctions to produce policy change varies with a number of factors. There are factors which argue that sanctions would be particularly effective in the case of Iraq. Other factors suggest Iraqi resilience in the face of sanctions. A review of these variables makes direct comparisons with other case studies of economic sanctions difficult. A brief listing quickly illustrates the complexity of predicting the effectiveness of sanctions in any given situation. Political scientists and economic analysts will need to develop further tools before policymakers and the public will know with any certainty what will work.

Factors Suggesting Iraqi Vulnerability to Sanctions

Diplomatic Environment. Iraq's invasion of Kuwait was recognized as an unmistakable threat to world order and the nation-state system. There was universal condemnation and an extraordinarily high degree of unanimity in passing UN resolutions and compliance with UN sanctions requirements.

Economic. Oil exports accounted for 95 percent of Iraq's foreign exchange earnings, suggesting that they were particularly vulnerable. Medical and other advanced services were operated by large numbers of expatriates who would depart in the face of international sanctions.

Psychological. The Iraqi people were aware that Iraq lost the Gulf War. The sanctions, war casualties, and nonreturning POWs left that message with many families. The military and security organizations also were aware of the material and human losses. This should have weakened the leadership's power.

Factors Contributing to Iraqi Resistance to Sanctions

Economic. The Iraqi economy was broad based, though not highly sophisticated, and was not dependent on imports. There was sufficient domestic production to meet the minimum needs of the population. Furthermore, because of its experience in the eight-year Iran/Iraq War, Iraqi procurement practices had long included overbuying spare parts and coping with patchwork repairs.

Iraq stripped Kuwait during its occupation of the emirate. This booty was available to the Iraqi leadership to use as rewards or as production inputs. To conserve resources, Baghdad severed large parts of the population from government services and the economy. Reconstruction was concentrated in the Baghdad area (population approximately 4 million). Basra and the South were neglected. The 3.1 million people in the North have been subjected to a total internal embargo. Some 750,000 people who fled Kirkuk and other cities during the spring 1991 uprisings have not been allowed to return to their homes.[24] By tapping private overseas monies to purchase humanitarian supplies, the Iraqi government found it could hold out even longer against sanctions.

Psychological. The Iraqi population viewed its rulers as totally ruthless. The leadership confirmed this perception in the indiscriminate way in which it put down the spring 1991 uprisings. Experience with the Iraqi police state has been shocking.

On the other hand, the Iraqi government has used nationalism to spur its core supporters to continued sacrifice. The leadership worked diligently to direct resources to core supporters in the Tikriti tribe, the multiple security agencies, and the military leadership.

The Iraqi people have become inured to economic hardship. For eight long years during the Iran/Iraq War, they confronted daunting economic and military sacrifice.

Conclusion

The United Nations Security Council made a conscious effort to weave humanitarian concerns into its design of the economic sanctions levied against Iraq. The Security Council recognized that these humanitarian concerns were part of maintaining the international consensus against Iraq. For its part, the Iraqi leadership over the last four years has demonstrated the qualities which have left it a pariah among nations. The Iraqi leadership's challenge to the moral conscience[25] and political unity of the world community remains. It has shown defiant resilience and a callous disregard for the well-being of its own people. As the international community ponders techniques of modifying the behavior of nation-states, the Iraqi example should be studied in further detail.

Notes

1. The views expressed in this chapter are those of the author and do not necessarily reflect the position of the U.S. Government.

2. The Security Council's response to the Iraqi invasion of Kuwait was virtually without precedent. Cameron Hume argues in his book *The United Nations, Iran,*

and Iraq: How Peacemaking Changed (Bloomington: Indiana University Press, 1994) that only in the late 1980s did the Security Council begin to act as a central authority for peacemaking, first to end the Iran/Iraq War and then as it progressively followed the steps laid down in Chapter VII of the charter after the invasion of Kuwait. See pp. 187–216.

3. UN Security Council membership in August 1990 comprised the five permanent members (China, France, USSR, UK, and USA) and Canada,* Colombia,* Cote de'Ivoire, Cuba, Ethiopia,* Finland,* Malaysia, Romania, Yemen, and Zaire. In January 1991 Austria, Belgium, Ecuador, India, and Zimbabwe replaced the above countries marked with *. *Report of the Security Council to the General Assembly* (Advance Version) A/46/2, November 29, 1991, p. 251. Further rotations occurred in January 1992, 1993, and 1994. Thus, a statistically significant number of nations have judged Iraqi compliance with the relevant Security Council resolutions.

4. One source for the text of the Security Council resolutions can be found in K. Matsuura, J. Muller, and K. Sauvant, ed., *Annual Review of United Nations Affairs* (Dobbs Ferry: Oceana Publications, published annually).

5. For an excellent study of the international law issues raised by each Security Council resolution, see Christopher Joyner, "Sanctions, Compliance, and International Law: Reflections on the United Nations Experience against Iraq," *Virginia Journal of International Law*, Vol. 32:1, Fall 1991, pp. 1–46.

6. *Annual Review of United Nations Affairs*, 1991, p. 210.

7. *Department of State Dispatch*, September 23, 1991, Vol. 2, No. 38, P. 696–97.

8. "Talks Fail at UN on Limited Oil Sales by Iraq," *New York Times*, October 7, 1993, p. A 14.

9. As discussed in Gary Hufbauer, Jeffrey Schott, and Kimberly Ann Elliott, *Economic Sanctions Reconsidered*, 2d ed. (Washington, DC: Institute for International Economics, 1990).

10. Paul Lewis, "In Iraq, Hunger Wins," *New York Times*, July 21, 1993, p. A 7.

11. "Looking for Trouble," *Newsweek*, October 17, 1994, pp. 24–27.

12. John Waterbury, "Strangling the Kurds: Saddam Hussein's Economic War Against Northern Iraq," *Middle East Insight*, July/August 1993, pp. 31–38.

13. See for example, "The Future of Humanitarian Assistance in Iraq," Hearings before the International Task Force of the Select Committee on Hunger, House of Representatives, March 18, 1992, pp. 192.

14. This figure is the current figure compiled by the Department of State and used in Department of State briefing materials for congressional appearances.

15. "Saddam's Other Victim," *New York Times*, June 26, 1993, sec. 1, p. 19. See also "Iraq: Background on Human Rights Conditions, 1984–1992," *Human Rights Watch*, August 1993 (Vol. 5, Issue 5).

16. See Chris Hedges, "A Firefight in the Reeds and An Escape into the Darkness," *New York Times*, November 16, 1993, p. A 10; or "Iraqi Regime Fights to Kill a Way of Life," *New York Times*, November 28, 1993, sec. 4, p. 12.

17. Kuwait Boundary Stirs Iraqi March," *New York Times*, November 21, 1993, p. 12.

18. Tim Trevan, "UNSCOM Faces Entirely New Verification Challenges in Iraq," *Arms Control Today*, April 1993, p. 11.

19. Ibid., p. 11.

20. Paul Lewis, "Iraq Agrees to Allow the UN to Monitor Weapons Industries," *New York Times*, July 20, 1993, sec. A, p. 1.

21. Paul Lewis, "Bowing to UN, Iraq Will Permit Arms Monitors," *New York Times*, November 27, 1993, sec. 1, p. 1. See also Tim Trevan, "Ongoing Monitoring and Verification in Iraq," *Arms Control Today*, Vol. 24, No. 4, May 1994, pp. 11–13.

22. Trevan, "UNSCOM Faces New Verification Challenges," p. 11.

23. Rolf Ekeus, "The Iraqi Experience and the Future of Nuclear Nonproliferation," *The Washington Quarterly*, Autumn, 1992, p. 73.

24. Statement by Deputy Assistant Secretary Melinda Kimble, *U.S. Department of State Dispatch*, March 23, 1992, Vol. 3, No. 12, p. 223.

25. The moral transgressions of the Iraqi leadership have been fully described elsewhere, but Kanan Makiya's book, *Cruelty and Silence: Qar, Tyranny, Uprising, and the Arab World (New York: W.W. Norton, 1993),* is a particularly thoughtful probing of the moral and ethical issues raised by Baghdad's behavior.

11

Economic Sanctions Against Iraq: Do They Contribute to a Just Settlement?

Bashir Al-Samarrai[1]

On August 6, 1990, the United Nations Security Council passed Resolution 661 imposing a trade and financial embargo against Iraq. The objective was to persuade Iraqi forces to withdraw from Kuwait. The embargo was the most comprehensive and effective economic measure the world had ever known. It totally isolated Iraq from the rest of the world, severing links from air, sea, and land routes. It had crippling effects on the Iraqi economy. More than 90 percent of imports and 97 percent of exports were cut off.[2] Iraq's financial assets abroad were seized, and food prices sharply inflated.[3] It is hard to imagine any blockade as thorough as this one.

Testifying before the Senate Armed Services Committee on December 4, 1990, the former Director of the Central Intelligence Agency, William Webster, stated that "at current rates of depletion, we estimate that Iraq will have nearly drained its available foreign exchange reserves by next spring."[4] All the evidence suggested that sanctions were choking off the Iraqi economy and that the embargo was having its intended effect. The Bush administration, however, showed no interest in the embargo and began to pursue the war option. The United States then began to aggressively lobby various members of the United Nations Security Council for their support of the war option. On November 29, 1990, the U.S. had managed to obtain UN Security Council Resolution 678 authorizing UN members to "use all necessary means" to bring about Iraqi withdrawal from Kuwait by January 15, 1991.

This was in marked contrast to the previous history of the UN where the U.S. had frequently opposed the UN playing an active role in peacemaking. When the UN attempted to play such a role in the past, the U.S. in most cases obstructed UN resolutions. The cases of Turkey's invasion of Northern Cyprus in 1974, Israel's invasion of Lebanon in 1982, Israel's 1967 occupation of the West Bank and Golan Heights—in defiance of UN Security Council Resolution 242—not to mention the U.S. invasion of Grenada and Panama, are just a few examples illustrating the hypocritical role of the United States in manipulating the United Nations.[5] The United States managed to obtain the necessary votes to escalate the conflict with Iraq through intimidation and bribery. Congressman Henry Gonzalez cites many examples as manipulations of the United Nations by the United States. Immediately after the November 29 vote in the UN authorizing force in Iraq, the U.S. administration released $140 million from the World Bank to China and agreed to meet with Chinese government officials, despite a congressional ban on such loans in the aftermath of the Tiananmen Square uprising. The former Soviet Union was promised $7 billion in aid from various countries and shipments of food from the U.S. Zaire was promised forgiveness of part of its debt and military assistance. A $7 billion loan to Egypt was forgiven. Yemen was threatened with termination of financial aid by the U.S.[6]

Having obtained the vote for its war option, and presumably to liberate Kuwait from Iraqi occupation, the United States led its allies to war against Iraq on January 17, 1991. But Iraq as a country (and not just Iraqi forces in Kuwait) became the target of the most relentless aerial bombardment in history. More than 100,000 sorties were flown, and 89,000 tons of explosives were dropped over Iraq.[7] Iraq was bombed into the Stone Age, with bridges, water purification plants, power grids, and sewage systems destroyed. In the aftermath of the war, a report issued by the United Nations mission, upon visiting Iraq in March 1991, described war-ravaged Iraq in these words: "Nothing that we had seen or read prepared us for this particular form of devastation that has now befallen the country." The United Nations report concluded with these chilling remarks:

> Allied bombing has wrought near apocalyptic results upon the economical infrastructure of what had been, prior to this war, a highly urbanized society. Now most means of modern life support have been destroyed or rendered tenuous. Iraq has for some years to come been relegated to a preindustrial age, but with all the disabilities of postindustrial dependency on an intensive use of energy and technology.[8]

This U.S.-led war against Iraq achieved its stated objective of forcing Iraq out of Kuwait. But in the process, the war resulted in a further destabilization of the Gulf region by destroying the balance of power, thus making future conflict not only possible but inevitable. Having successfully achieved its stated objective by forcing the withdrawal of Iraqi forces from Kuwait, the United States then shifted its goals to unilateral disarmament of Iraq and the removal of Saddam Hussein from power. The latter goal was not mandated by United Nations resolutions. In pursuit of its new goals, the Bush administration announced that the economic sanctions against Iraq would not be lifted until Saddam Hussein was removed from office. Ironically, before the war the Bush administration showed no interest in allowing the embargo to work, while after the war the United States found new merits in the embargo as an instrument of policy.

Because of this change, Iraq was not only subjected to the devastating treatments of war, but to the continued strangulation of the sanctions. The embargo has been maintained even though Iraqi forces were no longer in Kuwait, its military capabilities were decimated, and the disarmament of its weapons of mass destruction was nearly completed.[9] The economic sanctions continued to strangle the people of Iraq, and the country has been pushed to the verge of collapse, placing the life of its civilian population in great peril. Those whose lives have been spared from allied bombing have been faced with imminent danger from starvation and the lack of safe water, sanitation, and basic medical care. In this human tragedy, the innocent people of Iraq have been held hostage by both the U.S. policy of collective punishment and by Saddam Hussein's regime. The United States has insisted that Saddam Hussein must be removed from office before the sanctions can be lifted, while Saddam Hussein has vowed to stay in power at any cost. Several questions are raised by this dilemma. Where does the United Nations stand regarding the confrontation between the United States and Iraq? Are U.S. objectives compatible with those of the United Nations, in whose name the United States waged war?

However desirable that goal may be, no legal basis has been established linking the lifting of economic sanctions to the removal of Saddam Hussein. Moreover, in this goal the United States has pursued an agenda of its own which has nothing to do with the United Nations or international law. To the contrary, Article 54 of the Geneva Convention of 1977 states that "starvation of civilians as a method of warfare is prohibited." During the early months of the embargo, the president of the International Committee of the Red Cross warned that a total blockade of Iraq would be contrary to international law.[10]

Let us examine the logic of the U.S. policy. It seems that U.S. strategy has been based on the *faulty* assumption that if one maintains the economic sanctions long enough to cause enough hardship and suffering, people will revolt against their ruler. In other words, the aim is to starve the civilian population into revolution. Besides imposing sanctions, the United Nations imposed a series of punitive resolutions, at the bequest of the United States, that punish Iraq and its future generations for the behavior of a leader they did not elect. This policy has backfired by failing to draw a distinction between Saddam Hussein and the Iraqi people. The United Nations has played into Saddam Hussein's hands by making Iraq and the people of Iraq the targets of a hostile policy. This is despite repeated contentions by President Bush that the U.S. quarrel is not with the Iraqi people, but with Saddam only. But many Iraqis perceived that it was they, and not Saddam, who were the victims of the most severe food and medicine shortages.

Let us review a few examples of how sanctions have hurt the Iraqis and not Saddam Hussein and his regime. According to Dr. Eric Hoskins, a medical coordinator for the Gulf Peace Team and a member of the Harvard Study Team that visited Iraq five times, "it is likely that sanctions have resulted in more suffering and death of the civilian population of Iraq than the war itself." Dr. Hoskins stated that "we must decide whom the coalition forces fought this war against. We must also decide whether it is worth sacrificing the lives of thousands more innocent victims to achieve the removal of Saddam Hussein."[11] Another member of the Gulf Peace Team, Ann Montgomery, provided insight on the condition of children. Ms. Montgomery reported that forty babies were dying each day, not from any extraordinary illnesses, but because of a lack of milk and simple medications. She conveyed the angry plea of a doctor by stating, "please tell them not to make war on children."[12]

After visiting Iraq in April 1991, the Harvard Medical Team reported epidemics of cholera, typhoid, and gastroenteritis.[13] A study published by the *New England Journal of Medicine* entitled, "Effects of the Gulf War on Infant and Child Mortality in Iraq," concluded by stating that "these results provide strong evidence that the Gulf War and the trade sanctions caused a three-fold increase in mortality among Iraqi children under five years of age. We estimate that an excess of more than 46,000 children died between January and August 1991."[14]

The United Nations mission that visited Iraq in March 1991 recommended that the sanctions affecting food and medicine should be immediately lifted. The report of the UN mission stated,

> Sanctions in respect of food supplies should be immediately removed, as should those relating to the import of agricultural equipment and supplies. The urgent supply of basic commodities to safeguard the vulnerable groups is strongly recommended and the provision of major quantities of the following staples for the general population, such as, milk, wheat, flour, rice, sugar, vegetables, oil, and tea.[15]

It was partly in response to this report that the UN Security Council approved Resolutions 706 and 712 in August and September 1991 permitting limited oil sales from Iraq for the purchase of humanitarian supplies and for the expenses of UN missions in Iraq. Saddam Hussein has refused to accept the conditions attached to these resolutions.

Sanctions induced hyperinflation, and the prices of basic staple goods skyrocketed, placing most Iraqis outside the food market. For example, the price of bread increased by 2,857 percent, infant formula rose by 2,222 percent, flour went up by 4,531 percent, and eggs increased by 350 percent.[16] In addition to these massive increases in food prices, the purchasing power of most Iraqis was drastically reduced through inflation and loss of jobs. The Iraqi dinar depreciated. For instance, in 1980 one Iraqi dinar was equivalent to three U.S. dollars while in 1990, just before the latest war, four Iraqi dinars were equal to one U.S. dollar. By 1993 the Iraqi dinar had drastically depreciated, with thirty-five Iraqi dinars equaling one U.S. dollar. To illustrate the decline in the purchasing power of Iraqis, consider as an example the annual income of the average Iraqi physician (physicians being the highest paid professionals). As measured by U.S. dollars, in an analysis by Dr. Faik Al-Bazaz, M.D., University of Illinois Medical Center, the annual salary of an Iraqi physician has been radically reduced from $14,400 in 1980 to $1,400 in 1990 and to $270 in 1992.[17]

Economically and socially, the crippling impact of the continued sanctions produced, among other things, a situation where survival has been only for the fittest. Doug Broderic, the field director of Catholic Relief Services in Baghdad, commented, "What you get with prices like this is a Darwinian effect. The rich and the strong survive, the poor and the weak starve. In any society, the . . . weakest people are the children, so mostly it is the children that die."[18]

As a further illustration of the devastating impact of sanctions, *New York Times* correspondent Michael Kelly interviewed an Iraqi woman who said that while whole families are starving in Iraq, Saddam and his loyalists have been sheltered from the effects of the embargo: "Of course the people in the government do not live the way we live. They can get whatever they want. They have millions and they want to make millions more."[19]

Instead of achieving its intended objective of weakening Saddam Hussein's grip on power, the policy of economic strangulation has backfired. While most Iraqis oppose the regime of Saddam Hussein, they harbor a strong resentment toward the U.S. for destroying their country and starving its people. The sentiment voiced by the same Iraqi woman reflects the feelings of most people in Iraq. She expressed these sentiments by stating,

Saddam Hussein and George Bush have tried to defeat us, each in his own way. George Bush could have sent his army to Baghdad and killed this bastard Saddam, and he did not. It is as if both sides, the Americans and criminals of Saddam, are using us to work out their experiments, and they are interesting experiments. It is fascinating to see what it takes to bring about the total degradation of a people.[20]

There have been endless examples of the crippling effects of the continued economic sanctions on the people of Iraq. In contrast, there has been no evidence that the sanctions have weakened Saddam Hussein's grip on power. In effect, Saddam Hussein has used the embargo to keep the Iraqi people preoccupied with a constant search for something to eat instead of planning to overthrow him.

Conclusion

Economic sanctions have targeted the wrong party in Iraq, i.e., the poor, the helpless, and the children. Most Iraqis question the logic of this policy by wondering how it is possible for a helpless nation to overthrow one of the world's most ruthless dictators, when the U.S. and its allies could not, or would not, remove Saddam from power during the war. How much suffering must innocent Iraqis endure before the UN ends its strangulation policy or before Saddam is removed? Is the world willing to stand by and watch a whole nation being starved and strangled? To continue the present policy is analogous to blowing up an aircraft with all passengers aboard to kill the hijacker. In this standoff, eighteen million Iraqis are the passengers.

Notes

1. The views expressed in this chapter are those of the author and do not necessarily reflect the position of any organization or agency with which he is affiliated.

2. See William H. Webster's testimony before the Senate Armed Services Committee, "Sanctions in the Persian Gulf, Iraq: The Domestic Impact of Sanctions, December 4, 1990," in *Congressional Record*, January 10, 1991, pp. S123–24.

3. Ibid.

4. Ibid.

5. The United Nations record shows that since its inception, Israel has been condemned 66 times by the Security Council, and in addition, the United States used its veto power 29 times on behalf of Israel in obstruction of the United Nations role. See "Quatsch Watch" column, *Washington Report on Middle East Affairs*, Vol. XI, No. 8, March 1993, p. 60.

6. Michael Ratner, "International Law and War Crimes," in *War Crimes*, ed. Ramsey Clark and others (Washington D.C.: Maisonneuve Press, 1992), p. 42.

7. Rep. Les Aspin (D-Wis.) and Rep. William Dickinson (R-AL), *Defense for a New Era, Lessons of the Persian Gulf War* (Washington, D.C.: U.S. Government Printing Office, 1992), p. 7.

8. UN Security Council, *Report to the Secretary General on Humanitarian Needs in Kuwait and Iraq in the Immediate Post-Crisis Environment by a Mission to the Area Led by Mr. Martti Ahtisaari, Under Secretary General for Administration and Management,* 20 March 1991, p.5.

9. Rolf Ekeus, head of the United Nations Commission charged with eliminating Iraq's weapons of mass destruction, stated during a press conference on July 27, 1992, "We have, I think, with great success covered most of Iraq's weapons of mass destruction capability and missile area. We have, I think, successfully identified existing weapons and destroyed them. There may be a couple or a few left, but fundamentally all of them—most of them have been found and destroyed" "Excerpts from Remarks by Envoy and Bush," *The New York Times,* July 27, 1992, p. 6.

10. D.L. Bethlehem, ed., *The Kuwait Crisis: Sanctions and their Economic Consequences* (Cambridge: Grotius Publications Limited, 1991), p. 798.

11. Eric Hoskins, "The Truth Behind Economic Sanctions: A Report on the Embargo of Food and Medicines to Iraq," in *War Crimes,* ed. Ramsey Clark and others (Washington D.C.: Maisonneuve Press, 1992), p. 167.

12. Ann Montgomery, "The Impact of Sanctions on Baghdad's Children's Hospital," in *War Crimes,* ed. Ramsey Clark and others (Washington, D.C.: Maisonneuve Press, 1992), p. 100.

13. The Harvard Study Team, "Special Report: The Effect of the Gulf Crisis on the Children of Iraq," *New England Journal of Medicine,* Vol. 325, No. 13, September 26, 1991, pp. 977-80.

14. Alberto Ascherio, et al., "Effect of the Gulf War on Infant and Child Mortality in Iraq," *New England Journal of Medicine,* Vol. 327, No. 13, p. 931.

15. UN Security Council, *Report on Humanitarian Needs in Kuwait and Iraq,* by M. Ahtisaari, p. 5.

16. Michael Kelly, "Mob Town," in *The New York Times Magazine,* February 14, 1993, Section 6, p. 18.

17. Al-Bazaz, Faik, "The Effects of the Gulf War on Iraqi Physicians," (unpublished).

18. Ibid.

19. Ibid., p. 40.

20. Ibid., p. 50.

12

The Use of Sanctions
in Former Yugoslavia:
Misunderstanding Political Realities

Susan L. Woodward

The disintegration of Yugoslavia and the subsequent wars to define new borders and loyalties of national states posed a major challenge to the available instruments of international conflict regulation. Unwilling to use military force, Western powers employed a wide range of diplomatic tactics and economic sanctions as they sought to prevent war from breaking out and then to stop the military aggression, atrocities, and widespread violation of international norms. While it is still premature to assess the effectiveness of those sanctions, it is possible to analyze the appropriateness and potential effectiveness of such instruments in this case.

The literature on economic sanctions identifies, on the basis of statistical analysis, certain economic and political conditions of target countries and of the sanctions' characteristics, that increase the probability of success.[1] But there has been little attention paid to whether the kind of conflict, its causes, and the character of the political regime (apart from its stability) make a difference in the effectiveness of economic sanctions. The case of former Yugoslavia forces such consideration because it is a different kind of conflict than those usually addressed by this literature and the experience with economic sanctions. Moreover, as a kind of conflict that is likely both to appear again and to characterize the post–Cold War global order, assessment of the Yugoslav case has meaning far broader than its current intractability suggests.

This chapter argues first that economic sanctions, as applied, have only exacerbated the causes of war in the Yugoslav context and have dimin-

141

ished the resources and avenues to respond in ways expected by sanctioning powers. Sanctions have undermined the two conditions—the creation of democratic regimes within the territory, and regional economic integration—necessary to resolve the conflicts themselves. Second, the sanctions have had multiple and conflicting purposes, following from the particular international context of the conflict and the "law of the instrument," that have little to do with the nature of the conflict. The dilemma created by the international response between upholding international norms and solving the Yugoslav conflict has been resolved in favor of the former. Insofar as sanctions were addressed to the conflict itself, moreover, there seems to have been little attention paid to the political assumptions underlying economic sanctions. Once made explicit, it becomes clear that the political conditions assumed by the application of economic sanctions are missing in conflicts of the Yugoslav type. Economic conditions might give the economic sanctions force, but if the political assumptions about the expected behavioral response to such economic conditions are wrong or missing, then those sanctions may do great damage and potentially cause greater problems without bringing about the intended result. The character of the conflict even interferes with evaluating their effects.

The Four Phases of Sanctioning: April 1991 to April 1993

The use of economic sanctions to influence the Yugoslav conflicts have been applied in four phases. The first began in May 1991 when the United States attempted to bring Yugoslav politicians to the bargaining table and to resolve their conflicts peacefully by withdrawing economic and financial aid, and promising its reinstallation. At the same time, the European Community (EC) was attempting the same objective with the carrot before the stick by offering additional aid if Yugoslavia remained whole. When this failed to prevent Slovene and Croatian declarations of independence and the Yugoslav army's moves to secure the border between June 25 and June 28, the EC then adopted the U.S. tactics by withdrawing all economic and financial assistance to the country in July.

Second, after the wars began in Slovenia and then Croatia in July 1991, sanctions were imposed by the Economic Community on Yugoslavia as a part of its diplomatic efforts at mediation. This was done in an expression of disapproval for violation of a Helsinki principle, namely the use of military force to decide border issues. It was an attempt again, as stick and carrot, to bring these politicians to the table. The U.S. joined in imposing trade sanctions in December that year. Earlier, in September, the major powers (mainly the U.S., Britain, and France) sought UN Security Council action to impose a comprehensive arms embargo on all parties in Yugoslavia (Resolution 713, passed September 25) to uphold international norms against the aggressive use of force and to attempt to end the fighting in Croatia by hastening the moment when all sides would exhaust domestic military supplies.

The third phase occurred when trade sanctions were lifted on all parts of Yugoslavia except Serbia and Montenegro—which, as of April 27, 1992, were known as the Federal Republic of Yugoslavia (FRY). To counteract growing demands that the United Nations send peacekeepers to Bosnia-Herzegovina, where (as the secretary general argued) there was no cease-fire, a Security Council resolution (757) was passed on May 30, 1992, after two weeks' warning (Resolution 752). This resolution imposed on the FRY a universal, binding economic blockade under Articles 41 and 42 of the UN Charter.[2] It banned all economic trade and broke all scientific, cultural, and sports ties and diplomatic representations to Belgrade in an attempt to stop the war in Bosnia-Herzegovina. The argument was that while no fighting force in that republic was fully innocent, those contributing most to the war and its emerging atrocities and thus most responsible were Serbia and Serbs. They had failed to comply with Resolution 752 to cease fighting immediately, to cease all foreign assistance, to end ethnic cleansing, to stop interfering with the delivery of humanitarian relief to Bosnia-Herzegovina (Sarajevo in particular), and to stop interfering with the actions of the United Nations Protection Force (UNPROFOR) and other UN agencies. At the same time, the new Federal Republic of Yugoslavia (FRY) was denied the right to succeed the former Yugoslavia and was suspended from membership in the Conference on Security and Cooperation in Europe (CSCE). On June 18, 1992, humanitarian goods such as food and medicine were exempted (Resolution 760).[3]

In the fourth phase, by November 16, 1992, in light of widespread violations of the sanctions on both overland, river, and sea routes, certain actions were taken to make the sanctions more effective. Numerous monitoring activities, such as North Atlantic Treaty Organization (NATO) and Western European Union (WEU) ships in the Adriatic and U.S. customs inspectors monitoring on the Macedonian border with Serbia, progressively tightened the enforcement of sanctions. Pressures were placed on neighboring countries, particularly Romania, over Danube traffic, and there was a prohibition of transshipment through Serbia. The embargo itself was tightened beginning in April 1993 with a maritime exclusion zone; a freeze of all financial assets, buildings, and land overseas; and impounding of all means of transport outside the country. Again, the purpose was to stop the war in Bosnia-Herzegovina and to persuade its warring parties to sign a political settlement being negotiated by the United Nations–European Community envoys, Cyrus Vance and David Owen. The hope of Vance and Owen was that, by pressuring the leadership of Serbia to stop aiding and influencing the Bosnian Serbs, the latter would sign the Vance-Owen peace plan already accepted by Bosnian Croats and Muslim-dominated government forces. Only in the fourth phase could one identify a classic embargo as an instrument of diplomacy, with advance warning and relatively clear statements about the purpose of the sanctions and the behavioral changes expected, coordinated with other activities as a general policy. Until then, although the purposes could be surmised, there were many in the target countries who insisted that the only certainty of the sanctions was their "unknown objective."[4]

The Purposes of the Economic Sanctions

The purposes of the economic sanctions fall into three separate categories. The first was to avoid Western military engagement since Yugoslavia was considered to be of no strategic interest to the major powers. The outcome was, as the Bush administration said repeatedly, not in the U.S. national interest. Although the Europeans shared the belief that the Yugoslavian conflict was insignificant, they chose to use mediation of the conflict to demonstrate the possibility of European Union (EU) common foreign policy. Because the EU had no military force (once the U.S. objected to "out-of-area" NATO involvement) it had, by default, to rely on economic instruments in its attempts to stop the fighting and to persuade all parties to resolve their disputes through negotiation.

The judgment made early on that induced the application of sanctions was that the wars were largely caused by Serbian aggression. This consideration was made even before Slovenia and Croatia formally declared independence and the mediating efforts of the European Union erased the federal government and led *de facto* to the end of Yugoslavia and any internal solution, but it was then reinforced by the Slovene and Croatian portrayal of the Yugoslav army (assumed to be an instrument of Serbia), and Serbian policy to create a Greater Serbia (on the analogy of 1912),[5] and in the abundant reports that paramilitary gangs from Serbia were primarily responsible for the terror and atrocities against civilians in the early stages of the wars in eastern Croatia and eastern Bosnia-Herzegovina.[6] This second purpose of the sanctions, therefore, was to stop that aggression by persuading the Serbian leadership that the costs of isolation were too high. The UN sought to make it economically ever more difficult to continue outside assistance to Serbs in Croatia and Bosnia-Herzegovina, and to remove President Slobodan Milosevic, whom many accused of masterminding the wars, from power, either by his own resignation or by popular pressure.

As the wars continued, so did the flow of refugees into Europe. The publics of Europe, the United States, and some Islamic countries reacted with horror at the pictures of atrocities, news of widespread rape, detention camps, and practices of "ethnic cleansing." The blatant violations of the Geneva Conventions mounted. As these violations continued, the major powers sought to protect their domestic and international authority by appeasing these publics, who were morally outraged on behalf of the primary victims, the Muslims of Bosnia-Herzegovina. These major powers aimed also, however, to reassert international norms at a moment of global change, shore up unity and cooperation in the Atlantic Alliance and the Security Council, and deter others from such atrocities in the future.

Considering these purposes, the sanctions have failed thus far. They did not bring parties to the bargaining table in the spring of 1991. They did not influence the attempts to negotiate a cease-fire by Lord Carrington for the EU. They played no part in the cease-fire that froze the status quo of combatants in Croatia negotiated by Cyrus Vance in December 1991. As of late 1994, they had not been able to stop the fighting in Bosnia-Herzegovina.

In part, this can be attributed to the character of the sanctions. For example, their timing was set far more by the pace of domestic political pressure in Western capitals than by events in the former Yugoslavia. Timing related instead to coverage by the mass media, campaigns for national elections, the vote on European integration, turnover in administrations, and ruling party strength or weakness. The use of economic sanctions also sent a clear signal from the start that military means would not be used, encouraging those on the ground who would resort to military means that they would meet with no interference.

The sanctions themselves were not accompanied by a clear message or modest objective. Disagreements among Western powers led to long delays in implementing sanctions in the first year of war, thus diluting their strength, and giving parties on the ground room to use foreign patrons and exploit their competition. The "law of the instrument" was particularly detrimental because it set up a major conflict among the sanctions' purposes: protecting the instrument and international norms became more important over time than the actual outcome in Yugoslavia. No reassessment of the causes of the conflict as it evolved was possible once the sanctions were introduced. For example, recognition that it might be counterproductive to punish only one side of a multisided conflict came too late as the failure of later efforts by some to impose sanctions on Croatia as well demonstrates. Easing sanctions at certain moments might have brought the wars to a halt faster. In fact, the carrot at the end of the stick was not visible: no conditions were specified that would lead to a lifting of the sanctions, and no preparation was made for extricating Serbia from its isolation if Milosevic was removed. These difficulties were also a consequence of the kind of conflict to which the sanctions have been applied.

What Kind of Conflict?

The Yugoslav conflict reflects three separate processes. First, it represents a post–Cold War international transition that left security regimes, regional memberships, and the enforcement mechanisms for international norms undefined. This was exacerbated by the very slow creation of new institutions, responding to balance-of-power politics and crisis events rather than international leadership with a strategy for change. Second, Yugoslavia had been undergoing a decade-long process of economic, social, and political crisis to repay foreign debt and create a market economy. This process led to increasing social disintegration, constitutional stalemate, declining governmental capacity, and in the end, the collapse of domestic authority and the disintegration of the state. Finally, the conflict was a result of the transition away from the economic and political institutions of a communist-ruled regime to markets and democracy. In the Yugoslav case, one of many countries sharing these conditions, the consequence was a set of competing nationalist projects to create new states, according to the right of national self-determination, where borders, loyalties, and the claims to territory were all contested, and the territories of greatest contest were nationally and ethnically mixed. Part of the responsibility for these wars lies with the international community, especially the European Union and the U.S., which helped to dismember Yugoslavia by recognizing Slovene and Croatian independence before other areas were politically prepared, and without providing any basis for resolving the resulting conflicts over borders and populations. This oversight was based on the erroneous assumption that the former republics and provinces of the country were equivalent to nation-states. All parties have used military means in their quest for territorial control and have used expulsion, forced assimilation, intolerance, and propaganda to create nationally exclusive states out of a previously multinational environment. National loyalties and ethnic rights to residence and land were critical objects of the war, so that civilians were perceived as combatants even if they did not themselves see it that way. Moreover, these contests cannot be fully separated from the redefinition of regional alliances taking place.

The Outcome of Sanctions in Yugoslavia

If one looks at the causes of war in the former Yugoslavia, the sanctions made the situation worse, increasing the likelihood that war would continue and spread rather than cease. The conflict originated in an economic crisis from 1979 to 1989 that caused budgetary conflicts between the federal government and the republics, and created unemployment, hyperinflation, and a drastic fall in living standards. The further destruction of the economies of Serbia, Montenegro, Vojvodina, Kosovo, and neighboring states, as a result of economic sanctions, only made control of land and its physical assets more important and distributive conflicts, scapegoating, and social disorder worse. Under these conditions of economic and political collapse, it is extremely difficult to evaluate the separate effectiveness of the sanctions. It is, for example, impossible to determine what percentage of the decline in production has been due to the sanctions, to the collapse of the state and its economy, to the end of the communist system, or to the collapse of trade with the Eastern bloc and the Middle East.

The immediate cause of war was the independence of Slovenia and Croatia, and then of Bosnia-Herzegovina, without consideration for the rights of Serbs in Croatia and a constitutional solution for an independent Bosnia-Herzegovina which was composed of three nations—Muslims, Serbs, and Croats. Many of these Serbs did not want to leave Yugoslavia or to give up the equal right to national self-determination which they had in Yugoslavia. The imposition of sanctions against the one party that felt aggrieved by the breakup of its state was unlikely to be understood as just. All parties used military force to achieve their goals, including Slovenia, Croatia, and the Yugoslav army. Moreover, Croats in Bosnia-Herzegovina were also being aided from outside in their goal of creating a national state within the republic and linking up with Croatia. Thus, the Croatian government had substantial numbers of armed forces and paramilitary units in Bosnia,[7] whereas a majority of the Yugoslav army personnel, who remained loyal to a continuation of Yugoslavia, were from Bosnia. The unwillingness to impose sanctions against Croatia, along with Serbia and Montenegro, was incomprehensible to even the most pacific, nonnationalist Serbs.[8] Because the immediate cause was the breakup of a state, moreover, it was not easy to isolate the impact of sanctions on Serbia and Montenegro from that of other areas of the former country where economic links still existed. By normal measures of sanctions' effectiveness, the 50 percent trade dependence of Serbian production should have made it suitably vulnerable, but much of this trade came from other parts of the Yugoslav territory and from Eastern countries also reeling from the postcommunist transition and desperate for export revenues of their own.

The third cause of the wars was the quest for economic integration with Europe and the competition for membership in the European Union that accompanied the end of the Cold War. The distinction made in "readiness" for membership during 1989–90 between Central and Eastern Europe created a serious dilemma for Yugoslavia. Where Yugoslavia had open borders and association agreements with the EU long before other countries in the Eastern bloc, it now looked to be confined to the second tier. As former Habsburg territories with Roman Catholic populations, Slovenia and Croatia gambled that they could enter in the first tier if they separated from Yugoslavia. The other republics worried that their only chance to avoid being confined by the EU to the Balkans and to the fate of Turkey was to remain a single state. The sanctions on Serbia and Montenegro seemed to many to be reinforcing this new border around Europe, confirming their exclusion with economic isolation. The sanctions were seen as reflecting the long-standing interest of Germany and Austria to have clients in the Balkans and a weak Serbia, rather than imposing appropriate punishment for unacceptable behavior.

Economic sanctions depend on particular assumptions about the relationship between economic conditions and political behavior. The idea that increasing economic hardship would motivate Serbian citizens to protest Milosevic's policies in Bosnia and, if necessary, overthrow his rule altogether presumed a functioning democracy where people could organize to express their views and vote freely. It also assumed a free flow of information that meant Serbian citizens were acting on the same knowledge as the outside world, and a clear and uniform message about the reasons for the sanctions. Not only was Serbia in the initial process of creating a new state, but economic hardship had nurtured nationalist sentiments and the self-protective feelings that led to support for Milosevic in the first place. Further economic hardship would require individuals to spend more time on daily survival and less on political action. It reinforced the informal economic networks of family, tribe, or crime at the popular level and increased the power of the government and of Milosevic personally. The state gained greater authority in rationing goods and determining which enterprises would gain subsidies; which workers would therefore become unemployed; and whether farmers, veterans, pensioners, and the army would have income. Finally, the sanctions encouraged the exodus of those most able to protest and organize independent political action: the professional middle class.

The power to interpret the meaning of the sanctions rested with those who controlled the media, namely President Milosevic and his government. The nature of the sanctions regime made this increasingly easy because it forbad external assistance to create an independent media, cut the resources of opposition forces, made newspapers prohibitively expensive, effectively stopped the flow of information from outside, and increased problems of law and order that justified the police that girded his regime. Milosevic could rule more easily in conditions of isolation, and popular anger could just as easily be directed at the opposition if its anti-Milosevic arguments sounded like those of foreign powers. For many apolitical Serbs who might nonetheless oppose Milosevic, the sanctions violated their sense of fair play because other Yugoslavs were also guilty of the charges levied. Many other Serbs considered the sanctions just punishment, interpreted in religious terms of shame or guilt, but this required accepting the pain of absolution, not acting politically to get them removed.

Sanctions assumed democratic pressure from below to change the regime or its policies in a state that was still in formation, and where political avenues for debating the future of the Yugoslav states within the former country had been preempted by international mediation. Dire economic conditions that turned unpaid or unemployed workers into paid army recruits were now explicable by Western prejudice, reinforcing the governing myth Milosevic had created as martyr and protector of the Serbian nation, and the national myth of survival against external foes (whatever the odds). Sanctions also reinforced the conviction that Serbia was not internationally secure without its own state and military resources, and strengthened Milosevic's political base among criminals, police, and right-wing extremists. While middle-class liberals chose to leave the country, opposition forces who remained lost all means of influence, and the economic elite chose to wait out the sanctions, to demand subsidies, or to make huge profits on circumventing the embargo. The political elite continued to believe that the primary issue, as they saw it in Yugoslavia during 1986–90, was a matter of persuasion. Once the truth of their case was known, its injustice would be clear and the sanctions would be lifted. As for the realists, it was clear that Europe could not keep Serbia a pariah state forever and that, as the Germans began to insist in early 1992, some accommodation with the largest power in the Balkans (as they perceived it) would have to be made.

Finally, economic sanctions worked against finding alternatives to war and nationalism in the difficult process of replacing the socialist system with globally open market economies and democratic regimes. Their effects required the Serbian state to reimpose state monopolies, rationing, pricing, and centralized distribution of food, fuel, medicines, and transport, all of which had been abandoned. Private entrepreneurship abounded only in illegal activities, creating a criminal class that would not be easy to control for a long time. The effects of sanctions gave new life to the police and armed forces that were being cut, and it revived a search for Eastern alliances through religious, historical, or anti-Western sympathies—with Russian nationalists, with China, with Greek merchants and politicians, and with former communist networks in Romania and Bulgaria. At the same time, the goal of liberalization and open borders ran against the requirement to enforce the sanctions and the arms embargo, creating an additional dilemma between the assertion of international norms and a solution to the conflict.

Conclusion

From the outset there were two basic solutions to the wars in the former Yugoslavia: First, democratic regimes needed to be created throughout the territory. Second, regional economic integration (along the model of the Schumann plan for France and Germany and the subsequent European Community) would be necessary to compensate the devolution of power to smaller nation-states. Only with the resulting freedom of movement for people, ideas, and goods; restored sense of security for minorities; economic basis for overcoming the animosities of economic decline; and political stability would the new borders be acceptable and the new national dominant states be viable and stable. These solutions were prevented by the imposition and maintenance of economic sanctions. The embargo created a danger of greater impoverishment in the region beyond Yugoslavia that will require compensating funds to neighboring countries and could justify the continued division of Europe. Whether these costs were worth their remote and ambiguous influence over the war in Bosnia-Herzegovina will remain an open question. The major powers used economic sanctions because they were unwilling to use military force or to complete the diplomatic job they began with the recognition of independence for some parts of former Yugoslavia. The outcome of the sanctions was the opposite of that intended—it made Serbian president Milosevic the linchpin to a diplomatic resolution of the conflicts in both Croatia and Bosnia-Herzegovina, and it displaced attention away from those who chose to fight and would have to make peace. The use of an economic sanctions regime to resolve the conflicts created by the end of the Cold War and by competitive nationalism—and its use as a substitute for international mechanisms to peacefully negotiate the breakup of countries—raises new questions about the instrument that must be answered.

Notes

1. For example, the share of the target country's trade with sanctioning countries, the political stability of the regime, or foreign relations (friendly or hostile) between the target and the sanctioning countries. Peter A. G. van Bergeijk, "Success and Failure of Economic Sanctions," *KyKlos*, Vol. 42, sec. 3, 1989, pp. 385–404.

2. These articles permit sanctions against a state which "threatens peace, violates peace, or commits aggression," the legal basis for which resides in Article 39, "the right to intervene in the case of international peace and security."

3. A committee of the United Nations set up to oversee the arms embargo was delegated the task of monitoring, supplying information, and receiving and approving written requests for exemptions to the trade embargo. Preliminary evaluations have been critical, suggesting its ineffectiveness is largely due to its remoteness from Yugoslavia.

4. Dušan Zupan, "America, Serbia, and New World Order," *TANJUG*, April 19, 1992, reprinted in Foreign Broadcast Information Service, EEU-92-076, April 20, 1992, p. 38.

5. The Balkan Wars of 1910-12 were the culmination of struggles to define successor states to the Ottoman empire in the region. The independence struggle of Serbia, begun in 1803, had by midcentury become identified with a policy to unify Serbs in one country—a Greater Serbia—analogous to the simultaneous struggle for German and Italian unification. But major powers (particularly Austria in 1878 and 1908 and then the Versailles powers in 1918) attempted to prevent this Serbian project. Many in the West thus argued during 1991 that in their view, the wars in Croatia and in Bosnia-Herzegovina represented a resumption of Serbian ambitions which had been interrupted by the creation of Yugoslavia in 1918. The question for many was whether this "third Balkan war"—the subtitle to Misha Glenny's book on 1991–92, *The Fall of Yugoslavia: The Third Balkan War* (London: Penguin, 1992)—would lead, as in 1914, to an uncontrollable conflagration.

6. Fact-finding missions by the CSCE, the UN, the EC, and private organizations such as Amnesty International all came to this conclusion, although the success of Western public relations firms paid by the Slovenes, and especially by the Croatian and Bosnian governments, must be considered in this picture. Serb commentators speculated widely about the reasons why the report of Secretary General Boutros-Ghali to the Security Council, which was more balanced in its distribution of blame, was delayed until after the vote on sanctions on May 30, 1993. For a more nuanced understanding of multiple responsibility, see Misha Glenny's vivid reportage, *The Fall of Yugoslavia: The Third Balkan War.*

7. The numbers vary, but the most common number of official troops was 30,000.

8. The imposition of sanctions at the time of elections in Serbia (twice) was also considered by Milosevic sympathizers to be illegitimate interference, and by his opposition, counterproductive interference.

13

The Use of Sanctions in Former Yugoslavia: Can They Assist in Conflict Resolution?

Sonja Licht

After observing the impact of the sanctions against Serbia and Montenegro, one can formulate many questions concerning sanctions that should be answered before trying to evaluate their impact. Why did the international community allow violations of the Helsinki Accords to change existing international borders? Why did it need such a long time to impose an arms embargo on the former Yugoslavia, since it was well known that all the sides in the conflict were importing weapons even before the actual fighting started? Why was there no deliberate action after the Milosevic regime annulled the autonomy of Kosovo, which was accompanied by a very strong repression of the human rights of Albanians? Why were no sanctions imposed against Croatia, but only against Serbia and Montenegro, when it was well known that the regular army of Croatia has been consistently present in Bosnia-Herzegovina and involved in the ethnic cleansing of both Serbs and Muslims in western Herzegovina and central Bosnia?

Another set of questions is related to whether the sanctions were really working in a more narrow sense of the word. Were they weakening the regime in the new Yugoslavia, or just destroying the economic potential of the country? Were they targeted against the regime or the whole society? Were the sanctions imposed to punish Milosevic's nationalist, aggressive politics, or were they seen as a mechanism to punish the people of Serbia and Montenegro? Was there a real chance that the sanctions might help the people of the new Yugoslavia put an end to Milosevic's rule and finally start the process of transition toward democracy?

The Concept of Sanctions

It is necessary first to define the sanctions imposed by the United Nations. This is essential because even in well-informed international political circles, there are sometimes different explanations of the objectives and the nature of these measures. The United Nations, when imposing sanctions, made several assumptions, which may or may not have been completely accurate. First, it presumed that the Milosevic regime in Serbia was helping Serbs in Croatia and Bosnia-Herzegovina fight for their political and military goals. Second, it presumed that if there was no help from Belgrade, the Serbs in Croatia and Bosnia-Herzegovina would soon be defeated and the war would be over. Third, it presumed that the pressure on Serbia would be transferred to Serbs in Croatia and Bosnia-Herzegovina. Finally, as a side effect of the sanctions, the UN presumed that the dissatisfied people of Serbia would defeat the Milosevic regime (and thereby the primary causes of the war), and the possible danger of the conflict spreading would disappear.

The first presumption was partially correct, but one needs to consider two additional facts as well. First, Bosnia-Herzegovina was full of military storage facilities and military industries due to Tito's doctrine that guerilla war was to be fought in this region. Second, Croatia was also helping the Bosnian Croats, and some regular military units from Croatia had been fighting alongside them from the beginning of the war in Bosnia-Herzegovina.

The second presumption was not correct because the Serbian nation was separated into two different bodies. Serbs in Serbia and Montenegro achieved the establishment of their nation-states in the nineteenth century, but Serbs in Croatia and Bosnia-Herzegovina believed that their moment to do the same was upon them. They would continue their struggle even if there was no help from Serbia at all. This was a simple fact that could be verified through discussion with Bosnian Serbs. When Yugoslavia disbanded it became almost certain that Bosnia-Herzegovina would follow the same example. Bosnia-Herzegovina, which consists of ethnic Serbs, Croats and Muslims, had almost no chance of survival if the principle of self-determination was put above the principle of multiethnicity and democratic citizenship. Unfortunately, this happened in the former Yugoslavia, and has been wholeheartedly supported by many, including not only the nation-states of Europe and North America, but also transnational organizations and even several progressive peace and civic activists.

Through the conflict the Serbs, Croats, and Muslims of Bosnia-Herzegovina believed that their right to self-determination took precedence over all other rights. Most of these people did not believe in a civic Bosnian state, in part because it is hard to believe that Bosnia-Herzegovina could be the only exception when surrounded with authoritarian nationalist ethnic states. While the war was still going on, while feelings of fear and revenge were driving most of these people in a nationalist stampede, it seemed impossible to believe they would have the will and the energy to rid themselves of their nationalist leaders. As long as the war was going on, they would fight whether they received direct help from Serbia, Croatia, or anyone else. It is possible to wonder whether the Bosnian Serbs would have achieved less in the war without material and ideological help from Serbia. At this point, however, it is important to realize that what happened in Bosnia-Herzegovina was a civil war in which machine guns and mortars played a decisive role, and as long as there was ammunition for these weapons, the war raged on.[1] Of course, food and medical supplies were also essential, but even with very serious shortages, the fighting units usually continued. Most of the partisan units in World War II consisted of Croatian and Bosnian Serbs, and they were successfully fighting against a modern, much stronger German army for more than four years. Those of us who were convinced that the times have radically changed were forced to understand that most of those who are in the battlefields believe they are currently not only creating their own nation-states, but also ending the civil war that started in 1941.

The third presumption by the UN was only partially correct. Milosevic had a strong influence on Serb leaders in Croatia and Bosnia, but this influence was, most probably, not great enough to make them end their struggle for their nation-state which, after the disappearance of Yugoslavia, they considered vital for the protection of their people. The fourth presumption was totally incorrect. The traditional Serbian response to foreign pressure was to gather around their leaders and to resist. Actually, UN sanctions hurt Serbian democratic forces (which were quite strong and willing to challenge Milosevic's regime) more than the regime itself. The UN Security Council decided to impose sanctions against Serbia and Montenegro just one day before the people of these two republics were to go to the ballots to vote for the first Federal Parliament of the rump Yugoslavia. The democratic opposition in Serbia had long before decided to boycott these elections because it did not agree with the process by which this new Yugoslavia was established. The turnout was low but enough for Milosevic and his supporters to win. One main reason why more than 50 percent of the population took part in these elections was because of the shock of the UN decision to impose sanctions, which was very well manipulated by the state-controlled media. In less than a month after the UN Security Council decision, the democratic opposition organized a huge demonstration in Belgrade (starting on June 28, 1992) which lasted a total of eight days. There were from 50,000 to 300,000 people in the streets demanding the removal of Milosevic and other warmongers.[2]

Simultaneously, students started a protest movement that lasted for 42 days at all the universities in Serbia. This was probably one of the first mass protests without national symbols in the whole of Eastern Europe since 1989, a movement that embraced peace rather than resurgent nationalism and authoritarianism.

The Consequences of Sanctions

The economic consequences of the war and of sanctions have been terrible. Inflation skyrocketed.[3] Necessary agricultural supplies and fertilizers virtually disappeared, as did fuel, spare parts, and supplies for all industry. Production fell sharply while unemployment jumped.[4] Average salaries plummeted, although prices remained close to those in the European Community. By 1993 close to 80 percent of the population had fallen below the poverty line.[5]

There are hundreds of thousands of refugees, including Muslims, in Serbia and Montenegro without jobs and regular incomes. This situation became an enormous burden for the country.[6] The regime might have used them as a reserve army for breaking down social or political unrest or movements. The chances of a democratic alternative developing in Serbia and Montenegro depended strongly on the fate of refugees. This was even more important if one realized that at least half of these refugees would never be able to return to their homes, and that new refugees might have been expected from both Croatia and Bosnia-Herzegovina.

Most of these refugees found temporary residence in the most underdeveloped areas, Sandzak and Montenegro. Because of the sanctions and because Serbia and Montenegro were not internationally recognized, there are no bilateral agreements between the new Yugoslavia and other individual countries. Consequently, the amount of humanitarian aid arriving in the country has been more limited than that for Slovenia and Croatia. Thus, one paradox of the sanctions was that even the refugees, who were the direct victims of the war and had the bad luck of finding temporary residence in Serbia or Montenegro (such as the Muslims from Bosnia), were seriously hurt by the sanctions. According to the basic documents of the United Nations, all refugees should be protected, regardless of their race, nationality, or religion. For the democratic forces within the new Yugoslavia, it has been difficult to struggle against violations of UN principles when the UN sanctions themselves violate these principles.

The refugee problem particularly illustrates the basic problem with the UN sanctions. They were totally undifferentiated. Undifferentiated repression is an approach that should be avoided, not only by international organizations such as the UN, the European Community, and the Conference on Security and Cooperation in Europe (CSCE), but also by anyone who seriously considers the principles of emancipation, human rights, and democracy. For pragmatists seeking to end the war in the former Yugoslavia and to get rid of present and future Milosevic, it was extremely difficult to fight against the advocates of militant nationalism and right wing ideology when repression was perpetuated against everyone living in Serbia.

By 1993 in the new Yugoslavia there was no medicine; no food for babies; no spare parts for medical equipment; and no oil for heating hospitals, schools, kindergartens, or refugee camps. Some 90–95 percent of refugees were being sheltered in private homes[7] which, while a good way to prevent them from isolation within the society, also created many problems, especially when the vast majority of the population was living below the poverty line. International humanitarian organizations, such as the UN High Commission on Refugees (UNHCR), provided food for the refugees in collective centers, but there were many cases outside these centers where refugees did not receive any aid. This could lead to rising tensions and conflicts between these two populations. Elderly homes were without food, heating oil, and special equipment parts. Emergency health service, fire department, and humanitarian aid cars lacked gasoline. The disastrous situation in the health services might have a long-term effect on the health of the population, especially children. The incidence of diseases such as tuberculosis caused by poverty, malnutrition, and poor hygienic circumstances has already risen in some regions of the country. In parts of central Bosnia almost all the patients who were on dialysis have already died.

Culture, art, education, and the media were also seriously affected by the UN sanctions. There was simply no paper for books and newspapers, no cassettes, compact disks, video cassettes, films, art supplies, foreign books and newspapers, movies, and videos. Funding for science, art, education, and culture has declined, primarily because the national economy cannot provide for these activities. If the average salary was low, it was even less in the cultural field. Many young professionals have left the country, which means a terrible loss for the future. There was much debate on whether the UN sanctions required a complete severing of cultural and scientific cooperation. Many countries, including the U.S. and France, interpreted the sanctions in this way. Thus, individual artists and scholars very rarely succeeded in making a visit abroad. This will have a long-lasting negative effect on both cultural and scientific developments and on political life as well. In this way, the self-isolationist politics of the Milosevic regime were given new strength, as the potential and real forces of an open society were increasingly marginalized. As a result it has become more difficult to fight against the xenophobic nationalist rhetoric that declares: "We are endangered by everyone else," and "We are better than anyone else."

A very special problem concerns the fate of the independent media. In Serbia and Montenegro, despite the purges the regime conducted within official television and the universities, there were still several independent television and radio stations, one daily newspaper, and a few weekly journals. These outlets were very badly hurt by the sanctions, and it took almost half a year before they were exempted. Although they were the principal critics of the regime and of the politics of war, they could not receive any help from international organizations and private foundations until December 1992.

The Regime and the People

Life under sanctions forced a significant portion of society to live on the fringes of legality. The black market became a way of life. Of course, the war promoted criminal activity as well. Arms dealers and criminals were presented as patriots, which simply serves to increase their war profit. Although this grim picture has primarily resulted from the sanctions, it is also due to a catastrophic economic policy enacted by the Milosevic regime and its predecessors. The sanctions just deepened the already existing hardships, and most often were used as a cover-up for the inability and corruption of the government. With the sanctions in place, Milosevic was, in fact, provided with the best possible excuse, as all the misery and criminal activity could be attributed to the sanctions.

The character of the Milosevic regime was a mixture of communist heritage and a nationalist mafia that monopolized the still-existing resources. Only pro-regime newspapers had printing paper and ink, only official television had all its needed production materials, and only Milosevic's Socialist Party had sufficient facilities, money, organization, and the means of propaganda. Only banks that collaborated with the regime received fresh supplies of domestic currency out of the printing house to exchange for the hard currency exchanged on the black market. The political elite bought hard currency from people for worthless money, then deposited the real money in foreign private accounts. The sanctions, in reality, did very little damage to the Milosevic regime. The scarcity of resources resulting from the sanctions enabled his regime to thrive on the poverty of the people and to tighten its grip on power. It is difficult to say whether Milosevic and the politics that he represented would have collapsed without the imposition and maintenance of UN sanctions. However, it is certain that the sanctions did not help either to weaken Milosevic or to end the war.

Conclusion

The author of this chapter wants to make it clear that she is not unequivocally opposed to sanctions. On the contrary, they could and should be used more frequently, in all of those circumstances where states are violating international law and perpetrating aggressive actions against their own citizens and citizens of other countries. But sanctions should be differentiated and should always have clear objectives. If the UN sanctions against Serbia and Montenegro were intended to stop the war in Bosnia-Herzegovina, they should have been imposed against all of the sides of the conflict and especially against Croatia, whose soldiers were fighting in Bosnia-Herzegovina. If sanctions were a response to major violations of human rights, they should have been imposed against the Milosevic regime much earlier, and against all others who were involved in serious violations of these rights.

The experience of sanctions in Serbia and Montenegro proves that sanctions must be applied more discriminately to hit the intended target. They must affect the government and not the people. They should be aimed at war politics and military production, not the overall economic potential of the country and its prospects for development. They should target the political forces in power and not the genuine opposition, the media used for perpetrating the ideology of hatred and not the voices espousing democratic change. For example, when it became clear that Milan Panic, the first prime minister of the new federal Yugoslavia, was becoming a serious promoter of peace politics in the region and that he had turned against Milosevic and the warmongers, the UN and other international political organizations did nothing substantial to help him. This was a decisive moment of lost opportunity of the war in the Balkans.

A sanctions regime is a much better mechanism for conflict resolution than military intervention. This is true not only because sanctions are nonviolent and conducive to peace politics and common security, but because they could be an appropriate way to teach people democracy and tolerance in cases where positive incentives are not sufficient. Unfortunately, however, this is not how sanctions work today or how they were used in the former Yugoslavia. The international community was neither able nor willing to provide real positive incentives to those who were ready for a transition toward democracy and civic emancipation and promoted the values of a democratic political culture and tolerance. The international community used negative sanctioning as an instrument of undifferentiated punishment for all. In doing so, it strengthened the very power structures that it sought to challenge, and weakened or even destroyed the civil society and political opposition that were the only force capable of removing the regime and its war politics.

Notes

1. During a visit of a Helsinki Citizens' Assembly delegation to the Peace Conference on the former Yugoslavia in Geneva in January 1993, we were told by a number of international participants that they are aware of the fact that aircraft did not play an important role in this war, and that there were not too many flights during the last few months (most of them probably being Croatian aircraft). They stated that the no-fly zone has much more of a symbolic role than a real role to play in ending the war.

2. *Borba*, independent daily of Belgrade, discussed this in length on June 29, 1992, pp. 1–3. Coverage of this issue continued in *Borba* throughout July, 1992.

3. Peter Maass, "As Sanctions Bite, Serbs Look Warily Toward Winter," *The Washington Post*, August 18, 1992, sec. A, p. 1.

4. Stephen Kinzer, "Sanctions Driving Yugoslav Economy into Deep Decline," *New York Times*, August 31, 1992, International edition, sec. A, pp. 1, 5.

5. UN General Assembly, Forty-seventh Session, Permanent Mission of the Federal Republic of Yugoslavia to the United Nations, *Effects of Sanctions on the Yugoslav Economy and the Humanitarian Situation, Agenda Item: Strengthening of the Coordination of Humanitarian Emergency Assistance of the United Nations*, 1993, p. 2.

6. UN General Assembly, *Effects of Sanctions*, p. 2.

7. Ibid., p. 3.

14

The Use of Sanctions in Haiti: Assessing the Economic Realities

Claudette Antoine Werleigh

The case of sanctions against Haiti provides an opportunity to reflect deeply, to analyze and to question the use of economic sanctions as a means to resolve political problems. Often we were asked whether the embargo imposed on Haiti should be lifted or reinforced. As if the question was simple, the media usually expected a one-minute answer. Readers and viewers were led to such dichotomies as "one was either in favor of or against the embargo." The reality was far more complex than this. When questions about the embargo were raised in such a simplistic way, one tended to forget the reason economic sanctions were imposed in the first place. Also, one did not have the opportunity to evaluate the impact of the embargo in different parts of the country or its evolution over time. Most important, one could not explain such paradoxes as seeing the poor in Haiti, although hurt and deeply affected by the embargo, stand by it and exert pressure for strengthening its enforcement, while other groups in the Haitian society who were well-off and far less hurt by its impact press for its end.

When analyzing the embargo in Haiti, we must remember that the original sanctions underwent several permutations, most of which weakened the ability to exert sufficient leverage to persuade the coup leaders in Haiti to give up power. It was not until 1994, following the refusal of the military authorities to relinquish power, that full sanctions mandated by the UN Security Council were put in place, including a full naval blockade on all shipping and commerce save that of humanitarian aid. By this time, however, many felt that even these stronger measures would amount to little, since previous sanctions measures had fallen far short of their goal.

It might be helpful to think of the embargo as possessing three distinct moments. When the original sanctions were mandated there was great enthusiasm expressed by most Haitian people, who thought that the sanctions would hasten the departure of the coup leaders. The Haitian people were well aware of their own limitations, which rendered them defenseless against the repression unleashed by the Haitian armed forces and their paramilitary allies. During the second moment, while sanctions were not welcomed with particular enthusiasm, they were nevertheless accepted by most of the population because the coup leaders opposed them. The sanctions were also perceived as an act of solidarity from the international community. Although the sanctions hurt economically, they nevertheless seemed to succeed politically in isolating the coup leaders. The third moment arrived when it became clear to the Haitian people that not only had the embargo failed to achieve its stated goals, but new financial gains were being made by precisely those whom the sanctions were supposed to target.

Background of the Crisis

Although it was the first black republic in the new world and the first country where a slave revolt was successful, Haiti never fully became a nation. Haitian society has always been extremely divided. For many different reasons, internal as much as external, the economic structure of the country has remained the same since colonial rule. Coffee replaced sugar as the main export, and a new group of rulers, this time Haitians, replaced the former colonial masters. Even though it had become independent, Haiti's economic dependence on foreign countries continued to increase. When the U.S. Marines departed in 1934 after 19 years of total occupation of Haiti's national territory, they left behind the so-called "Garde d'Haiti" (Haitian Military Guard) which later became known as the "Forces Armées d'Haiti" to protect U.S. interests and to serve as the safeguard of the status quo.[1]

Well-to-do Haitians do not invest much in Haiti. For reasons that can be related to unstable political conditions, they prefer to transfer most of their money to private accounts in the United States or in Europe. Most Haitian people live in subhuman conditions: they have no water supply, little access to health services, and scarcely any food. As a traveler put it some years ago, "never was heaven on earth (the lifestyle of the rich) so close to hell (the living conditions of the poor)." The country has been mismanaged since the early days of its founding. While a tiny minority has been exporting wealth and living the *dolce vita*, Haitian peasants have been struggling hard to provide food for the local market, to maintain their families at a subsistence level of existence, and to produce goods for export. The conditions in which the Haitian peasant works—on tiny pieces of land, often on mountainous terrain, with obsolete tools and no access to credit; with no technical assistance or access to better seeds, pesticides, and fertilizers—have caused agricultural production to decline year after year. Meanwhile, the population has grown. The resulting heavy pressure on the land, added to all the above factors, could not but generate a profound crisis in the Haitian economy.[2]

During the 1980s, an attempt was made to diversify the economy. Appealing incentives were offered to foreign capital to encourage investments in light industry. But the lack of infrastructure (roads, electricity, and water) did not allow enough significant and meaningful investments to reverse the state of the economy. In addition, incentives mentioned above included a ten-year tax holiday, so the new factories did not significantly increase Haiti's internal revenue. International aid could have made a difference since a variety of projects were undertaken under bilateral and multilateral agreements. But a lack of vision and political will, combined with corruption among leaders, made it very difficult to obtain steady and tangible results. Growing discontent within the population brought political unrest to the country. As strikes multiplied, several factories closed their doors and moved quietly to the Dominican Republic or to Central America. This was easy since most of them did not make any investment in infrastructure. Primary materials were shipped to them from the United States and could easily be directed elsewhere. Investors had come to Haiti to take advantage of cheap labor and the so-called "stability" provided by dictatorial regimes. As these factors changed, so did their willingness to stay in Haiti.[3]

Nonviolent Struggle/Democratic Elections of 1990

After decades of dictatorship, the Haitian people sought to reverse their fate through nonviolent struggle. The elections of 1990 were recognized internationally as fair and democratic. With a massive participation of the population (90 percent of the electorate) Jean-Bertrand Aristide won with 67 percent of the vote.[4] The choice of Jean-Bertrand Aristide was first of all a vibrant no to the old order, with its macoutes, repression, extortion, and lack of accountability. It was a deliberate call for a new order, including rights such as equal opportunity for all to find employment, to send their children to school, and to have access to health facilities and justice. During the initial seven months of Jean-Bertrand Aristide's presidency, he did not have the time, nor could he have been able, to make these dreams of the Haitian people a reality. However, under his government, people regained their sense of dignity and confidence. The majority of the population felt that they had become active members of their society. Hope flourished anew. But while the elections of 1990 inspired hope for Haiti's impoverished majority, fear of losing their traditional privileges and power struck the nation's economic elite. For the first time they found that it was not they who influenced the choice of the new government, nor the new president who had long advocated on behalf of the poor. The rich were exhorted by President Aristide to share their wealth and to pay their fair share of taxes. Even this call was met with fear by a class long accustomed to evading any fiscal responsibility. Close oversight and the elimination of rampant corruption had for the first time made the state-owned enterprises profitable, bringing in much needed revenue to the Haitian state. The military coup d'état of 1991 brought this process to a halt.

Intervention of the OAS and Economic Sanctions

As he went into exile, President Jean-Bertrand Aristide made a call for help to the Organization of American States (OAS). He made it clear that he did not want any military intervention in Haiti. A meeting of the foreign ministers of the hemispheric nations was held in early October of 1991. The parties agreed to impose economic sanctions and to refrain from intervening militarily. The OAS message was directed as much to the armed forces of other countries in the region as to the Haitian army. The message was that in this new era of democracy, no military coup to overthrow a duly-elected government would stand.

Because the Haitian economy was very dependent on the outside world for fuel, industrialized products, and even for food, it was believed that the embargo on imported goods would force the coup leaders to agree to negotiations. The argument made sense in theory, but the OAS did not have the structure to implement and control the embargo. It had to rely on each member to respect it. Did all the countries really agree on the embargo? In principle they did, but political and economical groups in the respective countries were not all ready to sacrifice economic gain for the ideal of freedom and democracy in Haiti. Moreover, the Haitian military and their puppet governments used bribery and corruption to maintain the influx of goods.[5] It was enough for a boat to fly a Nigerian flag to be free to enter Haitian ports. Fuel was imported from the Dutch Antilles. Planes were landing every night at the international airport, and ordinary citizens would not, and in fact could not, risk their lives to identify either the planes' contents or countries of origin. Finally, products were channeled constantly to Haiti through the Dominican border.

In February 1992 the United States, yielding to pressure from the Haitian and American private sectors, partially lifted the embargo for goods related to the assembly industry (American-owned plants that assemble clothing, electronics, sporting goods, etc.). Countries in Europe, which of course were not members of the OAS, were not bound by the embargo. Some argued that the embargo contradicted some legal or technical aspects of the Lomé Convention between Haiti and the European Economic Community. Even countries that were full members of the OAS openly violated the embargo.[6]

At the outset of Haiti's political crisis, the government of the Dominican Republic turned a blind eye toward those violating the embargo. Indeed certain sectors in the Dominican business community began to profit handsomely from the illegal trade. Because the Dominican Republic is at a higher stage of development than Haiti, basic products are imported daily from Haiti's island neighbor. Politically speaking, the two governments have traditionally maintained very good relations, and the same is true for relations between the two military institutions. The Dominican government has constantly opposed the sanctions, citing humanitarian concerns. The freewheeling commercial traffic between the Dominican Republic and Haiti came to a halt only when Venezuela threatened to cut the discounted rate for petroleum sold to Santo Domingo.

Other political considerations came into play following the May 1994 general elections in the Dominican Republic, in which widespread allegations of fraud were made by a significant number of Dominicans and international observers. In its quest for international support amid these allegations, and in an attempt to defuse internal and external pressure, the Balaguer government (against whom the fraud charges were leveled) hastily complied with the OAS and UN sanctions by deploying more than 10,000 troops along the border with Haiti, enabling the Dominican authorities to call on the UN to provide technical support. The entire operation was *mise en scène*—pure theater. Trade continued to be carried out under cover of darkness at newly created trading points along the border, which provided a financial windfall to unscrupulous individuals in both countries.

Dominican officials and others who advocated a lifting of the sanctions argued that the embargo hurt the poor, and that it was destroying the economy of the poorest country in the hemisphere. It was true that the poor in Haiti had been deeply hurt. Clearly the economy of the country deteriorated further. But was the embargo really the cause of this situation? First, the embargo expressly excluded the very necessities of life, such as food or medicines. Second, as pointed out earlier, structural and conjunctural factors were the cause of the decline of the Haitian economy. Third, the greed to make money by any means, whether legal or illegal, combined with the lack of any price control or mechanism for protecting consumers, led to a skyrocketing of prices. Fourth, the embargo was an economic sanction in response to the perturbation of a democratic order.

Thus, the coup d'état and not the embargo was the root cause of any suffering. Fifth, the repression that prevailed since the coup d'état caused hundreds of thousands of people to leave their homes and working places. As a result, peasants could not work on their land, and many technicians could not develop and use their skills and knowledge properly. Sixth, to pay bribes to the military to avoid mistreatment or going to jail, peasants were often forced to sell everything they owned (cattle, land, etc.) at very low prices. The return after the coup of local section chiefs, able to terrorize and extort money from the population, wiped away any incentives to invest in economic activities.

Shortly after the embargo was first imposed in November of 1991, the country experienced an apparent scarcity of fuel. This "shortage" may actually have been the effect of hoarding or rationing by the major fuel distributors. Excepting this period, fuel and other goods were plentiful. For all practical purposes, there was no real embargo—it was a porous embargo. Even Augusto Ramirez-Ocampo, the first OAS special envoy to Haiti, echoing Aristide, noted that the embargo, which he had previously called the "major weapon" in the effort to restore democracy, was "violated systematically, evoking mockery and undermining the credibility and effectiveness of the measures" to return Aristide to power.

Effects of the Coup D'état

The embargo itself was a consequence of a coup d'état and therefore a component of a broader crisis. It would be inaccurate to attribute all the economic disruption to the embargo. An analysis of the crisis requires a very careful examination of the effects of the coup d'état and the real causes of the resulting economic disruption.

A few weeks after the military coup d'état, a scarcity of fuel had a strong and immediate impact on the flow of traffic. Prices of transportation doubled or tripled, causing some small farmers to keep their goods. This induced scarcity in Port-au-Prince, which is the main consumer of these goods, but it created a relative and very localized artificial surplus in some rural areas. For a short time, when the embargo was more strictly applied, people in the countryside had more food for their consumption than was usual. This phenomenon could have had a positive impact on the health conditions of the rural poor, but the surplus did not last long, in part because repression in Port-au-Prince and the major cities caused people to migrate to the countryside. While people in the countryside could not sell some of their products and therefore had to consume them, their access to manufactured goods (soap, oil, kerosene, etc.) became more difficult both because of the high price of transportation and because their revenues had diminished. The duration of the crisis exacerbated the state of an already fractured economy. The longer the crisis, the heavier was the toll on the economy, on the already vulnerable ecology, and on the country's infrastructure.

The coup d'état affected social groups in different ways. Most immediately affected were the industrial workers. More than 30,000 lost their jobs.[7] Even more workers belonging to the "informal" sector (shoe repairs, street vendors, etc.) had to cease or slow their activities. Shortages of seeds, fertilizers, and pesticides had a negative impact on farmers. In many places, the situation reached the point where peasants resorted to eating the seeds intended for use in the fields. For political reasons, the number of employees in the public sector increased from the September 1991 level. In the private sector, some businesses were negatively affected by the economic sanctions, with scarcity of fuel being the most crucial problem. The crisis caused a distortion of the Haitian economy.

The embargo was the pretext used by some businesses to increase their prices in anticipation of possible shortages. Price changes were made for products already in stock long before the economic sanctions were imposed. Even without shortages, prices rose considerably. The prices of products not included in the embargo, such as food and medicine, also increased.[8] Artificial shortages were created, and rumors about the unavailability of some products (mainly fuel) caused people to panic, buying and storing them at almost any price. All of the above phenomena decreased production (both agricultural and industrial) and caused the further deterioration of the local currency, the gourde. In September 1991, U.S. $1.00 equaled 7.65 gourdes. In July 1994 U.S. $1.00 equaled 14.50 gourdes.

For political reasons, the coup leaders expanded the public administration, creating new jobs for members of the political parties opposed to Jean-Bertrand Aristide. At the same time the *Office National des Impots* (Internal Revenue Service) collected fewer taxes from the wealthy. These simultaneous actions resulted in a deepening of the budget deficit. A common practice in the countryside was extortion by the local "chefs de section."[9] Arbitrary taxes were imposed on the rural population at vending posts, mills, and on the roads to market.

Political repression against grassroots organizations and local leaders forced skilled farmers to move. It is estimated that between 400,000 and 500,000 people were displaced, causing the further deterioration of agricultural production.[10] The military and its allies systematically destroyed or stole silos, tools, and equipment. Technicians were prevented from offering their services to the unskilled, and cooperatives were closed. Political repression significantly reduced agricultural production and earnings.[11]

The smuggling, bribery, and corruption that slowed during the seven months of Jean-Bertrand Aristide's presidency came back openly as a normal way of life.[12] Despite the embargo, new tanks, weapons, ammunition, military uniforms, and other imported products found their way to the military in Haiti. There was also a significant increase in drug trafficking.

While it lies beyond the purview of this discussion to fully assess the influence of international drug cartels within the global economy and on international politics, we would be mistaken not to consider the nature of these powerful actors whose activities exacerbated and contributed to the inefficacy of the international sanctions. The agreement by governments in the region to isolate the coup leaders was undermined by a shadowy network of narcotics traffickers that made Haiti one of eight major drug transshipment points in the world. An estimated four tons of drugs were channeled monthly through Haiti by sea and air, much of it cocaine. This earned the Haitian military over $100 million a year.[13]

Within such a context, it can be easily seen that the economic sanctions failed to reach their target because illicit income served as a cushion to ease the crunch of sanctions. Indeed, the military authorities who controlled all access to ports and airstrips increased their strength in three ways: politically by openly defying the international community, namely the OAS and the UN; militarily by acquiring more weapons and ammunition; and economically by consolidating their wealth.

In early 1993 the newly inaugurated Clinton administration, motivated by embarrassment over Clinton's reversal on the issue of Haitian refugees, put new emphasis on the restoration of democracy in Haiti. This led to a UN oil and arms embargo of Haiti being imposed on June 16 of that year. The imposition of a worldwide arms and oil embargo quickly brought the military to the negotiation table, which resulted in the Governors Island Accord being signed on July 3. The agreement called for the departure of the coup leaders, and President Aristide's return on October 30. Tragically it also allowed for the sanctions to be lifted before President Aristide's return. This set the stage for the military to break their commitments once the embargo was lifted and prevent a return to democracy.

Repression by the Haitian military spiraled in the wake of the dissolution of the Governors Island Accord. The Haitian military not only reneged on the agreement, but launched a renewed reign of terror against political opponents. In September 1993 Antione Izmery, a Haitian businessman close to President Aristide, was shot dead in broad daylight outside a Port-au-Prince church. In October, Justice Minister Guy Malary of the new constitutional government was assassinated. The arrival of military trainers agreed to in the July 3 accord was met by a crowd of unruly demonstrators—numbering around 150—who were amazingly successful in getting the U.S.S. *Harlan County* to reverse course and steam back to its U.S. port. Soon after that, the United Nations International Civilian Mission in Haiti (UNICMIH) was withdrawn, further contributing to the perception that the international community was unable to counter the intransigence of the coup leaders.

At the same time a concerted campaign to tarnish the exiled Haitian president began in earnest within the U.S. media. A widely circulated CIA report alleged that President Aristide was "mentally unstable," an assessment that the *Miami Herald* later disproved.[14] The *New York Times* reported that the CIA had relied upon information supplied by Haitian officers on the agency's payroll, including General Cédras himself, who was regularly depicted as urbane, well-mannered, and professional.[15] The perception of waning support for Aristide in Washington, combined with the junta's brazen success in flouting the Governors Island Accord, contributed to a growing sense of isolation and even betrayal within Haiti. For its part, the military was emboldened by its success. The character assassination against President Aristide, in particular, convinced the coup leaders that they had powerful friends in Washington who did not want the exiled president to return. Each new atrocity the coup leaders committed was met with a retreat by the international community. This added to the sense of the third moment, described above, in which international sanctions were seen as weak and ineffectual.

Conclusion:
Embargo, *Anbago* or *Anba Gwo*?

The Haitian people, with their keen political wit, made a pun from the sanctions experience. Instead of talking about the *anbago* (Creole for embargo), they said *anba gwo*, which meant "under the heel of the rich and powerful." Although it was perfectly clear that the historical exclusion and marginalization of the majority of the population led to the present poverty, it was far easier to blame the economic crisis on the embargo. Raising arguments about structured inequality was perceived to be "political" or "partisan," while blaming the embargo was considered "more scientific." In fact, politics and economics were intrinsically interrelated. The line between the two is hard to draw.

In Haiti's case, it is not possible to evaluate precisely what was due to structural factors and what was the effect of the political crisis; what was due to the unprecedented repression and what could be related to corruption and mismanagement. Another complicating factor is the lack of reliable data because, at the end, there were no longer local people who could monitor the effects of sanctions. Further, the embargo is a sensitive issue where personal, political, emotional, and class factors interfere with cold judgment. Also, there were firms paid to lobby and influence policy makers in the U.S. to advance their personal interests and deliberately spread disinformation about the sanctions. Equally important is the fact that economic sanctions had not been implemented seriously.

The key factor in resolving any problem is strong determination. In Haiti's case, this essential ingredient was consistently missing. The government of the U.S. in particular had little political will to apply economic sanctions for the goal of restoring democracy and returning Jean-Bertrand Aristide to power. The U.S. administration sent mixed signals to the coup leaders, unduly prolonging the crisis and contributing to the worsening of social, political, environmental, and economic conditions in Haiti.

Regarding Haiti, clearly the combination of economic and diplomatic measures could have been effective. Freezing the assets of the coup leaders, revoking their visas, and truly isolating the *de facto* government would have brought the military and coup leaders to the negotiating table in a matter of weeks, leading to a quick resolution of the crisis. All these developments contributed to a perception—correctly interpreted by both the Haitian people and the military—that the political will necessary to pressure the military to step down or to assist in returning Jean-Bertrand Aristide to the presidency did not exist.

Significant lessons may be learned from the ineffectual economic sanctions applied against Haiti. First, all parties responsible for implementing sanctions must clearly demonstrate a strong and decisive *political will*. Second, there must be a *clear and common objective*. In Haiti's case, the restoration of democracy and the return of President Jean-BertrandAristide, the ostensible goals of sanctions, stood in contrast to the concerns of other regional powers, namely the prevention of boat people reaching their shores. Third, there must be *complete cooperation* from neighboring countries. Otherwise, any embargo will remain porous and the sanctions will fail to bring about their intended results.

Notes

1. Georges A. Fauriol, "Haiti: National Security," in *Dominican Republic and Haiti, Country Studies, Library of Congress Federal Research Division Area Handbook Series*, ed. Richard A. Haggerty (Washington, D.C.: U.S. Government Printing Office, 1991), pp. 353–55.

2. United Nations Department of Public Information, *Yearbook of the United Nations, Vol. 46, 1992* (Boston: Martinus Nijhoff Publishers, 1993), pp. 236–37.

3. Michael S. Hooper, "How U.S. Policies Contribute to Haiti's Misery," *Utne Reader*, May/June 1987, pp. 58–59.

4. Washington Office on Haiti, *Report on the Elections of December 16, 1990,* (Washington, D.C.: Washington Office on Haiti, March 1991), p. 25.

5. Ambassador Jean Casimir, "Haiti after the Coup," *World Policy Journal*, Vol. 9, No. 2, Spring 1992, p. 572.

6. U.S. General Accounting Office, *GAO Evidence Regarding Non-Compliance with the OAS Embargo, GAO/NSIAD B-248828*, (Washington, D.C.: GAO, May 27, 1992).

7. Linda Robinson and Mike Tarr, "Striking out against Neighborhood Bullies," *U.S. News and World Report*, February 17, 1992, p. 32.

8. *Yearbook of the United Nations*, p. 236–37.

9. Mats Lundahl, "Commentary, Underdevelopment in Haiti: Some Recent Contributions," *Journal of Latin American Studies*, Vol. 23, 1991, pp. 416–17.

10. La Commission Permanente Sur L'Aide D'Urgence (CPAU), "Agriculture, Environment, and Rural Infrastructure, Situation before September 30, 1991," in *Aide D'Urgence: Diagnostic Lignes Strategiques Axes D'Intervention, Regroupement Inter-OPD* (Port-au-Prince: CPAU, Août 1992), p. 8.

11. Lundahl, "Commentary," pp. 426–28. See also "Fugitives from Injustice: The Crisis of Internal Displacement in Haiti," a report published by Human Rights Watch (formerly Americas Watch), in conjunction with Jesuit Refugee Service/U.S.A., and National Coalition for Haitian Refugees, Volume VI, Number 10, August 1994, p. 26–28.

12. *Haiti: A Country in Chaos* (Washington, D.C.: ACCESS Resource Brief, November 1992), p. 1.

13. David Corn, "Déjà Voodoo," *The Nation*, Vol. 257, No. 16, November 15, 1993, p. 559.

14. Chris Marquis, "CIA Report on Aristide was False," *Miami Herald*, December 2, 1990.

15. Tim Wiener, "CIA Formed Haitians' Unit, Later Tied to Narcotics Trade," *New York Times*, November 14, 1993, p. 1.

15

Sanctions and Apartheid: The Economic Challenge to Discrimination

Jennifer Davis

Writing about the role of economic sanctions in ending apartheid raises some thought-provoking questions about appropriate ends and effective means. I will attempt to ask and answer these questions in relation to the last forty-eight years of the struggle for freedom in South Africa. That is no arbitrary number, but reflects the years that passed between India's 1946 decision to ban all trade with South Africa, in protest against a society where all political, social, economic, and human rights were determined by skin color and the final transition to majority rule and multiracial democracy in 1994. As long ago as 1959, Nobel Peace Laureate Albert Luthuli, then president of the African National Congress, urged the international community to impose what he called an economic boycott of South Africa to "precipitate the end of the hateful system of apartheid." In 1990 Nelson Mandela reminded the world, as he left his prison cell after nearly three decades, that "sanctions were introduced for the purposes of the total elimination of apartheid and the extension of the vote to all people." When this goal was finally achieved four years later, sanctions were credited with helping to bring victory. What was the role of sanctions, and how did they contribute to the unraveling of apartheid?

Although I worked for sanctions since my arrival in the United States in 1966, and believe they were a potent force in the South African liberation struggle, I cannot claim for them either swiftness or overwhelming effectiveness. But I want to be clear. In the South African case, the fault lies not in the weapon but in the reluctance of those who controlled the weapon to use it. If analyzing the South African case is to be useful as a guide to the

173

possibilities of future international action, one must distinguish between the intrinsic potential effectiveness of economic sanctions in the South African situation, and the extent and nature of the international political will necessary to impose such effective sanctions. It is important to note that while I will focus on economic sanctions, the extensive international campaigns to achieve the isolation of South Africa in every arena, including sports, culture, science, and the academic and intellectual worlds, themselves drew strength from the economic campaigns and in turn contributed to their growth, creating a curve of growing energy and awareness.

Not by Sanctions Alone

It is vital to recognize the South African context within which sanctions were proposed. Never did serious sanctions supporters believe that sanctions *by themselves* could achieve the desired end of bringing human equality and political democracy to South Africa. Rather, economic coercion was seen as a strategy to provide direct support for an ongoing and very active liberation struggle. Cutting South Africa's supply lines from the outside world could weaken the regime, limit its physical capacity for survival, and ultimately undermine its psychological base. But the ability of antiapartheid activists in the United States to build broadbased citizen support for sanctions was very closely linked to an identification with the goals being sought in South Africa, and perhaps also to an uncomfortable recognition of the repressive forces in operation there. The contest between resistance and repression in South Africa directly effected mobilization in the United States. Intensified repression generated anger, but ultimately, the critical element in the sustained involvement of many Americans was their sense of engagement with a people themselves risking everything in a struggle to be free. Thus, the 1976 Soweto uprising and 1977 murder of Steve Biko led to a surge of U.S. campus activity. In the early 1980s, waves of South African resistance to a fraudulent "new dispensation" and the birth and banning of the United Democratic Front were reflected in a new explosion of U.S. public responsiveness, the passage of state and city sanctions legislation, and the achievement of the 1986 Comprehensive Antiapartheid Act, put in place by congressional override of a Presidential veto.[1]

A Vulnerable Economy

The effectiveness of economic sanctions varies enormously depending on a complex variety of factors. The paradox of the South African situation was that the U.S. and other major Western industrial nations kept on expanding their business with apartheid and opposing sanctions. This situation continued long after the arguments explaining why South Africa would be vulnerable to the pressures of sanctions had been clearly made and accepted by many member states of the United Nations, and by many citizens of those industrial nations.

Capital

The South African white-controlled economy was potentially very vulnerable to economic sanctions because it continued to rely heavily on foreign capital to power its expansion. Capital for the first growth industries, diamond and gold mining in the late nineteenth century, came from Britain and Europe. The United States arrived later, after World War II, playing a key role as manufacturing assumed increased importance. Despite some cyclical fluctuations and a brief period of capital withdrawal in the post-Sharpeville days, the 1960s and 1970s were boom years for the South African economy.[2] In the ten years from 1964 to 1974, foreign investment provided a yearly average 8 percent of new gross domestic investment, increasing to an average of 14 percent in the first five years of the seventies and peaking at 24.5 percent from 1975 to 1976, before collapsing to 2 percent in the post-Biko unrest.[3]

High Tech and Knowledge

Foreign investment brought with it the vital component of technical knowledge, to which some economists have attributed much of South Africa's growth, which averaged 4.5 percent and sometimes topped 5.5 percent annually in this period. Foreign capital flowed as direct investment into the private sector, with concentrations in mining, the oil and energy industry, and other manufacturing. South African Whites enjoyed a rapidly rising standard of living, benefits which were denied Blacks via the structure of repressive apartheid laws.

High Profits

U.S. direct investment grew rapidly and by 1981 totaled over $2.6 billion, nearly triple the book value of a decade earlier.[4] U.S. investors, like other foreign investors, had been drawn by very high rates of return. The rate of return to U.S. investors in South Africa was 29 percent in 1980 and 19 percent in 1981, several percentage points higher than worldwide average rates of return.[5] Much of the U.S. corporate involvement was concentrated in sectors of the economy that required sophisticated technology or access to materials not readily available in South Africa, such as oil, chemicals, and electronics. For instance, South Africa was almost entirely dependent on imports for its oil, and two U.S. corporations, Mobil and Caltex, controlled almost 40 percent of petroleum sales.

The Nature of Trade

When the UN General Assembly passed its 1962 resolution calling for a ban on exports to or imports from South Africa, three countries, the United Kingdom (U.K.), the United States, and Japan, were absorbing 51 percent of South Africa's exports, while the Federal Republic of Germany (F.R.G.), Belgium, France, and Italy accounted for another 19 percent.[6] South Africa's import sources were similarly concentrated. In 1967 the U.K., U.S., F.R.G., and Japan accounted for 61 percent of South Africa's total imports and 57 percent of exports. The U.K. alone accounted for 30 percent of exports and 26 percent of imports.[7] Twenty years later, a report by the U.S. General Accounting Office revealed a very similar pattern. Most of South Africa's foreign trade was still with six major industrial nations (the U.S., U.K., F.R.G., France, Italy, and Japan), which provided 79 percent of South Africa's $8.2 billion in imports and markets for 78 percent of its exports ($12.4 billion).[8] The content of trade remained similar throughout the 1960s, 1970s, and 1980s. South Africa imports capital equipment, machinery, high tech goods like computers, intermediate goods, chemicals, and oil. It exports primary products, mainly minerals and some agricultural products. Gold has always played a key role, often accounting for 40–50 percent of foreign exchange earnings. The fall in the price of gold from an annual average of $613 an ounce in 1980 and a high $800 an ounce in 1984 to an average hovering in the $350 range caused considerable pain.

The Citizen Campaign for Sanctions

Throughout the 1960s and 1970s, as repression intensified in South Africa, proponents of sanctions argued for international action through international *mandatory* sanctions. However, only the UN Security Council has the power to impose mandatory economic, diplomatic, and cultural sanctions, as provided for in Chapter VII of the Charter, and the three Western permanent members of the Security Council vetoed all such efforts. Only in 1977 did these powers finally agree to the imposition of a mandatory arms embargo, but they continued to block all economic action, comprehensive or targeted.

It was then left to the men and women in the streets of these countries to take up the issue. And increasingly they did, the form of their action reflecting the great variety of their circumstances. The breadth of these campaigns, the long-term involvement of many thousands of individuals in an incredibly drawn-out struggle not directly their own, is the more remarkable because it was achieved in the face of great obstacles. The press and media reported little on South Africa and less on actions in the small towns of Europe or North America. There were active antiapartheid movements in all those countries engaged in doing business with South Africa. In countries like the U.K., strong challenges were mounted to the British banks which stood at the center of South Africa's capital market. From the Netherlands, home of Shell Oil, came the impetus and direction for a powerful international "Boycott Shell" campaign. In many countries consumer boycotts were organized against easily identifiable South African products like Outspan oranges.

In the United States, early protest after Sharpeville focused on a consortium of banks led by Chase Manhattan, which provided South Africa with rescue loans when it was under severe pressure. There were few easily identifiable consumer products against which a boycott could be mobilized, but a very lively campaign was developed against the South African gold coin, the Krugerrand. An early, dramatically successful corporate campaign was waged by the workers of Polaroid, who risked their jobs to stop their employer from continuing to supply the South African government with film for its notorious identification system. As the movement to cut all economic links with apartheid grew, it began to focus major energy on ending U.S. corporate and financial engagement with apartheid. This choice was shaped by practicalities rather than the relative size of the several areas of U.S./South Africa economic involvement. By 1982, when the campaign was accelerating, total U.S. financial involvement in South Africa amounted to some $14 billion, excluding trade. Direct investment was being estimated at $2.8 billion, involving several hundred corporations. U.S. financial institutions had outstanding loans to South African borrowers totaling $3.7 billion, and U.S.-based investors were estimated to hold $8 billion worth of shares in South African mines.[9]

The most important campaign was the divestment campaign. This was expressed as the demand that individuals and institutions, such as universities, churches, unions, municipalities, and states, sell their holdings in all corporations that had direct investments in, or made bank loans to, South Africa. Through such a campaign, disinvestment advocates hoped to pressure U.S. firms to withdraw from South Africa. When the campaign started, there were many supporters who believed in its value as an educational technique that would heighten public awareness of the repressive apartheid system and therefore lay the ground work for eventual federal sanctions. But some thought it might achieve practical economic results as well, since the corporate permeation of U.S. life provided so many levers with which to exert pressure on the corporations. Every union had a pension fund, often controlled not by the union, but by employer representatives. This provided an avenue of challenge. Every university, even most colleges, had some form of accumulated funds often invested in "blue chip" corporations doing business in South Africa. On State university campuses and at Ivy League schools, students engaged administrators in intense debate about the morality of investing for profit in apartheid. Sparked by solidarity with the Soweto student uprising of 1976, the student movement grew. By 1982, more than thirty colleges and universities had divested more than one hundred million dollars from banks and corporations operating in South Africa, and divestment actions had brought new consciousness to hundreds of campuses.[10] The churches too were early participants in the debate and the campaign. Often church activists struggled year after year to get their own pension boards to divest. Sometimes churches chose rather to retain their stock and use it to exert pressure on the companies via shareholder resolutions. By the early eighties, however, major Protestant denominations had voted to withdraw funds from banks and do no business with corporations operating in South Africa. Many national, regional, and local churches took special action against Citibank, the largest U.S. lender to South Africa.

By the beginning of the eighties, the divestment campaign was beginning to win more than propaganda victories as engaged activists made new alliances and took their issue to city and state legislatures. In 1981 the American Committee on Africa organized the first of three conferences, bringing together legislators and activists to plan effective action against apartheid. By 1982, the legislatures of Massachusetts, Michigan, Connecticut, and Pennsylvania; and the city councils of Wilmington, Delaware, Grand Rapids, Michigan, and Philadelphia had all approved measures to mandate the divestment of up to three hundred million dollars. The movement surged again in the mid 1980s, in response to dramatic events in South Africa where the mass democratic movement, as represented by the United Democratic Front, rocketed to a membership of over a million and was then effectively banned. By the end of 1991 at least twenty-eight states, twenty-four counties, and ninety-two cities had taken economic action against corporations with investments in South Africa, reportedly causing some $20 billion of divestment.[11] A growing number of states, counties, and cities had intensified their pressure on the corporations by enacting selective purchasing policies that gave preference to companies not doing business in South Africa.

This local activity helped generate the thrust for a major victory in Washington, D.C. In 1986 the Comprehensive Antiapartheid Act was passed by the U.S. Congress over the veto of President Ronald Reagan. This Act imposed selective sanctions, including a ban on new investment, sales to the police and military, and new bank loans except for the purpose of trade. It included specific measures against trade, prohibiting the import of agricultural goods, steel, coal, iron, uranium, and the products of state-owned corporations. Federal sanctions were further extended with the passage of the Rangel Amendment to the Budget Reconciliation Act in 1987, which ended the ability of U.S. firms to claim tax credits for taxes paid in South Africa.

Measuring the Impact

In the 1960s, Union Carbide used to run an advertisement in South Africa saying, "We've been in South Africa a long time; we like it here." By the 1970s, no company dared say that publicly, and toward the end of that decade, companies were seeking to ward off citizen pressure by the adoption of a code of corporate good behavior called the Sullivan principles. Soon companies began to talk about "the hassle" factor. In 1982 General Electric pulled out of a $138 million joint venture with a South African mining company, admitting that pressure in its home base of Connecticut had influenced the decision.[12] Such examples multiplied, and corporations found themselves having to choose between doing business in New York City and California or South Africa. By 1989 key companies like Mobil were pulling out. At the end of the decade some 200 companies had disinvested from South Africa, although the manner of that disinvestment varied greatly, and many continued to do business through licensing, franchising, and distribution agreements.[13]

Despite the pressure on banks, U.S. lending to South Africa continued to grow in the early 1980s, and had reached $4.7 billion by the end of 1984, some 20 percent of South Africa's foreign debt.[14] Generally, the nature of foreign capital inflows had switched significantly in the first five years of the eighties, from direct investment, which seemed increasingly risky, to short-term loans. South African foreign debt grew from $16.9 billion at the end of 1980 to $23.5 billion in 1985, a year of political crisis and confrontation. At the same time South African bankers were living dangerously. They borrowed for the short-term in foreign markets, where cautious lenders, looking at rising risk factors, would no longer loan to them for the long-term. They then reloaned that money inside South Africa in long-term loans, confident that they could always go back for more. U.S. banks began to pull back, however. In 1980 states and cities began to develop policies restricting their business with banks that made loans to South Africa. By 1985 at least seven states and thirty cities had adopted policies that restricted their business with banks that made loans to South Africa.[15]

In December 1984 Seafirst adopted a policy of no new loans to South Africa. Bank of Boston, First Bank System, and North Carolina National

Bank Corporation followed within months.[16] At the end of July 1985 Chase Manhattan announced that it would not renew loans as they fell due. Bankers seldom explain their conduct, but this action seemed driven by a combination of concern about escalating risks (perhaps finally triggered by the declaration of a state of emergency in a turmoil-ridden society), the obvious slowing down of the South African economy, and the pressures back in the United States. Most U.S. banks, which had not already announced the no new loans policy, now followed the Chase example, causing a panic in South Africa. Of the $3.5 billion loans outstanding to U.S. lenders, $2.8 billion were for one year or less, and $13.6 billion of total outstanding loans were short-term. In September 1985 the government stepped in, declaring a debt standstill and reimposing exchange controls. Under the standstill new terms had to be renegotiated, which effectively extended the life of old loans. Ironically, the no new loans provisions of the Comprehensive Antiapartheid Act were set in place more swiftly by the play of political and economic pressures than by the slow deliberate passage of legislation.

It is difficult to quantify the cost of sanctions to the South African economy. The task is complicated by such factors as the serious fall in the gold price, which might have provided South Africa with a safety net. The long-vaunted high GDP growth rate of the 1950s and 1960s, still significantly over 3 percent annually in the 1970s, dropped to an average 1.3 percent in the 1980s and was negative in 1990 and 1991, dropping to minus 2.2 percent in 1992.[17] The arms embargo forced South Africa to pay markups of up to 100 percent for arms on the black market and left it with outdated equipment, particularly aircraft, which became a factor in South Africa's inability to carry through to victory its war in Angola. This occurred despite the many leaks in Western enforcement of the embargo. The oil embargo had a similar effect. Although the oil companies did not support it, and Western countries participated only at the end of the struggle, South Africa had to pay a premium of up to $2 billion a year to evade the ban by OPEC and other oil-producing countries.[18] In April 1986 President Botha acknowledged the payment of 22 billion Rand in oil premiums between 1973 and 1984.[19]

In 1990 *The Washington Post*, reporting the declining growth rate and 1986–88 capital outflows, said "South Africa had sustained net capital outflows of nearly $4 billion, not so much because of trade sanctions but because of a cutoff of U.S. and European investment and the calling in of outstanding loans."[20] The *Post* went on to cite a recent bankers' study showing that sanctions cost South Africa $32 billion to $40 billion between 1985 and 1989, "including $11 billion in net capital outflows and $4 billion in lost export earnings."[21]

Conclusion

It is indisputable that the myriad pressures generated by the many forms of sanctions imposed on South Africa forced the previously immovable and inflexible system of apartheid to recognize the necessity of change. Long-time sanctions opponent, Assistant Secretary of State for African Affairs Herman Cohen, conceded this reality in several mid-1989 interviews. "Sanctions are having a major impact on the psychology of the white community," he told *New York Times* columnist Anthony Lewis. "There is no capital inflow. There is disinvestment,"[22] In a similar vein *The Wall Street Journal* quoted his view that "Sanctions have a substantial impact on persuading white South Africans of the need for a negotiated settlement."[23]

South African arrogance was undermined. Succumbing to growing pressure "hardline" apartheid President Botha resigned in August 1989. He was replaced by F. W. de Klerk, who assumed the Presidency after September elections, in which he had pledged himself to reform.[24] De Klerk acknowledged openly the link between future economic prosperity and a reform of apartheid. "We recognize that credible constitutional reform has a very important role to play . . . in the normalization of South Africa's international economic relations and the development of a strong economy," he told a business conference in October, shortly after announcing the release of several major political prisoners.[25]

The die was cast. Early in 1990 Nelson Mandela was released from jail, and the final, though somewhat protracted process of negotiation for the end of apartheid was begun. Mandela himself was clear and explicit on the importance of maintaining and even intensifying international sanctions until "the complete eradication of apartheid" had been achieved. He made this call in his first public address after 27 years of imprisonment.[26]

Less than five years later, on May 10, 1994, I stood within one hundred yards of Nelson Mandela as he was inaugurated as the new president of South Africa, after the country's first ever nonracial, universal, democratic elections.

Later in the year, in a moving address to the Joint Houses of the U.S. Congress, Mandela underscored how much he attributed these profound changes to international action on sanctions. "We came to salute you for the place you have taken in the universal assault on apartheid . . . which has enabled us to repeat in this chamber the poetry of the triumph of the oppressed: 'Free at last, free at last, thank God Almighty we are free at last!'"[27]

Notes

1. See David B. Ottaway, "Africa Policy Seems in Disarray—State Department Left Picking Up Pieces After Sanctions Passage," *The Washington Post*, October 5,

1986, p. A22; Steven V. Roberts, "Senate, 78 to 21, Override's Reagan's Veto and Imposes Sanctions on South Africa," *The New York Times*, October 3, 1986, p. 1; Steven B. Roberts, "House, 313 to 83, Affirms Sanctions on South Africa," *The New York Times*, September 30, 1986, p. 1; Gerald B. Boyd, "President Vetoes Bill for Sanctions Against Pretoria," *The New York Times*, September 27, 1986, p. 1. For a discussion of the growth of democratic movement in South Africa and the U.S. antiapartheid movement see Richard Knight, "Sanctions, Disinvestment, and U.S. Corporations in South Africa," in Robert Edgar (ed.), *Sanctioning Apartheid* (Trenton: Africa World Press, 1990) pp. 67–89. For a review of U.S. federal sanctions, see "Sanctions and the Struggle Against Apartheid in a Changing South Africa," presented by the American Committee on Africa to the International Workshop on Sanctions, Oslo, Norway, March 8–11, 1990 (New York: American Committee on Africa, 1990).

2. On March 21, 1960, the Pan Africanist Congress led a peaceful protest against the pass laws. During the demonstrations, the South African police attacked a crowd at the small town of Sharpeville, near Johannesburg, killing 69 unarmed people and sending a shockwave around the world.

3. Jennifer Davis, "U.S. Dollars in South Africa: Context and Consequence" (New York: The Africa Fund, 1978) p. 1.

4. Figures on U.S. direct investment abroad are compiled by the U.S. Department of Commerce. Preliminary figures are published in the August issue of *Survey of Current Business* (U.S. Department of Commerce). These figures are subsequently revised and this paper uses the latest figures available at the time of writing. For a discussion of the growth of U.S. investment see Jennifer Davis, James Cason, and Gail Hovey, "Economic Disengagement and South Africa: The Effectiveness and Feasibility of Implementing Sanctions and Divestment," *Law and Policy in International Business*, Vol. 15, No. 2, 1983, pp. 529–63.

5. "Policies and Practices of Transnational Corporations Regarding Their Activities in South Africa and Namibia: Report of the United Nations Economic and Social Council to the Secretary General," E/C.10/1983/10, May 3, 1983; cited in Davis, Cason, and Hovey, "Economic Disengagement and South Africa." footnote 49, pp. 545–46.

6. International Monetary Fund, Washington, DC. The International Monetary Fund maintains a comprehensive database on world trade based on reporting by countries. These are published annually in *Direction of Trade Statistics* (Washington, D.C.: International Monetary Fund).

7. *Africa South of the Sahara, 1971* (London: Europa Publications, 1971) p. 712.

8. *South Africa: Trends in Trade, Lending, and Investment*, GAO/NSIAD-88-165, (Washington, D.C.: United States General Accounting Office, April 1988) p. 10.

9. Board of Governors of the Federal Reserve System, Federal Financial Examination Council, Statistical Release E.16.(126), "Country Exposure Lending Survey: December 1982," June 1, 1983; J. Anderson, "United States Understates Business Stake in South Africa," *The Washington Post*, July 30, 1983.

10. *Divestment Action on South Africa by U.S. Colleges and Universities*, (New York: The Africa Fund, December, 1986) p. 1; *Recent Stock Sales by Universities Score Victories for Student Activists*, press release, (New York: The Africa Fund,

1983) p. 1; Joshus Nessen, *Summary of Successful University Divestments* (New York: American Committee on Africa, April 1981) pp. 1–4. For more information on the student antiapartheid movement, see *Church and University Action Against Apartheid—A Summary of Withdrawals and Divestment* (New York: The Africa Fund, 1983); Jennifer Kibbe, *Divestment on Campus—Issues and Implementation,* (Washington, D.C.: Investor Responsibility Research Center, October, 1994); and *Student Antiapartheid Newsletter,* published between 1979 and 1985 by the American Committee on Africa and from 1986 to 1987 by The Africa Fund.

11. Richard Knight, *State & Municipal Governments Take Aim at Apartheid,* (New York: American Committee on Africa, 1991) p. 1–4. See also various issues of *ACOA Action News* published by the American Committee on Africa. The Investor Responsibility Research Center reports that when Mandela called for the lifting of sanctions in September 1993, some 172 states, counties, cities, and their agencies had divestment and/or selective purchasing policies in place, See "U.S. Companies in South Africa," *IRRC Fact Sheet* (Washington, D.C.: Investor Responsibility Research Center, October, 1994) p. 3.

12. "South Africa Draws Investors," *The New York Times,* November 3, 1982, sec. IV, p. 1; Bernard Simon, "S. Africa Venture by General Electric Off," *Financial Times,* October 12, 1982. While this action stopped a new investment, General Electric continued to have significant investment in South Africa until April 1986, when it sold its South African subsidiaries to local management. See Richard Knight, *Unified List of United States Companies Doing Business in South Africa,* 3d ed., (New York: The Africa Fund, 1990) p. 33.

13. Knight, *Unified List* pp. 1–85; Knight, "Sanctions, Disinvestment, and U.S. Corporations in South Africa," p.71.

14. Board of Governors of the Federal Reserve System, Federal Financial Examination Council, Statistical Release E.16. (126) "Country Exposure Lending Survey: December 1984," April 19, 1985, p. 1; South African Reserve Bank, *Quarterly Bulletin,* December, 1987, p. S-78.

15. Knight, *State & Municipal Governments Take Aim at Apartheid,* p. 3, 4.

16. Knight, *Unified List,* pp. 10, 11, 30, 54.

17. *Our Political Economy: Understanding the Problems,* (Johannesburg: COSATU Education, 1992) pp. 8, 9; South African Reserve Bank, *Quarterly Bulletin,* September 1994, p. S-128.

18. Jaap Walendorp, "The Oil Embargo Against South Africa: Effect and Loopholes," in R. Edgar (ed.), *Sanctioning Apartheid,* (Trenton: Africa World Press, 1990) p. 173. Walendorp was director of the Shipping Research Bureau in Amsterdam, which from 1980 to 1994 monitored the effectiveness of the oil embargo against South Africa. For a discussion of the U.S. corporate role see "Testimony of Richard Knight," Hearings on the Oil Embargo Against South Africa, United Nations Headquarters, April 12 and 13, 1989 (New York: American Committee on Africa, 1989).

19. *Windhoek Advertiser,* April 25, 1986, cited in Jaap Walendorp, "The Oil Embargo Against South Africa," p. 172.

20. William Claiborne, "South Africa's Quiet Revolution; Slowly But Surely, Black Resolve—and Economic Sanctions—Are Destroying Apartheid," *The Washington Post,* January 14, 1990, p. b1.

21. Ibid.

22. Anthony Lewis, "South African Possibilities," *The New York Times*, June 25, 1989, p. 25.

23. Roger Thurow and Robert S. Greenberger, "U.S. Signals About-Face on South Africa," *The Wall Street Journal*, June 30, 1989, p. A10.

24. Robert Pear, "U.S. Says South African Rulers Won 'A Mandate for Real Change,'" *The New York Times*, September 8, 1989, p. 8; and Christopher Wren, "De Klerk Calls for Gradual Change," *The New York Times*, September 21, 1989, p. 3.

25. Christopher Wilson, "De Klerk Says Apartheid Reform Is Vital for Stronger Economy," *Reuter News Reports*, October 26, 1989.

26. *Nelson Mandela—An Unbroken Spirit*, (New York: The Africa Fund, 1990) p. 2.

27. Address by the President of the Republic of South Africa, Nelson Mandela, to the Joint Houses of the Congress of the United States of America, October 6, 1994, p. 1.

PART FOUR

The Future of Sanctions

16

A Proposal for
a New United Nations Council
on Economic Sanctions

Lloyd (Jeff) Dumas

Despite all of the positive changes that have occurred with the ending of the Cold War, there are still tens of thousands of nuclear warheads deployed around the world on delivery vehicles ranging from small-scale artillery pieces to giant intercontinental ballistic missiles. The threat of nuclear war has clearly been reduced, yet as long as these weapons continue to exist, it will continue to hang over our heads like a dark cloud. If we persist in seeking security in such weapons, by accident or intention, we will someday light the spark that will spell the end of the human enterprise.

It would not take a general nuclear war to ruin the world's economy and take an enormous toll in human life and personal suffering. Even a relatively limited nuclear exchange could easily tear the highly interdependent system of production, trade, and finance to pieces. For that matter, worldwide conventional war, fought with modern nonnuclear weapons far more devastating than those of World War II, could well produce a long-lasting and severe global depression. And economic disaster is likely to lead to severe social and political disruption. Economic progress has made war larger and more destructive, and the growing destructiveness of war has made it an ever greater threat to an increasingly sophisticated, global, and interdependent economic system. Even the preparation for war threatens to undermine the economies of those nations engaged in high levels of military spending by diverting critical resources needed to maintain and improve their productive efficiency. When the military sector grows too large for too long, it weakens and ultimately destroys key parts of the economic system which support it, just as a parasite grown too large destroys the host on which its own life depends.[1] The progress of war threatens to end the progress of the economy. The question is: "Can the economy return the favor?" Is it possible to use economic relations to render war obsolete?

Using Economic Relations to Affect Political Behavior

One of the most central themes in market economics is the impact of incentives on voluntary behavior. The assumption is that there are always explicit or implicit goals that drive human behavior. It is therefore possible to affect behavior by creating conditions that affect the way in which those underlying goals can be achieved. For example, a tax credit for business investment will stimulate investment because it lowers the cost of buying equipment and therefore makes more investment an effective route to higher profits, the firm's underlying goal. Generally, it is further assumed that positive and negative incentives have symmetrical effects. Since they are both equally effective, it does not matter which approach is used. This follows from the first assumption, that behavior is instrumental, that it is driven by underlying goals that are rationally pursued. Instituting fines for firms that continue to exceed established pollution limits will have the same effect as providing comparable tax credits for those who do not. In either case, profits will be lower by the same amount if the firm continues current levels of pollution, so it will be just as likely to reduce pollution.

Economic sanctions are the main form of negative economic incentive used to influence international political behavior. As such, they fit easily into the usual political science paradigms of influencing behavior through threat or punishment. Even so, they do not have a good reputation among political scientists who often aver that they are relatively ineffective, especially as compared to the threat or use of military force. The historical record does not, however, appear to support this negative assessment of the effectiveness of economic sanctions. Applied in the right way under the right conditions, a sanctions regime can be an effective tool for influencing international behavior. To the extent that it is effective, there is little question that it would be greatly preferred to armed conflict.

Nevertheless, economic sanctions are still a part of the paradigm of threat, an attempt to influence behavior through punishment. As such, I do not believe they work as well as positive incentives in reinforcing desirable norms of international behavior. I take issue with both political scientists, who seem to think that economic sanctions are not powerful enough to compel compliance, and with economists, whose world view implies that sanctions are equivalent to positive incentives. An economic sanctions regime can be an effective and important tool for ending undesirable behavior. But establishing positive economic incentives that reinforce acceptable norms of behavior is even more effective, and costs much less.

In this chapter, the economic sanctions approach will be considered first, and suggestions made for institutionalizing the process of applying, monitoring, and enforcing them. Then, possibilities for restructuring international economic relations to strengthen positive economic incentives to avoid armed conflict and other violations of decent international behavior will be discussed.

Types of Economic Sanctions

There are three basic categories of economic sanctions: trade embargoes, financial boycotts, and the freezing of assets abroad. The strongest form of trade embargo is a total ban on exports to and imports from the target country. Tight export or import quotas, and the erection of very high, punitive tariff barriers are milder forms. Financial boycotts include divestment of the securities of the target country or firms from the target country, withdrawal of foreign investment in infrastructure or plant and equipment, and denial of foreign aid. If the target nation has substantial physical or financial assets abroad, those might be frozen. That is, although those assets would remain the property of the offending nation, it would be denied access to the assets themselves or earnings from those assets until it came into compliance with whatever conditions were specified by those initiating the sanctions.

There are two questions involved in the issue of whether sanctions work. The first is, are they effective on their own terms? For example, are trade embargoes really able to cut off trade or can the target country get around them by shifting trading partners? The second is, are they successful? In other words, do they ultimately have the desired effect on the behavior of the target nation? The answers to these questions are clearly interrelated. Sanctions that are not effective are unlikely to be successful, although success even in this instance is possible. It is conceivable that ineffective sanctions might still show that there is considerable public opposition to the offending behavior. That could cause the target nation to change its behavior, if it were particularly sensitive to world opinion. On the other hand, even very effective sanctions could fail to bring about the desired change, if the leaders and/or people of the nation in question believe they have enough at stake, and so are willing and able to suffer the punishment rather than give in. However, the ultimate criterion of how well sanctions work must be success, not effectiveness.

In their 1990 study of 116 cases of sanctions use, Gary Hufbauer, Jeffrey Schott, and Kimberly Elliott found a general success rate of 34 percent.[2] While that falls short of being an overwhelming endorsement of sanctions as a policy tool, it is very strong evidence against the often stated opinion that sanctions do not work. According to Hufbauer, Schott, and Elliott, there was a relationship between the cost that sanctions imposed on the target country and their degree of success. On average, successful sanctions cost the target country about 2.5% of its Gross National Product (GNP), while failed sanctions only cost 1% of GNP or less. A second important condition of success was that the sanctions had to be imposed for a relatively long time to succeed. Generally, an average of almost three years was required. Sanctions were also more likely to succeed when the target country was much smaller economically than those applying the sanctions. When sanctions are applied by more than one nation, the size of the bloc imposing the sanctions grows relative to the offending nation. Thus, all other things being equal, multilateral sanctions should work better for this reason alone.

It is not surprising that sanctions that inflict heavy costs on the target and relatively light costs on the imposers are more likely to succeed. When trade embargoes are placed on nations that are important trading partners, minimizing the cost to the imposers may require careful attention to alternate patterns of production or trade. For example, when the United Nations Security Council imposed a strict trade embargo on Iraq following Iraq's invasion of Kuwait on August 2, 1990, Saudi Arabia agreed to increase oil production to replace Iraqi oil in the world marketplace. This helped mitigate the effects of the embargo on all the oil-importing nations participating in the boycott. Finally, slow, hesitant, and incremental imposition of sanctions usually does not work well. Such a halfhearted approach often reflects conflict or ambiguity of purpose of the imposers. For example, U.S. sanctions against Panama put into effect by the Reagan administration in 1988 sought to drive the leader of Panama (Manuel Noriega) from power. But at the same time, the U.S. seemed intent on not inflicting real pain on the Panamanian economy. Sanctions were applied incrementally, then weakened by a series of exemptions. This is not a recipe for success. Sanctions are more likely to be successful when they are applied quickly and in full force.

Institutionalizing Economic Sanctions

As the world economy has become more interconnected, the likelihood that economic sanctions can be successfully applied by any one nation has diminished. There are simply too many alternate trading partners, and too many ways of bypassing sanctions with the assistance of nations that disagree with their imposition. Furthermore, the spread of democratization has emphasized more participatory forms of decision making, and the end of the long Cold War has given new hope to the age-old dream of a more just and demilitarized world order. Taken together, these trends imply that nations are ready to develop a new, multilateral approach to global security.

One such approach could be the creation of a Council on Economic Sanctions and Peacekeeping (CESP) within the framework of the United Nations. Though the activities of the CESP would have to be coordinated with those of the UN Security Council and its sanctions committee, and a working relationship established, there are many reasons why it seems worthwhile to create a new entity. First, the membership of the Security Council is quite small and it would be better if the CESP were more inclusive. Second, the five permanent members of the Security Council (Britain, France, Russia, China, and the U.S.) have the power to veto any resolution by simply voting against it. The small size of the Security Council combined with the absolute veto power of its permanent members has the feeling of the few imposing their decisions on the many. This is not consistent with the more cooperative, participatory spirit of the CESP. Finally, the task of imposing, monitoring, and enforcing sanctions is large and complex enough to justify creating an entity wholly focused on doing these important functions well. Organizing these functions separately emphasizes the commitment the world community to a less militarized style of international relations.

Just how inclusive should the membership of the CESP be? It could be a committee of the whole, with every country in the UN being represented. However, this structure, although inclusive, immediately raises questions about voting procedures. If every member nation has one vote and there is to be no veto allowed, then the large number of smaller nations in the UN would dominate the council's decisions and could impose their will on the world's largest and most powerful countries. This is not only undesirable, it is completely impractical. An equitable weighted voting scheme of some type would have to be developed. For example, each nation might be given several votes, roughly in proportion to its economic size. Using some fairly objective measure like GNP, several rough categories of economic size could be established. Each nation in any particular category would have the same number of votes as every other nation in the same category. Those that fall into larger size categories would have more votes than those in smaller size categories. Using comparatively few categories defined by broad ranges of size, with some reasonable relative number of votes assigned to each category would prevent any given large country (or handful of countries) from completely dominating.

Who could introduce a resolution to institute sanctions? Certainly the Security Council, by voting, must be able to request the CESP to institute sanctions. But how else can such a request be made? One approach would be to allow any member of the UN to introduce a sanctions resolution. It might, however, be better to require that a certain number of member nations agree to cosponsor sanctions before the CESP would consider a request to impose them. If the number was kept small, for example, six to ten members, this would avoid "frivolous" resolutions without putting an undue restriction on any nation's ability to raise important grievances. After all, if a resolution could not attract that limited a number of cosponsors, it would have virtually no chance of succeeding anyway.

Certain acts could be defined in advance as so unacceptable that sanctions would automatically be imposed against any nation committing them. For example, it could be agreed in advance that any nation engaging in military combat in which its own forces have invaded or attacked the territory of another nation would be subject to an immediate and total trade embargo by all member nations. The embargo would continue until the attacks ceased or the forces were entirely withdrawn and a UN peacekeeping force deployed to monitor compliance with the cease-fire or withdrawal. Only participation in UN–authorized military actions (including those set in motion to help an attacked nation repel the attack or invasion) would be exempted from this provision.

How should the CESP determine the level of sanctions to be imposed? Certainly, the resolution requesting that sanctions be instituted could specify the sanctions requested, but there is no inherent reason why it would have to do so. Whether or not the initial resolution requested particular sanctions, there would still need to be some mechanism for agreeing upon the type and severity of sanctions to be implemented. The usual democratic process of discussion, debate, and vote should be used. The debate and vote should always be in two stages: first, whether to impose sanctions; second, if sanctions are to be imposed, what kind should they be? The first vote should include a clear statement about what behavior the target nation would have to change to cause the CESP to lift whatever sanctions it was imposing. Regarding trade embargoes, the second vote should include explicit consideration of whether basic items of food and medicine should be exempted from the boycott, and if so, how they should be delivered to the people of the nation being sanctioned.

This two-step procedure parallels the common practice of having an innocence/guilt phase and a punishment phase of capital murder trials. Separating the condemnation of the offending behavior from the debate on sanctions helps avoid situations where the parties are so far apart on punishment that they become deadlocked and do nothing at all for a time. This would delay and thus weaken the impact of a clear, joint condemnation of the behavior, a matter about which all might strongly agree. Furthermore, it is possible in advance to specify ranges of appropriate punishment for certain general types of offenses, as is done in domestic criminal law. A yes vote on imposing sanctions would thus be an implicit agreement to inflict at least the minimum prescribed punishment. It would narrow the subsequent punishment debate. The disadvantage of prescribing ranges of punishment in advance is the loss of flexibility and the possibility that more minor offenses may cease to be deterred if offenders are assured that punishment will be light even if they are caught.

Once the CESP has agreed to impose sanctions, it must have means available to monitor them. The CESP should have direct access to and priority with a permanent UN Monitoring Organization (UNMO), which might be a successor to the current cluster of Sanctions Committees. It would include a variety of analysts, from those who are skilled at gathering and interpreting economic data on financial and trade flows to those who operate, maintain, and interpret data from special dedicated UN satellite surveillance systems. In a way, the UNMO would be the internationally controlled equivalent of the headquarters of a national intelligence gathering agency, minus the secrecy (and minus any covert operations). It is worth operating the UNMO as a separate entity because there are a variety of other functions it could perform that are of vital interest to the world community. The UNMO could be used to help monitor compliance with certain types of arms reduction and disarmament treaties, and provide economic data useful for research, planning, and development.

How are sanctions to be enforced? The present state of the legal and political environment is such that it is not possible to rely on an overarching authoritative and enforceable system of international law or governance with any real degree of confidence. There is no system for enforcing the tenets of international law or treaty agreements comparable to the police, court, and prison systems that enforce domestic law. In this context, international laws and treaties work best when they are perceived as mutually beneficial by the parties involved. An important force that leads the parties to comply is the possibility that their violation of the agreement will cause the agreement to collapse, and thus, the benefits they receive from the agreement to be lost. This may seem like a weak force, but it can be strong enough to achieve compliance. We hear so much about violations of international law that we tend to forget that they are the exception. Some international treaties, like those governing the mails and aviation, have been extremely successful. Others, like the law of the seas, are violated too often but are still much more often obeyed. And after all, with all their enforcement mechanisms, are not domestic laws violated on a daily basis in virtually every country on earth? The fact that enforcement is far from perfect does not mean that it is ineffective.

Having an organization like the CESP engaged in enforcing established norms of international behavior makes sense precisely because it is of great mutual benefit to the nations of the world. The multilateral CESP sanctions

approach to world order and global security is more democratic, less
dangerous, much cheaper and more stable, just, and effective than continuing to rely so heavily on the brute force of national militaries applied
unilaterally or by small numbers of countries in alliance. By virtue of their
membership, the nations participating in the CESP would have publicly
declared their belief that it was an agreeable alternative. As always, of
course, the real test of the strength of their belief and commitment comes
when the CESP votes to do something with which they strongly disagree.
Will they accept the cost of their complying with a particular decision they
do not like to retain the ongoing benefits of keeping the CESP strong?

As a general principle, any nation that violates CESP sanctions should
automatically and immediately be subject to the same sanctions. Since
sanctions would be automatic, potential violators would know about
them in advance and would further know that there would be no debate
about imposing them. Violators would be certain that they would be
punished if their violations were discovered. Occasionally where the
nature of the sanctions would make them inappropriate or irrelevant to
the violator, the CESP could vote to institute alternate sanctions against
the violator if they are at least as severe as those originally imposed.

Military forces should be employed to monitor and/or enforce compliance with the sanctions. Military intelligence and surveillance systems
could be of great help in monitoring movements of planes, railroad trains,
truck convoys, and ships—systems that are critical to sanctions involving
trade embargoes. It is perfectly possible that national governments would
agree to a set of sanctions that private profit-seeking interests or subnational
political groups would then try to violate. Most of the enormous amount
of smuggling that goes on in the world, after all, is not a government
enterprise. Naval blockades, no-fly zones, and other forcible interdictions
of the movement of people and goods may be necessary. Military or
paramilitary forces are useful and perhaps indispensable here. Partial
boycotts are even more difficult to enforce. It is easier to stop all ships from
entering target country ports than it is to allow certain types of cargoes to
pass through while stopping others. Total boycotts do not require board-
ing and inspection of cargo, but partial boycotts do. The only way to get
around this problem with partial embargoes is to have the UN itself, or
another appropriate international group (the Red Cross for example), put
together shipments of the goods that are not being interdicted (like food
or medical supplies) and deliver them in vehicles over which they have
total control. Nonetheless, there would have to be some way to stop the
movement of other vehicles, by force if necessary. Military forces would
still be very useful for this.

All military or paramilitary forces involved in enforcing CESP sanctions should always be clearly identified as UN forces. They should fly UN

flags, use UN decals and so forth so they are easily identifiable as UN forces. A flotilla of UN–flagged ships blockading the harbors of the offending nation would have a very different psychological impact than ships flying the colors of any nation or group of nations. Along with reducing the postboycott antipathy of the target nation's population to any particular country or set of countries, it would be a clear and unmistakable symbol of the world community's condemnation of the acts that led to the imposition of trade sanctions in the first place.

It is important to point out that the type and magnitude of military forces used as an adjunct to other means of enforcement of trade sanctions do not justify maintenance of anything like present-day arsenals of the major military powers. Nuclear, chemical, or other weapons of mass destruction are clearly of no value for this purpose. Long-range offensive forces are similarly irrelevant. What is needed is the capacity for comprehensive border patrol. And since CESP actions are, by definition, very multilateral, the forces of many nations would be available to put together the combined military capability required.

Like other approaches to dealing with violations of the norms of decent national and international behavior, sanctions will not always succeed. At what point should they be declared a failure, if they are not working? What should be done then? One thing is clear: Economic sanctions rarely work quickly. The shortest average duration of successful sanctions in the Hufbauer, Schott, and Elliott study was fourteen months; the longest was five years. They are not tools for quickly achieving total surrender. They are, however, a means for applying strong, sustained pressure to move the target nation increasingly in the direction of compliance. Economic sanctions should be used jointly with continuing attempts at diplomacy and other nonmilitary means of conflict resolution. It is, in fact, much easier to couple sanctions with diplomacy than it is to effectively use diplomacy and offensive military force together. While it is difficult to specify how long a sanctions regime should be allowed to operate before it is declared unsuccessful, it is a tactic that requires patience. Unless the offending behavior is so dramatic and difficult to reverse as to compel more drastic approaches—as would be the case, for example, where the offending nation is engaged in systematic genocide—sanctions should be given at least a year, if not a few years, to produce reasonable progress. CESP staff should prepare evaluations of both the effectiveness and success of each ongoing case of sanctions every six months. Any time after a year, the CESP may consider a resolution to declare the original sanctions a failure. If the CESP declares that the imposed sanctions are not working, it may either vote to increase their severity or to refer the case to the Security Council for further action.

On the other hand, sanctions should be lifted immediately upon certification by the CESP that the offending nation has met the required conditions. The required conditions would be either those specified in the original sanctions resolution, or modified conditions subsequently negotiated and approved by an official CESP vote. At the same time, the CESP would evaluate whether the target nation has directly done significant damage to another nation (or readily defined subnational group) in concert with its offending action. If the nature and extent of the damage are judged sufficient to warrant consideration of reparations, the CESP will refer the case to the International Court of Justice for final judgement. What should be done if another nation militarily attacks a nation being sanctioned to take advantage of its weakened condition? Such an action should be met by the same automatic response that would accompany offensive military action in any other case—the immediate imposition of severe sanctions against the attacker.

Beyond all of its functions in relation to imposing, monitoring, and enforcing various economic sanctions, the CESP could and should play an important additional role in international conflict resolution. The CESP needs a staff of negotiators and conflict resolution specialists anyway, in concert with its sanctions function. Since the CESP's basic purpose is to provide a less violent and destructive alternative to military action, it would be perfectly consistent for it to dispatch those specialists to any place in the world where serious, potentially violent international conflict may be brewing. The UNMO could be given the added responsibility of notifying the CESP about any such situations that its monitoring activities detect. The Security Council could also direct the CESP to send mediators anywhere in the world to try to head off a developing crisis before it erupts into violence.

Beyond Sanctions

Economic sanctions are important. Their potential contribution to a more civilized system of enforcing reasonable norms of national and international behavior should not be underestimated. Yet the greatest contribution economic relations can make to global security lies not in their use for punishing, but in their potential for strengthening positive incentives to keep the peace. Elsewhere, I have analyzed some principles and institutions that could help make the use of economic relations successful as a means to this end.[3] These are not so much a set of tools for reacting to military crises as a possible way of preventing conflicts from degenerating into military crises and war. There are four basic principles involved in creating an international peacekeeping economy.

Principle I: Balance Relationships

Economic relationships in which the flow of benefits is primarily one way generate hostility, conflict, and war. They anger those being exploited and produce strong incentives for them to disrupt the relationship and injure the exploiter. This, in turn, forces the exploiters to continuously expend resources to stay in control. This is expensive, and creates a stressful atmosphere of continual tension and fear. Mutually beneficial, balanced relationships do just the opposite. They bind the parties together out of mutual self-interest. Everyone has strong incentives to resolve any conflicts that arise to avoid losing or even diminishing the benefits that the relationships provide. The people of the dozen member nations of the European Community have fought many wars with each other over the centuries. They still have many disagreements, some of them quite serious. But now they are bound together in a web of balanced multilateral economic relationships so mutually beneficial that they no longer even think in terms of attacking each other militarily. They debate, they shout, they argue, but they don't shoot.

Principle II: Balance Independence and Interdependence

Economic independence reduces vulnerability and therefore the feeling of insecurity that vulnerability produces. Insecurity often leads to defensive, belligerent behavior. The problem is that economic independence runs counter to the idea of tying nations together in a web of mutually beneficial relationships, as discussed above. However, it is possible to strike a sensible balance between independence and interdependence by increasing independence where vulnerability is most frightening, and increasing interdependence everywhere else. This implies that critical goods such as staple foods, water, and basic energy supplies should be exempt from the general principle of maximizing interdependence.

Principle III: Emphasize Development

There have been about 150 wars since the end of World War II, nearly all of them fought in the less developed countries.[4] Poverty and frustration can be a fertile breeding ground for conflict, yet one cannot fight poverty and frustration with bullets. Without sustained improvement in the material conditions of life of the vast majority of the world's population living in the Third World, there is little hope for a just and lasting peace. It is also much easier to establish balanced relationships among nations at a higher and more equal level of development. They have more to offer each other.

Principle IV: *Minimize Ecological Stress*

Competition for depletable resources has been a source of conflict over the millennia of human history. Environmental damage also generates conflict.[5] It does not recognize or respect the arbitrary political borders that people have created. Acute environmental disasters such as those of the Persian Gulf War or the nuclear power accident at Chernobyl make this clear, as do chronic ecological problems such as acid rain. Developing renewable energy resources, conserving depletable resources by recycling and a whole host of other environmentally sensible strategies are thus not only important for ecological reasons, but because they also help reduce the strain on our ability to keep the peace.

Conclusion

It is always an interesting and gratifying intellectual exercise to invent new structures, institutions, and strategies for better dealing with the problems that face us. But the times call for more than just an intellectual exercise. We are living in a time of extraordinary opportunity, a time in which the character and operation of national and international systems are undergoing profound, structural changes. Such times are always turbulent and difficult. They call upon us to take action to guide the change that is undeniably occurring in progressive directions. Guiding change means both developing a clearer vision of where we want to go and a practical strategy for getting there from here. The vision that underlies this analysis is that of a demilitarized world, a world in which international conflict is more justly and peacefully resolved. We humans are a contentious and quarrelsome lot. It will be a long time, if ever, before we learn to treat each other with the caring and respect with which we would all like to be treated. But as cantankerous and conflictual as we may be, there is no reason we cannot learn to manage and resolve our conflicts without these all-too-frequent spasms of mass organized brutality we call war. In this increasingly interconnected world, war has become too dangerous and the preparation for war too expensive to allow it to continue as an accepted social institution. It is an idea whose time has gone.

The institutions and procedures described and discussed here are far from utopian. The economic sanctions approach as institutionalized in the CESP and the UNMO does not represent an ideal way of handling international conflict. It is, however, a great deal better than what we have now. And it is practical. The idea of a peacekeeping international economy is still more appealing. It too is practical. But it will undoubtedly take even longer to establish. This is a time to dream. But we must do more than dream. We must take the tools in our hands and begin to build. We will probably never have a better chance than we have now.

Notes

1. Lloyd J. Dumas, *The Overburdened Economy: Uncovering the Causes of Chronic Unemployment, Inflation and National Decline* (Berkeley, Calif.: Univ. of California Press, 1986).

2. Gary Clyde Hufbauer, Jeffrey J. Schott and Kimberly Ann Elliott, *Economic Sanctions Reconsidered*, 2d ed., (Washington, D.C.: Institute for International Economics, 1990) p. 93.

3. Lloyd J. Dumas, "Economics and Alternative Security: Toward a Peacekeeping International Economy" in *Alternative Security: Living Without Nuclear Deterrence*, ed. Burns Weston (Boulder, Col.: Westview Press, 1990), pp. 137–75.

4. Ruth L. Sivard, et al., *World Military and Social Expenditures, 1993*, (Washington, D.C.: World Priorities, 1993), p. 20.

5. For examples, see Thomas Homer-Dixon, "On the Threshold: Environmental Changes as Causes of Acute Conflict," *International Security*, Vol. 16, No. 2 (Fall 1991), pp. 76–116.

17

Research Concerns and Policy Needs in an Era of Sanctions

David Cortright and George A. Lopez

The essays in this volume illustrate how economic sanctions have played the sometimes contradictory roles of multilateral peacebuilder and foreign policy panacea in the post–Cold War era. This duality results in part from the difficulty of applying an instrument that may not be fully understood to the varied and complex economic, military, and political dynamics of a contemporary world which itself defies full comprehension. The chapters in this book demonstrate that our knowledge of the imposition, maintenance, effectiveness, and context of sanctions use lags far behind the needs of policymakers. It comes as no surprise then that academic and policy discussions are dominated by stock phrases—"sanctions are blunt instruments," "sanctions are a response to domestic pressure to 'do something,'" "sanctions are halfway measures," and more recently, "sanctions harm the wrong people"—that do little to clarify the utility of sanctions use in particular circumstances.

We believe that the academic and policy communities can now move beyond these standard responses to chart a new agenda for research and dialogue regarding the place of sanctions in national foreign policy and in multilateral peacebuilding. Accordingly, in this chapter we outline three broad areas of inquiry where the emerging research agenda of scholars and analysts might meet the needs of policymakers.[1] These three areas include understanding the policy context of sanctions, assessing methods for improving the impact of sanctions, and investigating incentives as a means of persuasion.

Understanding the Policy Context of Sanctions

Of the multiple concerns which policymakers have regarding sanctions the most prominent will always be, "do sanctions work?" While much of the focus in this volume has provided rather clear, albeit conditioned, answers to this query, we offer some concluding observations for how research might make further progress on this essential question.

In thinking about whether a national or multilateral sanctions policy will work, two related research concerns emerge. The first involves a more thorough analysis of context, i.e. the diversity of circumstances in which sanctions have been and are likely to be invoked in the contemporary era. The data from recent sanctions cases shows that—Serbian behavior notwithstanding—sanctions have been somewhat effective when used to punish military aggressors and those who violate other widely held international norms. Yet sanctions have been absolutely ineffective in bringing about a change of government leadership within a target country.

Beyond this we know little about how success in sanctions cases varies with the specific foreign policy issue at stake or the international policy outcome desired.[2] In light of the diversity of situations in which sanctions might be employed in the future, researchers must investigate the extent to which key variables—such as the amount of international cooperation and compliance, the degree of economic impact on the target, etc.—vary with the sanctions situation at hand.

It is a policy-relevant and empirically testable proposition whether sanctions are more effective against a target (or alternatively, attract greater international support and cooperation) when invoked to punish violators of international human rights standards, *or* to persuade states to denuclearize, *or* to convince the leaders of a country (such as Libya or Sudan) to change their policy on harboring suspected international terrorists. Further, as we will suggest later, analysts should investigate the relative effectiveness of sanctions as compared with other diplomatic instruments, including their inverse, economic incentives. Thus the "bottom line" is that researchers need to contextualize sanctions as diplomatic instruments in a more detailed manner in order to assist policymakers in determining whether sanctions are a useful course of action.

Related to understanding how sanctions success will vary according to the issue at hand is our second major concern with the context of sanctions. As they have come to be discussed and implemented in the post–Cold War world, sanctions seem to move freely—even *simultaneously*—between the world of preventive diplomacy and the world of coercive diplomacy. Some analysts, most notably Jack Patterson in this volume, strongly believe that sanctions should not be understood as having such versatility, nor should coercion be their primary feature. For Patterson, policymakers should understand and impose sanctions as a technique for crossing "the threshold of peace" in the best tradition of preventive diplomacy and conflict resolution rather than as a means of forceful coercion that can make sanctions a "trap-door to war." Whether the intention is coercive or preventive, sanctions measures will be most successful when they are part of a larger and coherent strategy which includes other diplomatic means of persuasion and conflict resolution.

Recent sanctions episodes show that different nations will have quite different motives and understandings in imposing sanctions. Yet the stability of a sanctions coalition may depend on the extent to which the partners share a similar view of the policy context and meaning of the particular episode. Achieving such consensus is often difficult.

The findings we have about the effectiveness of sanctions pose further dilemmas for those who seek sanctions as a strong, yet nonviolent and preventive policy. If sanctions are to be effective in achieving their goal, i.e. halting objectionable policies by a particular nation, they must be harsh, comprehensive, immediate and multilateral. The "logic of the instrument," in its most effective form, leans heavily toward a hard and fast policy.

However, the political psychology of both coercion and persuasion calls for a more graduated application of pressure. Schelling provided the classic argument for this approach, calling for incremental application of force, combined with the threat to inflict more pain in the future. The escalatory nature of the actual policies, combined with the threat of further action, would leave the target with a sense of impending "pain beyond endurance."[3] Faced with this prospect, according to Schelling, the target will change its behavior before a full scale application of coercion (i.e., delivering on the threat) occurs.

This notion of the advantage of incremental actions is also shared by those who emphasize peaceful conflict resolution and preventive diplomacy. Recasting the frame of reference of a dispute and implementing policies in a trial and error mode are often essential to successfully resolve a dispute without violent confrontation.[4]

However appealing the gradual imposition of economic sanctions may be theoretically, history shows that the strength of economic coercion may be sapped by such gradualism. Scholars and policymakers are thus left with uncertainty. Swift, comprehensive sanctions may be more effective for some purposes, while gradual pressures may be more appropriate for others. Differentiating the conditions suitable for each approach remains a central challenge for future scholarship.

Assessing the effectiveness of sanctions is made more problematic by the strong tendency for policymakers to oversell what sanctions can deliver from the target. Political leaders often seek to maximize claims as to what sanctions policy can accomplish, while minimizing actual political commitments and economic costs. This situation means that scholars and policymakers will need to be more critically self-conscious about the intent, tone, and direction of a sanctions policy, and the often unstated

assumptions about the wider political framework involved. Suc̶
ments will limit the tendency to view sanctions as a panacea for resolv̶
every crisis and may lead to a more realistic appreciation of their utility as
an important but still insufficiently understood tool of international
peacemaking.

Assessing Methods for Improving Sanctions

A number of the authors in this volume address ways in which the
international community can tighten the grip of sanctions once they are
implemented and better assess their impact. Jeff Dumas' proposal to
create a Council for Sanctions and International Peacekeeping and United
Nations monitoring organization is the most conspicuous and ambitious.
The advantages of an international monitoring agency were underscored
by James Ngobi, who noted that the United Nations must rely solely on its
member states for the enforcement and monitoring of sanctions. Scholars
can render an important service by evaluating and refining such specific
policy proposals. They can also help to generate additional recommendations.

In January 1995 UN Secretary General Boutros Boutros-Ghali proposed
the creation of a new "mechanism" for sanctions monitoring within the
UN Secretariat. In his position paper, "Supplement to an Agenda for
Peace," Boutros-Ghali urged the Security Council to create a body that
could a) assess the potential impact of sanctions, before they are imposed,
on the target country and third countries, b) monitor the implementation
of sanctions, c) measure their effects, so that they can be fine tuned to
maximize political impact and minimize collateral damage, d) ensure the
delivery of humanitarian assistance to vulnerable groups, and e) explore
ways of assisting third countries under Article 50.[5] Such an agency is
needed, according to the Secretary General, to minimize the unintended
adverse consequence of sanctions, including the imposition of suffering
on vulnerable groups and the creation of a rally effect within the target
country. The proposed new mechanism would improve the ability of
sanctions to bring about the desired modification of political behavior in
the target state. Boutros-Ghali's proposal deserves careful consideration
among policymakers and researchers alike.

Scholars also should turn their attention to assessing how policy elites
can strengthen the economic impact of sanctions in a way that increases the
prospect of producing the desired political outcome in the target state.
Researchers have generated a number of suggestions for such improvement.[6] One is to devote much greater attention to the myriad financial
sanctions available to nations and multilateral organizations. Scholars and
policymakers need to explore ways of targeting sanctions more precisely

against those who are responsible for the objectionable policies that have created the dispute. We know that freezing overseas national and personal assets; blocking currency transactions; cancelling loans, grants and aid packages; and declaring a moratorium on direct investment are all powerful tools for pressuring wealthy elites in a target country. Yet these are seldom used in sanctions, or, when employed, are enacted long after trade restrictions have given ruling elites the chance to make adjustments that will minimize the personal impact of such financial measures. As noted in this volume, the cases of Haiti and the former Yugoslavia illustrate how financial sanctions would have greatly strengthened the impact of other economic pressures.[7]

A central concern for the future of multilateral sanctions is finding ways to assist states that wish to maintain sanctions but who find themselves paying a high economic price for such international cooperation. Almost a decade ago Margaret Doxey raised this issue as crucial, and Ngobi and Kaempfer have revisited it in this volume.[8] Boutros-Ghali identified this as a major concern in his "Supplement to an Agenda for Peace." Scholars must address both mechanisms of compensation for vulnerable partners in multilateral sanctions policies, and study how imposing "secondary" sanctions against states which violate a sanctions regime may help to strengthen such a regime.

The Yugoslav, Haitian, and South African cases demonstrate that any strategy for improving the effectiveness of sanctions must examine how sanctions assist or hinder the work of opposition groups in the targeted country. This is not a new concern for analysts of sanctions, yet the manner in which it unfolds from case to case has become more complex. Those who impose sanctions must be sensitive and astute enough not to generate a rally-around-the-flag effect in the target state that might weaken resident groups opposed to the government's objectionable policies. Sanctions also should not adversely constrain the transnational contact, travel, and resources that sustain opposition groups, especially their leadership, in the target country. Exactly how to achieve these outcomes will demand serious research on a case-by-case basis.

Investigating Economic Incentives

One additional area appears ripe for policy research. This involves a thorough analysis of the utility of economic incentives, or "sanctions in reverse," as a mechanism for changing the behavior of target states. Much like the research areas mentioned above, the idea of "positive sanctions" is not new, having its roots as early as Galtung's study of Rhodesia, as well as being a matter for discussion by Baldwin.[9] Yet the predominant concern with economic tools of foreign policy has been on punitive measures. Now that we have a sufficient number of studies on the limits and successes of sanctions, a greater focus on the possibilities of reward-based strategies seems very much in order. Our own belief, corroborated by the work of visiting scholars who participated in the 1994 "Bombs, Carrots, and Sticks" project at the Kroc Institute,[10] is that incentives may be more effective than sanctions in achieving goals such as nuclear nonproliferation. Whether the announced resolution of the 1994 U.S./North Korean standoff over nuclear verification substantiates this view remains to be seen. But greater research into this area of economic statecraft is essential.

New studies are needed not merely for scholarly curiosity but because various financial and economic agencies are already employing financial incentives as a means of affecting political behavior, especially in the area of nuclear nonproliferation. In 1993 we learned that officials of the European Bank for Reconstruction and Development were circulating a proposal outlining a "debt for denuclearization" swap with republics of the former Soviet Union. The central idea was that Western nations holding the debt obligations of these new sovereignties might trade them for a more rapid commitment to dismantle the inherited Soviet nuclear arsenal.[11] Motivations of a similar nature, with the United States and other nations offering substantial economic and diplomatic commitments in exchange for a commitment to denuclearize, led to the crucial decision of the Ukrainian parliament in 1994 to accede to the Nuclear Nonproliferation Treaty as a nonnuclear state.

International lending institutions and major foreign aid providers are beginning to consider employing positive incentives to encourage demilitarization policies within recipient countries. At the 1991 World Bank Conference on International Economic Development, former Bank President Robert McNamara argued that the World Bank and the International Monetary Fund should explicitly consider policies of military reduction in their criteria for assessing a nation's "worthiness" for a loan.[12] Two of the wealthiest industrial countries, Germany and Japan, are also moving ahead to implement demilitarization criteria in their international aid packages. Such financial assistance will take into account a recipient nation's level of military spending, its involvement in the arms trade, and its commitment to the nonproliferation of weapons of mass destruction. Of the two, Japan has moved more rapidly to full implementation of these criteria, codifying them in its official development assistance charter in June 1992.[13] This new policy was applied soon thereafter when Tokyo announced in 1993 that it would provide recognition and economic aid to North Korea only if that nation offered assurances that it had dismantled its plutonium reprocessing center at Yongbyon.

Concluding Comment

Other scholars and policymakers no doubt will add to our listing of research priorities and policy needs. We have not focused, for example, on the dilemma noted by our Russian colleagues in chapter 4, that for continued implementation of multilateral sanctions in the ;, nations will need clear criteria regarding how and when sanctions are to be lifted. Similarly, now that a majority-ruled, democratic South Africa and a democratizing Haiti have emerged, detailed research on post-sanctions situations becomes very important. Has the return of trade, investment, loans, and other economic linkages which were suspended under the sanctions regime been satisfactory? What motivates some economic actors to reestablish presanctions arrangements, while others do not renew such connections?

Throughout this volume we have shown that the somewhat awkward, imperfect, and often slow acting instrument that is economic sanctions has become a mainstay of the post–Cold War world. Because world politics finds itself still caught between the temptation to use brutal means for redressing grievances, and inclinations toward multilateral peacebuilding in the best tradition of the UN system, continued and serious investigation of economic sanctions must be a high priority. In the post–Cold War world we are engaged in the politics of inventing, sometimes by trial and error in policy, and sometimes through scholarly research. Economic sanctions represents one of the high-profile areas where the two must dynamically reinforce one another. Whether sanctions will be only a panacea or a constructive tool of peacemaking will be determined by how we invent, assess, and reinvent in the years ahead.

Notes

1. Our thinking here is to bridge scholarship with policy needs in the manner outlined by Alexander George, *Bridging the Gap: Theory and Practice in Foreign Policy* (Washington, D.C.: The United States Institute of Peace, 1993), especially pp. 105–45.

2. There have, of course, been serious attempts at classifying sanctions episodes so as to shed some light on this question. The analysts from the Institute for International Economics examined the success rate of sanctions from 1918 to 1990 across five major diplomatic goals such as changing the target's behavior, destabilizing the target, etc. And Lindsay posited five distinct goals of those imposing sanctions, such as compliance, subversion, deterrence, etc. However useful these studies are, they may not be as issue-specific as policymakers demand. See Gary Clyde Hufbauer, Jeffrey J. Schott, and Kimberly Ann Elliott, *Economic Sanctions Reconsidered* (Washington, D.C.: Institute for International Economics, 1990), pp. 92ff; and James M. Lindsay, "Trade Sanctions As Policy

Instruments: A Re-Examination," *International Studies Quarterly*, (June, 1986), pp. 166–67.

3. See especially the chapter "The Diplomacy of Violence" in Thomas Schelling *Arms and Influence* (New Haven, Conn.: Yale University Press, 1966), pp. 63ff.

4. A good example of recent research in this mode is Louis Kriesberg, Terrell A. Northrup and Stuart J. Thorson *Intractable Conflicts and Their Transformation* (Syracuse, New York: Syracuse University Press, 1989).

5. *Supplement to an Agenda for Peace: Position Paper of the Secretary-General on the Occasion of the Fiftieth Anniversary of the United Nations*, A/50/60, January 3, 1995, pp. 17-18.

6. In developing these ideas we are much indebted to two of our young colleagues who are pursuing just these lines of inquiry in their own dissertation work. See Brenda A. Markovitz, *The Utility of Economic Sanctions: A Case Study of United States' Sanctions Against the Republic of Panama, 1987–1989*. Ph.D. Dissertation, Department of Government and International Studies, University of Notre Dame, forthcoming; and, Jaleh Dashti-Gibson, *Sharpening the Bite: Improving Economic Sanctions in the Post-Cold War World*. Ph.D. Dissertation, Department of Government and International Studies, University of Notre Dame, forthcoming.

7. Another rationale for greater attention to financial sanctions also emerges from the essays in this volume. Because financial sanctions hit the ruling elites much harder than general trade embargoes, such measures minimize the moral dilemma created by broadly cast economic sanctions that impose their heaviest, if not disproportionate, toll on economically vulnerable "average" citizens.

8. Margaret Doxey, *International Sanctions in Contemporary Perspective* (New York: St. Martin's Press, 1987).

9. Johan Galtung, "On the Effects of International Economic Sanctions: Examples From the Case of Rhodesia," *World Politics*, (April, 1967), pp. 378–416; and, David Baldwin, *Economic Statecraft* (Princeton, New Jersey: Princeton University Press, 1985).

10. We are indebted to the work of Amitabh Mattoo (India), Haider Rizvi (Pakistan), Zeev Eytan (Israel), and Gehad Auda (Egypt). Copies of the working papers of these scholars are available from the Joan B. Kroc Institute for International Peace Studies at the University of Notre Dame.

11. As discussed by European Bank officials in interviews with David Cortright, autumn 1993. See also René Karsenti, "The Future of European Finance: Swapping Debt for Nuclear Warheads—and Peace," *The Journal of International Securities Markets*. (Spring, 1992) Vol. 6, pp. 5-9.

12. As discussed in Nicole Ball, "Levers for Plowshares: Using Aid to Encourage Military Reform," *Arms Control Today*, (November, 1992), p. 12.

13. Ibid., p. 13.

Bibliography

Books

Adler-Karlsson, Gunnar. 1968. *Western Economic Warfare, 1947-1967: A Case Study in Foreign Economic Policy.* Stockholm: Almqvist and Wiksell.

Africa South of the Sahara. 1971. London: Europa Publications.

Ahtisaari, Martti. 1991. *Report on Humanitarian needs in Kuwait and Iraq.* New York: United Nations Security Council.

Alerassool, Mahvash. 1993. *Freezing Assets: The USA and the Most Effective Economic Sanction.* New York: St. Martin's Press.

American Friends Service Committee. 1993. *Dollars or Bombs: The Search for Justice through International Economic Sanctions.* Philadelphia.

Baldwin, David A. 1985. *Economic Statecraft.* Princeton, N.J.: Princeton University Press.

Barros, James. 1982. *Britian, Greece and the Politics of Sanctions: Ethiopia, 1933-1936.* London: Swift Printers for the Royal Historical Society, Atlantic Highlands, N.J.: Humanities Press.

Becker, Abraham S. 1984. *Economic Leverage on the Soviet Union in the 1980s.* R-3127-USDP. Prepared for the Office of the Under Secretary of Defense for Policy. Santa Monica, Calif.: Rand (July).

Becker, Charles M. and Jan H. Hofmeyr. 1990. *The Impact of Sanctions on South Africa.* Washington: Investor Responsibility Research Center.

Bethlehem, D.L., ed. 1991. *The Kuwait Crisis: Sanctions and their Economic Consequences.* Cambridge: Grotius Publications Limited.

Blechman, Barry M., and Stephen S. Kaplan. 1978. *Force Without War: U.S. Armed Forces as a Political Instrument.* Washington: Brookings Institution.

Burton, John. 1990. *Conflict: Resolution and Provention.* New York: St. Martin's Press.

Campbell, Barry R., and Danforth Newcomb, eds. 1990. *The Impact of the Freeze of Kuwaiti and Iraqi Assets on Financial Institutions and Financial Transactions.* London: International Bar Association Series.

Carter, Barry E. 1988. *International Economic Sanctions: Improving the Haphazard U.S. Legal Regime.* Cambridge: Cambridge University Press.

Committee on Economic Sanctions. 1932. *Boycotts and Peace.* New York, London: Harper and Brothers.

Commonwealth Group of Eminent Persons. 1986. *Mission to South Africa: The Commonwealth Report.* London: Commonwealth Secretariat.

Damrosch, Lori Fisler, ed. 1993. *Enforcing Restraint: Collective Intervention in Internal Conflicts*. New York, N.Y.: Council on Foreign Relations Press.

Damrosch, Lori Fisler, and David J. Schaffer, eds. 1991. *Law and Force in the New International Order*. Boulder, Colo.: Westview Press.

Daoudi, M.S. and M.S. Dajani. 1983. *Economic Sanctions: Ideals and Experience*. London: Routledge and Kegan Paul.

Davis, Jennifer. 1978. *U.S. Dollars in South Africa: Context and Consequence*. New York: The Africa Fund.

Doxey, Margaret P. 1980. *Economic Sanctions and International Enforcement*. 2d ed. New York: Oxford University Press for Royal Institute of International Affairs.

———. 1987. *International Sanctions in Contemporary Perspective*. New York: St. Martin's Press.

Dumas, Lloyd J. 1986. *The Overburdened Economy: Uncovering the Causes of Chronic Unemployment, Inflation and National Decline*. Berkeley, Calif.: University of California Press.

Elagab, O.Y. 1988. *The Legality of Non-Forcible Counter Measures in International Law*. Oxford: Clarendon Press.

Ellings, Richard. J. 1985. *Embargoes and World Power: Lessons from American Foreign Policy*. Boulder, Colo.: Westview Press.

———. 1991. *Private Property and National Security: Foreign Economic Sanctions and the Constitution*. Washington. D.C.: National Legal Center for the Public Interest.

Ferencz, Benjamin B. 1983. *Enforcing International Law: A Way to World Peace, A Documentary History and Analysis*. London; New York: Oceana Publications.

Freedman, Robert Owen. 1970. *Economic Warfare in the Communist Bloc: A Study of Soviet Economic Pressure Against Yugoslavia, Albania, and Communist China*. New York: Praeger.

Funigiello, Philip J. 1988. *American-Soviet Trade in the Cold War*. Chapel Hill, N.C.: University of North Carolina Press.

George, Alexander. 1991. *Forceful Persuasion: Coercive Diplomacy as an Alternative to War*. Washington: U.S. Institute of Peace Press.

Glenny, Misha. 1992. *The Fall of Yugoslavia: The Third Balkan War*. London: Penguin.

Guichard, Louis. 1930. *The Naval Blockade: 1914-1918*. New York: D. Appleton.

Hale, Terrel D. 1993. *United States Sanctions and South Africa: A Selected Legal Bibliography*. Westport, Conn.: Greenwood Press.

Hanlon, Joseph and Roger Omond. 1987. *The Sanctions Handbook*. Harmondsworth: Penguin.

Hanlon, Joseph, ed. 1990. *South Africa: The Sanctions Report: Documents and Statistics*. Independent Expert Study Group on the Evaluation of the Application and Impact of Sanctions Against South Africa. London: Commonwealth Secretariat.

Hayes, J.P. 1987. *Economic Effects of Sanctions on Southern Africa*. Brookfield, Vt.: Gower.

Higgins, Pearce. 1910. *The Binding Force of International Law*. Cambridge: Cambridge University Press.

Hirschman, Albert O. 1980. *National Power and the Structure of Foreign Trade.* Expanded edition. Berkeley: University of California Press.

Hufbauer, Gary Clyde, Jeffrey J. Schott, and Kimberly Ann Elliott. 1983. *Economic Sanctions in Support of Foreign Policy Goals.* Institute for International Economics, Washington. Cambridge, Mass.: Distributed by MIT Press.

————. 1990, 2d ed. *Economic Sanctions Reconsidered: History and Current Policy.* Institute for International Economics, Washington. Cambridge, Mass.: Distributed by MIT Press.

Hume, Cameron. 1994. *The United Nations, Iran, and Iraq: How Peacemaking Changed.* Bloomington: Indiana University Press.

Jack, D.T. 1941. *Studies in Economic Warfare.* New York: Chemical Publishing.

Kaempfer, William H. and Anton D. Lowenberg. 1992. *International Economic Sanctions: A Public Choice Perspective.* Boulder, Colo.: Westview Press.

Kalshoven, Frits. 1987. *Constraints on the Waging of War.* Geneva: International Committee of the Red Cross.

Knight, Richard. 1990. *Unified List of United States Companies Doing Business in South Africa.* 3rd ed. New York: The Africa Fund.

————. 1991. *State and the Municipal Governments Take Aim at Apartheid.* New York: American Committee on Africa.

Knorr, Klaus. 1975. *The Power of Nations: The Political Economy of International Relations.* New York: Basic Books.

Larmore, Charles E. 1987. *Patterns of Moral Complexity.* Cambridge: Cambridge University Press.

Leyton-Brown, David, ed. 1987. *The Utility of International Economic Sanctions.* London: Croom Helm, New York: St. Martin's Press.

Lipton, Merle. 1988. *Sanctions and South Africa: The Dynamics of Economic Isolation.* Special Report No. 1119. London: The Economist Intelligence Unit.

Losman, Donald L. 1979. *International Economic Sanctions: The Cases of Cuba, Israel, and Rhodesia.* Albuquerque: University of New Mexico Press.

Lowenfeld, Andreas F. 1983. *Trade Controls for Political Ends.* New York, N.Y.: M. Bender.

Malloy, Michael P. 1990. *Economic Sanctions and U.S. Trade.* Boston: Little Brown.

Martin, Lisa L. 1992. *Coercive Cooperation: Explaining Multilateral Economic Sanctions.* Princeton, N.J.: Princeton University Press.

Medlicott, W.N. 1952. *The Economic Blockade.* 2 vols. London: Longmans, Green.

Mersky, Roy M. 1978. *Conference on Transnational Economic Boycotts and Coercion.* Dobbs Ferry, N.Y.: Oceana Publications.

Mitrany, D. 1925. *The Problem of International Sanctions.* London: Oxford University Press.

Miyagawa, Makio. 1992. *Do Economic Sanctions Work?* Houndmills, Basingstoke, Hampshire: Macmillan; New York: St. Martin's Press.

National Academy of Sciences. 1987. *Balancing the National Interest: U.S. National Security Export Controls and Global Economic Competition.* Report of the Panel on the Impact of National Security Controls on International Technology Transfer, Committee on Science, Engineering, and Public Policy. Washington: National Academy Press.

Nelson Mandela—An Unbroken Spirit. 1990. New York: Africa Fund.

Nincic, Miroslav, and Peter Wallensteen, eds. 1983. *Dilemmas of Economic Coercion: Sanctions in World Politics.* New York: Praeger.

Orkin, Mark, ed. 1990. *Sanctions Against Apartheid. Community Agency for Social Enquiry.* New York: St. Martin's Press.

Our Political Economy: Understanding the Problems. 1992. Johannesburg: COSATU Education.

Pax Christi International. 1993. *Economic Sanctions and International Relations.* Brussels: Pax Christi International.

Renwick, Robin. 1981. *Economic Sanctions.* Harvard Studies in International Affairs No. 45. Cambridge, Mass.: Harvard University Center for International Affairs.

Rode, Reinhard, and Hanns D. Jacobsen. 1985. *Economic Warfare or Detente: An Assessment of East-West Relations in the 1980s.* Boulder, Colo.: Westview Press.

Royal Institute of International Affairs. 1938. *International Sanctions.* London: Oxford University Press.

Sarna, Aaron J. 1986. *Boycott and Blacklist: A History of Arab Economic Warfare Against Israel.* Totowa, N.J.: Rowman and Littlefield.

Shepherd, George W., Jr., ed. 1991. *Effective Sanctions on South Africa: The Cutting Edge of Economic Intervention.* New York: Greenwood Press.

Stanley Foundation. 1993. *Political Symbol or Policy Tool: Making Sanctions Work.* Muscatine, Iowa: The Stanley Foundation.

Stewart, Alva W. 1989. *U.S.-Soviet Trade: A Brief Checklist.* Monticello, Ill.: Vance Bibliographies.

Strack, Harry R 1978. *Sanctions: The Case of Rhodesia.* Syracuse, N.Y.: Syracuse University Press.

United Nations. 1990. *Transnational Corporations in South Africa: Second United Nations Public Hearings.* New York.

U.S. Congress. Office of Technology Assessment. 1983. *Technology and East-West Trade: An Update.* Washington.

U.S. Department of Commerce. 1990. *Bureau of Export Administration. 1990 Annual Foreign Policy Report to the Congress.* Washington.

U.S. General Accounting Office. 1983. *Administration Knowledge of Economic Costs of Foreign Policy Export Controls.* Report to Senator Charles H. Percy. Washington.

———. 1988. *Trends in Trade, Lending, and Investment.* GAO/NSIAD-88-165. Washington.

———. 1992. National Security and International Affairs Division. *Economic Sanctions: Effectiveness as Tools of Foreign Policy.* Washington.

U.S. Library of Congress, Congressional Research Service. 1988. *U.S. Economic Sanctions Imposed Against Specific Foreign Countries: 1979 to the Present.* CRS Report for Congress 88-612 F. Washington.

von Alting, Geusau, A.M. Frans, and Jacques Pelkmans. 1982. *National Economic Security: Perceptions, Threats and Policies.* Tilburg, the Netherlands: John F. Kennedy Institute.

Voorhes, Meg. 1988. *Black South Africans' Attitudes on Sanctions and Disinvestment.* Washington: Investor Responsibility Research Center.

Walzer, Michael. 1977. *Just and Unjust Wars: A Moral Argument with Historical Illustrations* New York: Basic Books, Inc.

Weintraub, Sidney, ed. 1982. *Economic Coercion and U.S. Foreign Policy: Implications of Case Studies from the Johnson Administration.* Boulder, Colo.: Westview Press.

Wolf, Charles. 1980. *International Economic Sanctions.* Santa Monica, Calif.: Rand Corp.

Woodward, Bob. 1991. *The Commanders.* New York: Simon and Shuster.

Wu, Yuan-Li. 1952. *Economic Warfare.* New York: Prentice Hall.

Young, Oran. 1979. *Compliance and Public Authority: A Theory with International Applications.* Baltimore: Johns Hopkins University Press.

Articles

Abbot, Kenneth W. 1981. "Linking Trade to Political Goals: Foreign Policy Export Controls in the 1970s and 1980s." 65 *Minnesota Law Review*: 739–89.

Ascherio, Alberto, et al. 1992. "Effect of the Gulf War on Infant and Child Mortality in Iraq. 327:13 *New England Journal of Medicine* (September 24).

Askin, Steve. 1989. "The Business of Sanctions Busting." *Africa Report* (January-Febuary): 18.

Auerbach, Stuart. 1993. "Are Sanctions More Harmful than Helpful?" *The Washington Post* (March 28): sec. H.

Baldwin, David A. 1971. "The Power of Positive Sanctions." 24 *World Politics* (October): 19–38.

———. 1984. "Economic Sanctions as Instruments of Foreign Policy." Paper presented at the Meeting of the International Studies Association, Atlanta (March).

Barber, James. 1979. "Economic Sanctions as a Policy Instrument." 55 *International Affairs* (July): 367–84.

Bayard, Thomas O., Joseph Pelzman, and George Perez-Lopez. 1983. "Stakes and Risks in Economic Sanctions." 6 *The World Economy* (March): 73–87.

Becker, Gary S. 1983. "A Theory of Competition Among Pressure Groups for Political Influence." 98 *Quarterly Journal of Economics* (August): 371–400.

———. 1985. "Public Policies, Pressure Groups, and Dead Weight Costs." 28 *Journal of Public Economics* (December): 329–47.

Bienen, Henry, and Robert Gilpin. 1979. "Evaluation of the Use of Economic Sanctions to Promote Foreign Policy Objectives." Boeing Corp., unpublished (April 2).

Bierman, John. 1989. "The Challenge to Sanctions." *Maclean's* (March 13): 24.

Binder, David. 1991. "U.S. Suspends Trade Benefits for Yugoslavia." *The New York Times* (December 7): 5, 7.

Bradsher, Keith. 1991. "Two Democrats Offer Bill Requiring Trade Sanctions." *The New York Times* (November 5): C2, D10.

Brembeck, Howard S. 1991. "A Nonviolent Solution to the Persian Gulf Crisis." *Inforum* (January): 1, 2.

Brembeck, Howard S. and David Cortright. 1994. "Prescription for a Civilized World." *Inforum.* (Summer): 1–4.

Carter, Barry E. 1987. "International Economic Sanctions: Improving the Haphazard U.S. Legal Regime." *California Law Review* (July): 1159–1278.

Casimir, Ambassador Jean. 1992. "Haiti after the Coup." 9 *World Policy Journal* (Spring): 572.

Chase, Eric L. 1992. "To End Terrorism, Punish Its Sponsors." *The New York Times* (January 28): A17, A21.

Christiansen, Drew and Gerard F. Powers. 1993. "Unintended Consequences." 49:9 *The Bulletin of the Atomic Scientists.* (November): 41–45.

Cockburn, Alexander. 1991. "Servants to Murder: The Press, Bush and Iraq Today." *The Nation* (November 25): 658–59.

"Conference on Extraterritoriality for the Businessman and the Practicing Lawyer." 1983. 15 *Law and Policy in International Business*: 1095–1221.

Contreras, Joseph. 1991. "Is It Time to Lift Sanctions? An Interim Report Card on South Africa's Reforms." *Newsweek* (July 1): 37.

Crosette, Barbara. 1992. "U.S. Plans to Sharpen Focus of its Sanctions Against Haiti." *The New York Times* (February 5): A8, A10.

DeKieffer, Donald E., ed. 1983. "Incentives: Economic and Social." 15 *Case Western Reserve Journal of International Law.* (Spring).

DeKieffer, Donald E. 1988. "Foreign Policy Trade Controls and the GATT." 22 *Journal of World Trade* (June): 73–80.

Dowty, Alan. 1994. "Sanctioning Iraq: The Limits of the New World Order." 17 *The Washington Quarterly* (Summer).

Doxey, Margaret. P. 1972. "International Sanctions: A Framework for Analysis with Special Reference to the UN and Southern Africa." 26 *International Organization*: 532–35.

———. 1983. "International Sanctions in Theory and Practice." 15 *Case Western Reserve Journal of International Law* (Spring).

———. 1983. "International Sanctions: Trials of Strength or Tests of Weakness." 12 *Millenium* (May): 79–87.

Dumas, Lloyd J. 1990. "Economics and Alternative Security: Toward a Peacekeeping International Economy." in *Alternative Security: Living Without Nuclear Deterrence.* ed. Burns Weston. (Boulder, Colo.: Westview Press): 137–75.

———. Lloyd J. 1993. "Organizing the Chaos." 49:9 *The Bulletin of the Atomic Scientists.* (November): 46–49.

The Economist. 1989. "How Do South African Sanctions Work?" (October 14): 45.

———. 1990. "The Sanctions Card." (May 26): 17.

———. 1990. "Food For Some." (September 22): 48.

———. 1990. "In the Eye of the Storm." (December 8): 46.

Eland, Ivan. 1993. "Sanctions: Think Small." 49 *The Bulletin of the Atomic Scientists.* (November): 36–40.

Elliott, Kimberly Ann. 1989. "International Sanctions in Contemporary Perspective." Book Review. *American Political Science Review* (June): 691–92.

———. 1993, "A Look at the Record." 49:9 *The Bulletin of the Atomic Scientists.* (November): 32–35.

Førland, Tor Egil. 1993. "The History of Economic Warfare: International Law, Effectiveness, Strategies." 30 *Journal of Peace Research:* 151–62.

Finney, Lynne Dratler. 1983. "Development Assistance—A Tool of Foreign Policy." 15 *Case Western Reserve Journal of International Law* (Spring).

French, Howard W. 1992. "As Haiti Erodes Politically, So Do Farmland and Health." *The New York Times* (January 28): A1, A3.

Friedberg, Aaron L. 1991. "The Changing Relationship Between Economics and National Security." *Political Science Quarterly* (Summer): 265.

Galtung, Johan. 1967. "On the Effects of International Economic Sanctions: With Examples from the Case of Rhodesia." 19 *World Politics* (April): 378–416.

Gavin, Joseph G., III. 1990. "Should Economic Sanctions Be Part of Foreign Policy?" *USA Today* (September): 24.

Gordon, Michael. 1990. "Navy Begins Blockade Enforcing Iraq Embargo." *New York Times* (August 17): sec. A, p. 10.

The Harvard Study Team. 1991. "Special Report: The Effect of the Gulf Crisis on the Children of Iraq." 325:13 *New England Journal of Medicine* (September 26): 977–80.

Hatch, John. 1991. "Sanctions Must Stay." Interview with African National Congress President Nelson Mandela. *New Statesman and Society* (September 27): 12.

Hecht, Jeff. 1992. "Sanctions Hit Iraq's Ancient Sites." *New Scientist* (February 29): 13.

Hedges, Chris. 1992. "Outlook in Libya: Adapt, Improvise; Malta Becomes Transit Point as Travel by Sea Replaces the Banned Flights." *The New York Times* (April 17): A5.

Hendrickson, David C. 1993. "The Ethics of Collective Security." 7 *Ethics and International Affaires:* 10–15.

Hoskins, Eric. 1991. "Starved to Death." *New Statesmen and Society* (May 31): 15.

———. 1992. "Killing is Killing—Not Kindness." *New Statesman and Society* (January 17): 12.

———. 1992. "The Truth Behind Economic Sanctions: A Report on the Embargo of Food and Medicines to Iraq." *War Crimes*, ed. Ramsey Clark and others (Washington D.C.: Maisonneuve Press): 167.

Human Rights Watch. 1993. "Iraq: Background on Human Rights Conditions, 1984–1992." (August).

Ibrahim, Yossef M. 1990. "OPEC To Increase Oil Output to Offset Losses from Iraq." *New York Times* (August 30): sec. A, p. 1.

Johnson, James Turner. 1991. "Just War Tradition and the War in the Gulf." *The Christian Century* (February): 6–13.

Joyner, Christopher. 1984. "The Transnational Boycott as Economic Coercion in International Law: Policy, Place, and Practice." 17 *Vanderbilt Journal Of Transnational Law.*

———. 1991. "Sanctions, Compliance, and International Law: Reflections on the United Nations Experience Against Iraq." 32:1 *Virginia Journal of International Law* (Fall): 1–46.

Kaempfer, William H. and Anton D. Lowenberg. 1986. "A Model of the Political Economy of International Investment Sanctions: The Case of South Africa." 39:3 *Kyklos.*

Kaempfer, William H. and Michael H. Moffet. 1988. "Impact of Anti-Apartheid Sanctions on South Africa: Some Trade and Financial Evidence." *Contemporary Policy Issues* (October): 118–29.

Kaempfer, William H. and Anton D. Lowenberg. 1988. "Theory of International Economic Sanctions: A Public Choice Approach." 78 *American Economic Review* (September): 2.

———. 1992. "Using Threshold Models to Explain International Relations." 73 *Public Choice* (June): 419–43.

Kapstein, Jonathan. 1989. "South Africa: The Squeeze Is On." *Business Week*. Industrial/Technology Edition. (September): 44–48.

Khan, Haider Ali. 1988. "The Impact of Trade Sanctions on South Africa: A Social Accounting Matrix Approach." *Contemporary Policy Issues* (October): 130–40.

Kimmitt, Robert M. 1991. "Economics and National Security." Address Before the American Bar Association. U.S. Department of State Dispatch (June 3): 398.

Kinzer, Stephen. 1992. "Sanctions Driving Yugoslav Economy into Deep Decline." *New York Times* (August 31): sec. A, pp. 1–5.

Konovalov, Alexander, Sergei Oznobistchev, and Dmitri Evstafiev. 1993. "Saying Da, Saying Nyet." 49:9 *The Bulletin of the Atomic Scientists* (November): 28–31.

Kozyrev, Andrei. 1992. "Renewal of the Kafkian Metamorphoses." *Nezavisimaya Gazeta* (August 20).

———. 1993. "There are More Internal Enemies than External Ones." *Kuranti* (April 16).

———. 1994. "The Lagging Partnership." 73 *Foreign Affairs* (May/June): 61.

Kreisberg, Louis. 1988. "Positive Inducements in U.S.—Soviet Relations." 2 *The Syracuse University Program on the Analysis and Resolution of Conflict (PARC) Newsletter* (March).

Kuran, Timur. 1987. "Chameleon Voters and Public Choice." 53 *Public Policy*: 53–78.

———. 1987. "Preference, Falsification, Policy Continuity, and Collective Conservatism." 97 *Economic Journal* (September): 645.

The Lancet. 1991. "Starvation in Iraq." (November 9): 1179.

Lederach, John Paul. 1991. "From War to Peace." 10 *Mennonite Central Committee U.S. Peace Section Conciliation Quarterly Newsletter* (Winter).

Lenway, Stefanie Ann. 1988. "Between War and Commerce: Economic Sanctions as a Tool of Statecraft." 42 *International Organization* (Spring): 397–426.

Leich, Marian Nash. 1990. "Foreign Assets Control and Economic Sanctions." *American Journal of International Law* (October): 903–07.

Leidy, Michael P., William H. Kaempfer, and Anton D. Lowenberg. 1989. "The Theory of International Economic Sanctions—A Public Choice Approach: Comment, Reply." *American Economic Review* (December): 1300–06.

Lewis Paul. 1990. "Soviets Seek Meeting of UN Military Panel." *New York Times* (October 11): sec. A, p. 19.

———. 1990. "U.S. Seeks to Revive Panel that Enforces UN Decrees." *New York Times* (September 19): sec. A, p. 11.

Lief, Louise. 1991. "On the Street Where He Rules." *U.S. News and World Report* (September 30): 47.

———. 1991. "Even in Hussein's Hometown, The Sanctions are Biting." *U.S. News and World Report* (September 30): 51.

Lillich, Richard B. 1975. "Economic Coercion and the International Legal Order." 51 *International Affairs* (July): 358–71.

Lindsay, James M. 1986. "Trade Sanctions as Policy Instruments: A Re-examination." 30 *International Studies Quarterly* (June): 153–73.

Lopez, George A. and David Cortright. 1993. "Sanctions: Do They Work?" 49:9 *The Bulletin of the Atomic Scientists.* (November): 14, 15.

Lundahl, Mats. 1991. "Commentary, Underdevelopment in Haiti: Some Recent Contributions." 23 *Journal of Latin American Studies*: 416–17.

Marcuss, Stanley J., and Eric L. Richard. 1981. "Extraterritorial Jurisdiction in United States Trade Law: The Need for a Consistent Theory." 20 *Columbia Journal of Transnational Law*: 439–83.

Marcuss, Stanley J., and D. Stephen Mathias. 1984. "U.S. Foreign Policy Export Controls: Do They Pass Muster Under International Law?" 2 *International Tax and Business Lawyer* (Winter): 1–28.

Maren, Michael. 1989. "Fortress South Africa." *Africa Report* (March/April): 31.

Mass, Peter. 1992. "As Sanctions Bite, Serbs Look Warily Toward Winter." *The Washington Post* (August 18): sec. A, p. 1.

———. 1993. "Serbian People Politicians Scoff at West's Threats to Sanctions." *The Washington Post* (March 31): sec. A, p. 25.

Massing, Michael. 1991. "Can Saddam Survive?" *The New York Review of Books* (August 15): 59.

Meldrum, Andrew. 1989. "Finding a Meeting Point." *Africa Report* (March/April): 38.

Montgomery, Ann. 1992. "The Impact of Sanctions on Baghdad's Children's Hospital." *War Crimes*, ed. Ramsey Clark and others (Washington, D.C.: Maisonneuve Press): 100.

Moyer, Homer E., Jr., and Linda A. Mabry. 1983. "Export Controls as Instruments of Foreign Policy: The History, Legal Issues, and Policy Lessons of Three Recent Cases." 15 *Law and Policy in International Business*: 1–171.

Mylroie, Laurie. 1991. "Trial and Error: The Way to Fell Saddam." *The New Republic* (June 3): 17.

Nanda, Ved P. ed. 1991. "The Iraqi Invasion of Kuwait: The UN Response." 15 *Southern Illinois University Law Journal*: 431.

The Nation. 1989. "Real Sanctions." Editorial (October 9): 372.

Neff, Stephen C. 1988. "Boycott and the Law of Nations: Economic Warfare and Modern International Law in Historical Perspective." *British Yearbook of International Law 1988* (Oxford: Oxford University Press): 135–45.

Nelan, Bruce W. 1990. "Measuring the Embargo's Bite: Even if Some Countries Relent and Send Emergency Food and Medicine to Baghdad, Saddam Still Faces a Cash Crunch." *Time* (September 17): 32.

The New Republic. 1990. "Disabled Weapons." (September 3): 11.

The New York Times. 1992. "An Incentive for Saddam Hussein." Editorial. (March 3): A14, A22.

Norton, Robert E. and Lee Smith. 1990. "War's Cost to the Economy." *Fortune* (December 31): 67.

Nossal, Kim Richard. 1989. "International Sanctions as International Punishment." *International Organization* (Spring): 301–22.

Olson, Richard Stuart. 1979. "Economic Coercion in World Politics: With a Focus on North-South Relations." 31 *World Politics* (July): 471–94.

Peltzman, Sam. 1976. "Toward a More General Theory of Regulation." 19 *Journal of Law and Economics* (August): 211–40.

Pennar, Karen. 1990. "Will the Embargo Work? A Look at the Record." *Business Week* (September 17): 22.

Perlow, Gary H. 1983. "Taking Peacetime Trade Sanctions to the Limit." 15 *Case Western Reserve Journal of International Law* (Spring).

Reed, Stanley. 1990. "Iraq May Not Starve, But Its Industry Will." *Business Week* (September 17): 28.

Rich, Paul B. 1990. "Sanctions and Negotiations for Political Change in South Africa." *African Affairs* (July): 451.

Robinson, Linda and Mike Tarr. 1992. "Striking Out Against Neighborhood Bullies." *U.S. News and World Report* (February 17): 38.

Rubenstein, Ed. 1990. "Can Sanctions Work?" *National Review* (December 31): 12.

Schmitt, Eric. 1991. "A Move to Block U.S. Aid to Amman; Jordan Suspected of Violating the Embargo Against Iraq, Administration Says." *The New York Times* (December 8): 10, 12.

Schreiber, Anna P. 1973. "Economic Coercion as an Instrument of Foreign Policy: U.S. Economic Measures against Cuba and the Dominican Republic." 25 *World Politics* (April): 387–413.

Smeets, Maarten. 1990. "Economic Sanctions Against Iraq: The Ideal Case?" *Journal of World Trade*, Switzerland (December): 105–20.

Smith Jeffery R. 1993. "Iraq Shipped Oil to Iran, U.S. Alleges." *Washington Post* (March 31): sec. A, p. 1.

Spencer, Gary. 1991. "UN Official Discusses Sanctions' Viability." *New York Law Journal* (January 24): 1.

Stigler, George J. 1971. "The Theory of Economics Regulation." 2 *Bell Journal of Economics and Management Science* (Spring): 3–21.

Talbott, Strobe. 1991. "Fiddling While Dubrovnick Burns." *Time* (November 25): 56.

Trevan, Tim. 1993. "UNSCOM Faces Entirely New Verification Challenges In Iraq." *Arms Control Today* (April): 11.

Tsebelis, George. 1990. "Are Sanctions Effective? A Game-Theoretic Analysis." *Journal of Conflict Resolution* (March): 3.

Uhlaner, Carole Jean. 1989. "Relational Goods and Participation: Incorporating Sociability into a Theory of Rational Action." 53 *Public Choice* (September): 253–85.

van Bergeijk, Peter A. G. 1989. "Success and Failure of Economic Sanctions." 42:3 Kyklos: 385–404

Wallensteen, Peter. 1968. "Characteristics of Economic Sanctions." 5 *Journal of Peace Research*: 248–67.

Werleigh, Claudette Antoine. 1993. "Haiti and the Halfhearted." *The Bulletin of the Atomic Scientists.* (November): 20–23.

Woodward, Susan. 1993. "Yugoslavia: Divide and Fail" 49 *The Bulletin of the Atomic Scientists*. (November): 24–27.

Wren, Christopher S. 1991. "African-Americans, Visiting Mandela, Back Sanctions Plan." *The New York Times* (November 3): 4, 14.

Zupan, Dusan. 1992. "America, Serbia, and New World Order." *TANJUG* (April 19) and *Foreign Broadcast Information Service* (April 20): EEU-92-076.

Index

About the Book

As the challenge of preventing military conflict has become increasingly complex in the post–Cold War era, economic sanctions are being applied with growing frequency. Sanctions are being used to enforce international law, to deter aggression and terrorism, to defend democracy and human rights, and to prevent nuclear proliferation. In this timely book, some of the world's leading scholars and policymakers critically address questions about the utility, appropriateness, and success or failure of sanctions as well as their impact on the poor and innocent.

This volume takes up two broad areas of inquiry: It assesses the general aspects of sanctions—their history, purpose, effectiveness, political and economic impact, and their relation to other forms of peacekeeping and international diplomacy. It also examines specific case studies, focusing on recent conflicts in Haiti, Iraq, and the former Yugoslavia, as well as the impact of sanctions in South Africa's climate of political change. Finally, the book analyzes the experiences of some of the pivotal actors who have invoked sanctions—the United States, Russia, and the United Nations—and concludes with a discussion of the future of sanctions research and policy.